Internet Standards and Protocols

Dilip C. Naik

Microsoft Press

Published by Microsoft Press
A Division of Microsoft Corporation
One Microsoft Way
Redmond, Washington 98052-6399

Library of Congress Cataloging-in-Publication Data
Naik, Dilip.
     Internet Standards and Protocols : The Professional Desktop
   Reference / Dilip C. Naik.
        p.   cm.
     Includes index.
     ISBN 1-57231-692-6
     1. Computer network protocols--Standards.   2. Internet (Computer
   network)   I. Title.
   TK5105.55.N35   1998
   004.6'2--dc21   98-22927
                                                              CIP

Printed and bound in the United States of America.

1 2 3 4 5 6 7 8 9   QMQM   3 2 1 0 9 8

Distributed in Canada by ITP Nelson, a division of Thomson Canada Limited.

A CIP catalogue record for this book is available from the British Library.

Microsoft Press books are available through booksellers and distributors worldwide. For further informa-tion about international editions, contact your local Microsoft Corporation office or contact Microsoft Press International directly at fax (425) 936-7329. Visit our Web site at mspress.microsoft.com.

Macintosh is a registered trademark of Apple Computer, Inc. Intel is a registered trademark of Intel Cor-poration. ActiveX, Authenticode, Microsoft, NetShow, Visual Basic, Windows, and Windows NT are either registered trademarks or trademarks of Microsoft Corporation in the U.S.A. and/or other countries. MD5 is a trademark of RSA Data Security. Other product and company names mentioned herein may be the trade-marks of their respective owners.

Companies, names, and/or data used in screens and sample output are fictitious unless otherwise noted.

Acquisitions Editor: David Clark
Project Editor: John Pierce

To the memory of my father, C. D. Naik

About the Author

Dilip C. Naik has a master's degree in electrical engineering and is also a Microsoft Certified Systems Engineer. He has over 15 years of experience in the computer industry and has spent nearly 10 of those years at Microsoft working in various capacities, including software development and program management. Dilip has lived on four continents and worked on three. His motto is "Have Brain, Will Train." This book is the outcome of one such training effort.

Contents

PART V Multimedia

PART VI Appendixes

Acknowledgments

The scope of this book is beyond the resources of a single individual. I would like to record my deep gratitude to John Pierce, my editor at Microsoft Press, who cajoled and drove me to finish this work. I am also indebted to David Clark at Microsoft Press and, of course, to the people there who toiled on this book, most notably Barb Runyan, Cheryl Penner, Travis Beaven, Linda Ebenstein, Stuart Greenman, and Pamela Hafey. Some of my colleagues contributed their thoughts and ideas, enthusiastically recommending that a book such as this was viable and necessary and helping to review the contents.

Introduction

Internet Standards and Protocols is intended to aid readers in keeping abreast of the ever changing technologies of the Internet. Obviously this is a difficult task because some of the topics covered rate more than a single volume by themselves—Transmission Control Protocol is just one example. However, I expect this book will prove useful to a wide range of readers, including:

- Novices attempting to gain insight into a technology behind a medium that is becoming increasingly important in life and commerce.
- People who have in-depth knowledge of one particular aspect of the Internet and who need to obtain an overview of other Internet technologies.
- People who are simply seeking a source that can act as a quick refresher course or who want to locate topics to investigate futher.
- People who need a general knowledge of various aspects of the Internet in their professional lives, such as someone preparing for a job interview, a sales engineer calling on an information technology professional, or even an information technology professional expecting a call from a sales engineer.

This book might best be described as a glossary with a difference. Start with a glossary that covers various terms related to the Internet, and arrange the terms functionally rather than alphabetically. For example, I've included a chapter about electronic mail, one about directory services, and one about multimedia. I've also taken some latitude in deciding which topics to include and which not. Some of the topics I cover might seem outdated, but I've included them because they are still an integral part of the Internet. Other topics are about relatively new technology. Given the leeway to make these decisions, I've expanded important topics to five pages, rather than the five sentences that glossaries often allow.

A glossary simply summarizes material that is available elsewhere. In that respect, this book is no different from a glossary. Given enough time and resources, one can locate all of the material covered in this book in a multitude of places. The value of this book is in providing a single handy reference that unifies and summarizes all these various sources.

Organization of This Book

In Part I, "Plumbing," of this book, I describe the network plumbing that constitutes the modern-day local area network (LAN), to some extent the modern day wide area network (WAN), and the Internet. Most of this section covers the physical layer, the data-link layer, and the network layer of the International Organization for Standardization/Open Systems Interconnection (ISO/OSI) seven-layer model. I provide an overview of the ISO/OSI model in Chapter 1, "The ISO Open Systems Interconnection Model." Security, in terms of guarding passwords and data, is considered part of the plumbing because it has moved to the core services of a network and is no longer considered part of an application.

In Part II, "Locating Information," I describe mechanisms for locating information. Some of these, such as Wide Area Information Server (WAIS), are technologies that once held promise but now seem fated to become irrelevant (if not already relegated to being so). Some of the other technologies covered in this section, such as Lightweight Directory Access Protocol (LDAP), are technologies that show a lot of potential, with a promise of more widespread adoption and deployment.

Part III, "Information Retrieval," describes the various standards and tools that have evolved to retrieve information. This includes electronic mail and file transfer protocols.

In Part IV, "The Web," I describe technologies related to the World Wide Web (WWW). In one sense the Web acts as a tool to locate information as well as to retrieve that information. With the rapid advances in Web-related development and the attention focused on it, the Web deserves a section all to itself.

Finally in Part V, "Multimedia," I cover multimedia on the Internet, including audio, video, and VRML (Virtual Reality Modeling Language).

This is a book about technologies and not about products. Where appropriate, certain products are mentioned as examples that implement a particular technology. No inference about product quality or popularity should be drawn if a particular product is mentioned and another one is not or from the order in which products are mentioned.

Standards Bodies

Various organizations are involved in the development and control of the Internet, primarily with regard to the software protocols and interfaces used. The list of organizations that follows is meant only to be representative and is by no means exhaustive.

Internet Society

The Internet Society (ISOC) is a society of Internet professionals and experts that coordinates the viability and scaling of the Internet. One of the main services ISOC provides is developing Internet standards and protocols, which it accomplishes in cooperation with other organizations.

Internet Architecture Board

The Internet Architecture Board (IAB), formerly known as the Internet Activities Board, is the technical advisory group for ISOC. IAB oversees the architecture and evolution of Internet protocols, providing the process to create Internet standards, managing the Request for Comments (RFC) document series, and administering the various Internet-assigned numbers. IAB also works with other organizations concerned with standards and technical issues related to the Internet. IAB has two principal subsidiary task forces, the Internet Engineering Task Force, and the Internet Research Task Force.

Internet Engineering Task Force and Internet Engineering Steering Group

The Internet Engineering Task Force (IETF) is the protocol engineering and development arm of the Internet. IETF consists of groups that contribute to the technical evolution of the Internet. They refine existing standards and develop new ones, mostly through various working groups. IETF members share technology with Internet Research Task Force members and recommend standards to the Internet Engineering Steering Group (IESG), which works with IAB.

IETF is divided into nine areas: applications, internet services, network management, operational requirements, routing, security, service applications, transport, and user services. Each area has one or more working groups responsible for creating a standard or resolving a problem. A working group often begins as the result of an informal Birds of a Feather (BOF) session at an IETF event.

Internet Research Task Force and Internet Research Steering Group

The Internet Research Task Force (IRTF) is a task force of IAB. It consists of various research groups that work in the areas of Internet protocols, applications, architecture, and technology. IRTF is managed by the IRTF chair and the Internet Research Steering Group (IRSG), which consists of various research group chairpersons and other researchers.

The duties of IETF and IRTF look similar; however, IRTF tends to focus on longer-term research issues (using fewer people in a less formal structure, doing more research-oriented work), whereas IETF focuses on shorter-term issues of creating standards (using more people in a more rigid bureaucracy, which is needed to create formal standards).

Internet Network Information Center

The Internet Network Information Center (InterNIC) handles the registration of Internet domain names and manages the database of these names. This process is currently undergoing changes. One possibility being reviewed is to have more than one registration provider. Also, some lawsuits are pending as to whether a fee may be charged for registration and who would be the entity authorized to collect the fee.

Internet Assigned Numbers Authority

The Internet Assigned Numbers Authority (IANA) maintains the Internet Protocol (IP) numbers of the Internet, ensuring that each domain is unique. In addition to IP addresses, IANA is the central registry for other Internet-related numbers and data. IANA is located at the Information Sciences Institute of the University of Southern California.

World Wide Web Consortium

Tim Berners-Lee invented the WWW while working at the European Laboratory for Particle Physics (CERN). Now he works at the Massachusetts Institute of Technology (MIT) and is director of the World Wide Web Consortium (W3C).

W3C is an international, vendor-neutral industry consortium funded by commercial members, which works with vendors and other standards bodies to develop the Web-related protocols of the Internet, such as HTTP, HTML, and URLs.

W3C is hosted in the United States by the MIT Laboratory for Computer Science (MIT LCS), in Europe by the Institut National de Recherche en Informatique et en Automatique (INRIA), and in Asia by the Keio University Shonan Fujisawa campus.

Other Standards Organizations

In addition to the ISOC and its related organizations, other standards organizations have an influence on the Internet, as they have on other aspects of the computer (and most other) industries. These include the International Organization for Standardization (ISO), American National Standards Institute (ANSI), European Computer Manufacturers Association (ECMA), Institute of Electrical and Electronics Engineers (IEEE), Open Group, Open Software Foundation (OSF), X/Open, and others. Among these, ISO has a wide variety of working groups that conduct research on a broad spectrum of topics, such as paper sizes and photographic film, although electrical and electronic engineering aspects of research problems are specifically excluded from the ISO charter.

Commercial Companies

In addition to the standards bodies involved in the evolution of Internet protocols, corporations have an influence, which is not surprising given the increasing commercial viability of the Internet. Companies such as Microsoft, Netscape, and Sun Microsystems have large stakes in protocols and interfaces used on the Internet. Sometimes these interfaces are de facto standards, sometimes they remain proprietary, and sometimes they are given to standards bodies.

Microsoft has given the core ActiveX technologies to the Active Group, working under the Open Group. It is directed by a steering committee of twelve vendors. Netscape worked with the ECMA to create a standardized version of JavaScript, called EcmaScript. Sun Microsystems is currently working to get Java recognized as an ISO standard.

RFCs and Internet-Drafts

Internet technical documents are available in two main formats: RFC documents and Internet-Drafts. RFC documents have existed since 1969 and the days of ARPANET. They are the primary technical document series for the Internet development community. RFCs detail network protocols and interfaces and other computer topics related to the Internet; RFCs can also include meeting notes and, sometimes, humor (April Fool's Day and Christmas RFCs are traditional).

The RFC series of documents is named numerically. For example, RFC 2000 is IAB's "Internet Official Protocol Standards" document. An updated document doesn't use its old numeric name but is given a new name. For example, RFC 2000 replaces (makes obsolete) these RFCs: 1920, 1880, 1800, 1780, 1720, 1610, 1600, 1540, 1500, 1410, 1360, 1280, 1250, 1200, 1140, 1130, 1100, and 1083. When reading an RFC-based standard, be sure you have the latest document.

All RFCs are not alike. RFCs go through a review and feedback process, and during that time they are given various categorizations. The maturity level of an RFC (in decreasing order) can be standard, draft standard, proposed standard, experimental, informational, or historic. The requirement level of an RFC can be required, recommended, elective, limited use, or not recommended.

Internet-Drafts are another series of Internet technical notes. Internet-Drafts are working documents, mainly for the various IETF working groups. These draft documents are valid for six months, after which they are updated, replaced, or made obsolete.

Internet-Drafts are not numbered like RFCs; rather, they have unique filenames, often in the form of *draft-<Author>-<WorkingGroup>-<Topic>-<Version>.txt*.

In addition to RFCs and Internet-Drafts, a company with its own Internet protocol or interface will publish this information either on its Web site or through its developer information channel.

References

http://info.isoc.org/index.html

http://www.isi.edu/iab

http://www.ietf.org

http://www.irtf.org

http://www.internic.net

http://www.iso.ch

http://www.iana.org/iana

http://www.w3.org

http://www.ietf.org/1id-abstracts.html

http://ds.internic.net/rfc

http://ds.internic.net/rfc/rfcXXX.txt (where XXX is the RFC number)

http://www.isi.edu/rfc-editor

RFC 1800, "Internet Official Protocol Standards"

RFC 1796, "Not All RFCs Are Standards"

Plumbing

P
A
R
T

I

1

The ISO Open Systems Interconnection Model

THIS CHAPTER INTRODUCES the seven-layer International Organization for Standardization Open Systems Interconnection (ISO/OSI) data communications model. The ISO/OSI model divides the field of networking and network-aware applications into seven layers. The reasons for doing so include defining standards and reference models for each layer; breaking up the problem of network communication into smaller, more manageable problems; encouraging interoperability between vendor implementations; and easing development by creating the possibility that one could develop a particular layer and reuse existing implementations of other layers.

Figure 1-1 shows the seven-layer model.

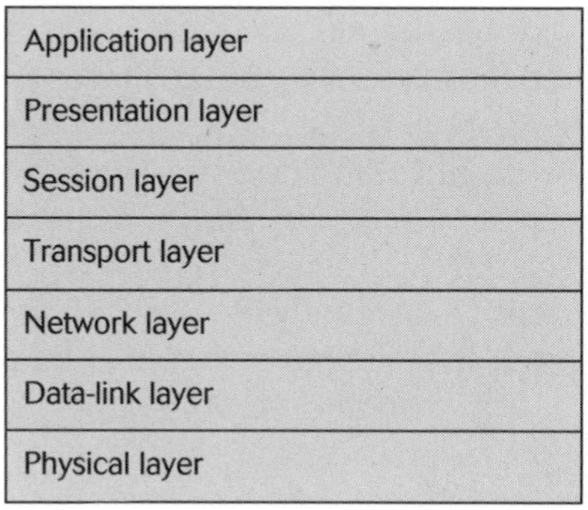

Application layer
Presentation layer
Session layer
Transport layer
Network layer
Data-link layer
Physical layer

Figure 1-1   *The ISO/OSI seven-layer data communications model.*

Conceptually, each layer interacts with its peer layer on a remote computer. In practice, except for the physical layer, each layer communicates with the layer above and below it. Each layer provides services to the layer above and uses the services of the layer below. Note that in actual practice, a computer might be running multiple, independent implementations of any one layer—for example, a computer could have multiple network cards running Ethernet or multiple cards running Ethernet and token ring, and so on.

In an ideal world, the ISO/OSI architecture would have been defined first, and the various pieces would have been built by commercial, research, and standards organizations next, with each piece being neatly categorized as belonging to some particular layer within the architecture. However, what actually happened was that a number of the technologies were developed first, and the seven-layer model followed. In some cases, new technologies were launched after the seven-layer model was designed, and they did not completely adhere to the model. But in spite of its less than ideal evolution, at the very least, the model has succeeded in accelerating the pace toward interoperability and the benefits that interoperability brings.

Let's look more closely at each of the seven layers and how they are used.

Physical Layer

The physical layer describes physical properties such as the electrical and mechanical characteristics of any media and the signals that transport information. This includes physical characteristics of cables and connectors, voltage levels, electrical current levels, and so on. For example, the physical layer describes the specification for untwisted wire pair (UTP) cable. Details of the physical layer are generally outside the purview of this book.

Data-Link Layer

The data-link layer transports data across the physical media. This layer is further divided into two separate layers: a logical link control (LLC) layer and a media access control (MAC) layer. This separation allows a single LLC layer to use different MAC layers. The MAC layer deals with physical addresses such as those used by Ethernet and token ring. These addresses are burnt into the network cards by the manufacturer. Physical addresses should be distinguished from the logical addresses, such as IP addresses, that the network layer deals with. For the sake of completeness, descriptions of some data-link layer implementations, such as Ethernet and token ring, are included in Chapter 2, "Basic Transports and Plumbing."

Network Layer

While the data-link layer is concerned with physical addresses, the network layer deals with logical addresses. The network layer provides connections and routing between two nodes on a network.

The network layer also provides connection-oriented services such as X.25, or connectionless services such as Internet Protocol (IP), that are used by the transport layer. An example of a major service provided by the network layer is routing.

Examples of protocols at the network layer include IP and Internet Control Message Protocol (ICMP).

Transport Layer

The transport layer provides services that are quite similar to the network layer. Some network layers provide a quality of service that ensures reliability. However, not all network layers do. Part of the functionality that the transport layer provides is to guarantee reliability. One justification for the existence of the transport layer is that in some situations, the bottom three layers (physical, data-link, and network) are provided by a telecommunications carrier. The subscriber can ensure reliability by running an appropriate transport layer protocol in such situations.

Transmission Control Protocol (TCP) is a widely used transport layer protocol.

Session Layer

The session layer provides functionality to establish, manage, and disconnect sessions. A session is a logical connection between two different end points. The session layer doesn't always need to be used; for example, when applications use a connectionless transmission model, a session layer protocol is obviously absent. In a connectionless model, every data packet that an application sends has complete destination information, similar to a letter that one mails using the postal service. In a connection-oriented model, some work is performed to set up a logical connection or circuit before actual data transmission takes place. When the data transmission is complete, more work is performed to terminate the session. The best example is a telephone call. Some work is performed to establish a connection when you dial, and then the telephone rings at the other end. The data transmission begins when one party says "Hello." After one of the parties hangs up, the telephone company again performs some work to disconnect.

The session layer also tracks which end of the session transmits data, a functionality called "dialog management."

Simple Mail Transport Protocol (SMTP), File Transfer Protocol (FTP), and Telnet are examples of popular protocols that span the session, presentation, and application layers.

Presentation Layer

The presentation layer provides the means for two protocol stacks to negotiate the syntax of data that each end will transmit to the other. Because there is no guarantee of a common data syntax, the presentation layer also provides data translation services when required.

Application Layer

The application layer is the highest layer in the ISO/OSI model, and it uses the services of the presentation layer (and indirectly the other layers) to execute a specific application. The application could be electronic mail exchange, file transfer, or any other network-aware application.

Figure 1-2 shows the ISO/OSI model and some of the popular protocols that operate at the different layers.

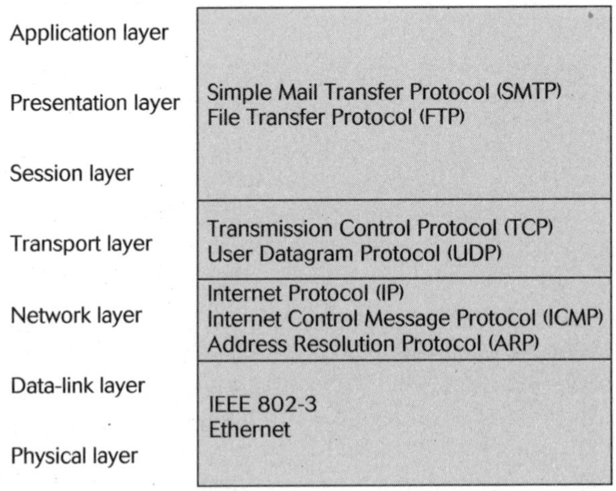

Application layer	
Presentation layer	Simple Mail Transfer Protocol (SMTP) File Transfer Protocol (FTP)
Session layer	
Transport layer	Transmission Control Protocol (TCP) User Datagram Protocol (UDP)
Network layer	Internet Protocol (IP) Internet Control Message Protocol (ICMP) Address Resolution Protocol (ARP)
Data-link layer	IEEE 802-3 Ethernet
Physical layer	

Figure 1-2   *The ISO/OSI seven-layer model and some popular protocols.*

Terminology

It would be a gross but effective oversimplification to say that the Internet consists primarily of seven kinds of devices. Most of these devices work at the physical, data-link, or network layers of the ISO/OSI model. The terms representing these devices are used throughout the book, so I'll take some time to provide a brief overview of them here.

Repeaters

Repeaters operate at the physical layer of the ISO/OSI model and are primarily used on local area networks (LANs) to extend the segment length. A repeater simply echoes a signal it receives, boosting the signal strength. Repeaters are also used in bus topologies to extend the length of a bus. Figure 1-3 shows a typical configuration in which a repeater is employed.

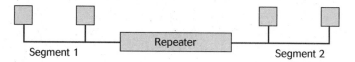

Figure 1-3   *A repeater and segments.*

In Figure 1-3, the repeater extends the length of the LAN bus from the length of segment 1 to the length of segment 1 plus the length of segment 2.

Repeaters are transparent; in other words, other devices (such as host computers, routers, and so on) cannot detect their presence. A repeater can translate data from one physical medium to another, for example, from Ethernet to Fiber Distributed Data Interface (FDDI), but the two segments connected by a repeater must have identical LLC implementations. They can both be Ethernet or both be token ring, for example, but they cannot be a mix of the two. This is because repeaters have no idea how to make use of data-link layer services.

Bridges

Bridges operate at the data-link layer. As mentioned earlier in this chapter, part of the data-link layer is the MAC layer. Each node has a network interface card (such as an Ethernet or token ring network card) that has a unique MAC address. Bridges operate by recognizing the MAC addresses in the data frames they receive and selectively forwarding the frames over different ports. Consider Figure 1-4 on the following page.

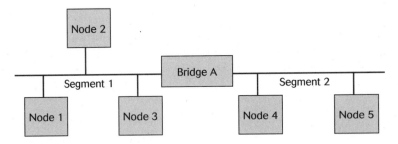
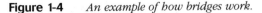

Figure 1-4   *An example of how bridges work.*

Frames sent from a node to another node on the same side of the bridge are not forwarded. For example, frames sent from node 1 to nodes 2 or 3 are not forwarded. Frames sent from a node to a node on the other side of the bridge are forwarded by the bridge. For example, frames from node 1 are forwarded to node 4.

A bridge can have multiple ports. In other words, a bridge can connect more than two LAN segments. A bridge forwards packets by building a table that associates each given MAC address with a bridge port or a LAN segment. A bridge can also operate by examining each frame, which might contain instructions as to how the frame should be routed.

One important advantage provided by bridges is that they reduce unneccesary traffic on LAN segments by dividing the collision domain on a LAN from one large domain to multiple smaller subdomains. This increases network capacity for data transmission and reduces data collisions that occur as a result of multiple nodes transmitting at the same time.

A bridge can also act as a store and forward device, completely receiving a frame before forwarding it over a port. This allows a bridge to perform calculations to validate the frame, using the cyclical redundancy check (CRC) contained within the frame. Bad frames are dropped and not forwarded. This helps in network utilization because only a single LAN segment carries the bad frame, and other segments are spared the useless exercise of transporting a bad frame.

Bridges come in two broad types. A *local bridge* connects two local segments of a LAN. A *remote bridge* connects two LAN segments across a wide area network (WAN). The way a bridge works is similar to a router, the difference being that the bridge accomplishes the connection at the data-link layer rather than at the network layer, as routers do.

Bridges are capable of translating data between different MAC layers. For example, a bridge could take an Ethernet frame and forward a token ring frame over a different port, as shown in Figure 1-5.

Figure 1-5 illustrates computer 1 sending a frame to the bridge. The frame wends its way through the physical layer (layer 1) and the MAC part of the data-link layer (layer 2) and into the LLC part of the data-link layer (layer 2). From there, the data is sent to different data-link and physical layers, and then on to computer 2.

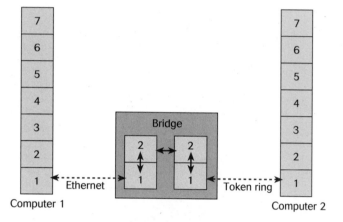

Figure 1-5   *A bridge translating data between two different media.*

Routers

Routers operate at the network layer. In contrast to bridges, which forward packets based on tables that store physical addresses (such as Ethernet addresses), routers forward packets based on tables that store logical addresses (such as IP addresses). Routers are extremely complicated beasts, and a number of large companies derive a considerable portion of their revenue by selling routers. One often comes across the term *multiprotocol router,* which simply indicates that a router can understand multiple network layer protocols, such as TCP and Internetwork Packet Exchange (IPX).

Switches

There is some confusion about what exactly a *switch* is. The classical definition is that at the data-link layer a switch operates very much like a bridge. In this definition, the difference between a bridge and a switch is that a bridge operates like a store and forward device, whereas a switch does not. As soon as a switch decodes the destination address, the switch starts transmitting the frame over the appropriate port. This can happen even while the rest of the frame is being received. The advantage in such a scheme is that a switch can operate faster than a bridge. The disadvantage is that a switch will forward all frames, including bad frames. Strictly speaking, this type of a switch is called a LAN switch, but a lot of old literature refers to it simply as a switch.

That was the definition of a switch as applied primarily to LANs. The modern day definition of a switch, especially when applied to the Internet, is radically different. The modern day switch is a WAN switch rather than a LAN switch. A switch is still a device that operates primarily at the data-link layer, but the same switch also has some limited knowledge of the functionality at the network layer. Because of this additional functionality, it would be more appropriate to compare a modern day switch to a router than to a bridge.

To summarize this, the modern day switch competes with a router to be a faster replacement for the router. The classical switch competed with a bridge to be a faster replacement for the bridge.

A modern day switch decodes a data packet to extract the network layer address. The network layer address is somehow (for example, by using Address Resolution Protocol) mapped to a port on the switch. Subsequent data packets sent between the same source and destination are switched at the data-link layer rather than at the network layer, which is used by routers to accomplish the same task. Switches also do not participate in any routing protocols, such as Routing Information Protocol. Another advantage of modern day switches is that they provide for other applications, such as Virtual Lans.

Gateways

A *gateway* is usually a combination of software and hardware that connects two different networks that use different protocols. Gateways typically operate at the network layer and above. Some gateways, called *application gateways,* forward data from one network to another but also accomplish protocol translation while doing so. An example would be an e-mail gateway that converts two different forms of e-mail protocols. At times the term *gateway* is applied to a situation in which no protocol translation is involved, but data is simply forwarded from one network to another. The gateway in that case is the piece of software and hardware that joins the two networks. One characteristic of a gateway is that it will have multiple network layer addresses, for example, multiple IP addresses.

Hosts

A *host* is usually a computing device running a network protocol such as TCP/IP. A host typically also has some application software that causes TCP/IP packets to be sent and received. A host usually exchanges data with other host computers, and a lot of activity on the Internet comes from managing the information flow among host computers. Examples of a typical host are routers, PCs, servers, proxy servers, gateways, and so on.

Nodes

The term *node* is simply a shorthand way of saying "repeater, bridge, router, switch, gateway, or host."

2

Basic Transports and Plumbing

IN THIS CHAPTER, I'LL DESCRIBE SOME OF the basic transport protocols and devices used on the Internet, including modems and network standards.

Modems

A *modem,* short for modulator/demodulator, is a communications device that converts digital signals into analog signals and vice versa, thus enabling computers (which use digital signals) to transmit information over standard telephone lines (which use analog signals). After the digital signals generated by a computer to be sent to another computer are converted, the modem feeds the analog signals into the basic telephone system (also called the plain old telephone system, or POTS). At the receiving end, another modem changes the analog signals it receives from the telephone system into digital form and transfers them to the recipient computer.

CCITT, a French acronym for the International Telegraph and Telephone Consultative Committee, has established a number of standards for data communications, including protocols for modems, networks, and facsimile transmission. In 1993, CCITT changed its name to the International Telecommunications Union, and it is now known by the acronym ITU. The table on the following page summarizes some of the ITU's protocols for modems. The table is not exhaustive. Especially absent are entries related to vendor-specific protocol implementations. Also, the term *bps* stands for *bits per second.* A character consists of 8 bits, plus a start bit and a stop bit—in other words, it takes 10 bits to transmit one character.

Protocol	Data Transfer Rate
V.34	28800, 26400, 24000, 21600, 19200, 16800, or 14400 bps
V.32 bis	14400, 12000, 9600, or 7200 bps
V.32	9600, 4800, or 2400 bps

An initiating modem attempts to connect at the highest possible protocol and then falls back to the next protocol if the modem at the other end of the connection does not support the higher protocol. For example, in the case of the modulation protocols above, the fallback order is as follows: the initiating modem attempts to use the V.34 protocol. If that attempt fails, the modem tries V.32 bis and then V.32 if its second attempt fails as well. Once it has settled on a particular protocol, the modem attempts to transmit at the highest possible speed within the protocol and fall backs to a lower speed if the line is noisy and errors are encountered.

Modems also use error detection protocols and correction protocols. These protocols permit detection of garbled data and, in some cases, the computation of the original data without requiring that the data be retransmitted. Once a modulation protocol has been negotiated, modems negotiate an error detection and correction algorithm in a similar manner. Examples of error detection protocols are Microcom Networking Protocol (MNP) levels 1, 2, 3, and 4 and V.42, also referred to as Link Access Protocol for Modems (LAPM). In this case, the fallback order is from V.42 to MNP 4 to MNP 3 to MNP 2 to MNP 1. Note that the use of modem error detection protocols and correction protocols does not obviate the need for error checking at a higher level—within a file transfer protocol, for example. Error checking within a file transfer protocol is necessary because data might be lost between the computer and the modem, perhaps due to buffer overruns, and that loss will not be detected by a modem's error detection and correction protocol.

Modems also attempt to compress the data they transmit. The table below summarizes a few of the transmission standards.

Transmission Standard	Comments
MNP level 3	Removes start/stop bits by making the transmission synchronous; data is organized into blocks.
MNP level 4	Data is organized into blocks (as with MNP 3), but block size depends on line quality. More efficient than MNP 3.
MNP level 5	Similar to MNP 4, but with added data compression. Efficiency depends on data.
V.42 bis	Efficiency depends on data.

The fallback scheme proceeds from V.42 bis to MNP 5, MNP4, MNP3, and so on and then to no compression method.

56-Kbps Modems

A recent development regarding modems has been the introduction of the 56-Kbps (kilobits per second) modem, which transmits over the Public Switched Telephone Network (PSTN). The PSTN began as an end-to-end analog system, transmitting sound in analog waveform from one end of the telephone connection to the other. Gradually, elements of the connection began using digital lines, and at those points the analog waveform was converted to digital signals by using sampling techniques. The trunk lines between exchanges were the first to go digital. Now, almost all of the PSTN's parts, except for the proverbial last mile from the local exchange to the consumer, have become digital.

Classical modems generate an analog signal that the PSTN digitizes by sampling (at a rate of about 8000 times per second). The digital signal is transmitted to the server or Internet Service Provider (ISP), where it undergoes a digital-to-analog-to-digital transformation. 56-Kbps modems work on the assumption that the connection at the server or ISP is a digital connection. This is illustrated in Figure 2-1.

Figure 2-1   *A 56-Kbps modem connection.*

The 56-Kbps modem's higher speed results from the fact that no analog-to-digital conversion occurs, and thus no sampling errors are introduced. In practice, the modem's speed is reduced from a theoretical 64 Kbps to about 56 Kbps because some digital values cannot be used for transmission—their resulting analog tones are lost or distorted on some lines—and because federal regulations limit the capacity of a telephone line. Finally, 56-Kbps modems are asymmetrical in that they provide up to a 56-Kbps transfer speed in one direction and a 28-Kbps transfer speed in the other direction. This is because there are two analog/digital conversions in one direction, but only one in the other direction.

Two major variants of this technology exist: K56flex, developed by Rockwell Semiconductor Systems, and x2, developed by U.S. Robotics (now part of 3Com). U.S. Robotics modems are based on digital signal processor chips. They depend on hardware for basic processing, and the rest of the processing is performed by software. This means that these modems are relatively easier to upgrade than modems based on Rockwell Semiconductor Systems chips. These variants are currently incompatible with each other and thus require that the two nodes communicating use the same technology. A new standard, called V.90, has been developed, which unifies these two technologies. It is rather early to tell, but preliminary trials with V.90 indicate that not all V.90 modems are equal and that the performance (in terms of transmission speed) achieved between two V.90 modems will be highly dependent on the exact software and hardware used within the modems. Although efforts are being made to reconcile the two technologies, that reconciliation is far in the future at the time that this book is going to press.

Ethernet

This section uses the term *Ethernet* in a generic sense to represent all of its flavors. Ethernet, developed by Xerox, is a widely used standard for LANs. Ethernet LANs are suitable for use with applications that require periodic data transmission at high rates. Ethernet workstations use what might seem to be an undisciplined approach to transmitting data. An Ethernet workstation transmits data when it determines that no other workstation is transmitting data on the wire. While transmitting, the workstation also listens to the line in case another workstation has also started transmitting. If a collision is detected, each workstation waits for a random amount of time before transmitting again. Varying algorithms are proposed if further collisions are detected on subsequent retransmissions. One algorithm calls for waiting an exponentially increasing amount of time. This scheme of regulating communication line traffic is called Carrier Sense Multiple Access with Collision Detection (CSMA/CD).

Ethernet network access cards are made by a wide variety of manufacturers. A standards body assigns a range of addresses to each manufacturer. This helps ensure that each Ethernet card has a unique address. Ethernet transmission of data occurs in variable-length frames, such as the one depicted in Figure 2-2.

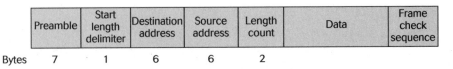

Preamble	Start length delimiter	Destination address	Source address	Length count	Data	Frame check sequence
Bytes 7	1	6	6	2		

Figure 2-2 *An Ethernet frame.*

Each frame has a source and a destination address. However, Ethernet is a broadcast technology in that every workstation receives every frame transmitted on the cable connecting the workstations. Although a workstation is expected to ignore those frames destined for other workstations, this process works on an honor system. Legitimate users (such as protocol analyzers) and not-so-legitimate users (such as network hackers) might operate a workstation in what is called *promiscuous mode,* whereby the workstation passes every frame to its upper layer software instead of ignoring those frames addressed to other workstations.

Ethernet workstations are typically connected in either a bus or star topology. Ethernet switches and bridges are used to connect multiple buses (or LANs). The switches and bridges forward frames that are destined for a workstation on a different LAN. Effectively, switches and bridges reduce the size of collision domains and ensure that a larger percentage of network resources is used for meaningful transmissions (those that do not result in frame collisions). Various types of cables are used to connect Ethernet nodes. The table below lists some of those cable types and their maximum segment lengths.

Cable Type	Maximum Segment Length
10Base5	500 meters
10Base2	500 meters
10BaseT	100 meters

Token Ring

Token ring technology comprises two major standards. The first, IBM's Token Ring network, continues to be positioned by IBM as a prime LAN technology. The other, developed by the Institute of Electrical and Electronics Engineers (IEEE), is the IEEE 802.5 standard. In practice, the IEEE 802.5 standard closely resembles the IBM Token Ring standard, although the two standards, of course, do have some differences. The main difference is that the IBM Token Ring specification requires a star topology and twisted-pair wiring, while the IEEE specification does not.

An IEEE token ring LAN is configured in a ring topology and uses a short message, called a *token,* to determine which node is allowed to transmit information. (A frame on the network consists of a token and associated data, either user data or control information for token ring management.) The token is passed around the ring, and only a station that has the token can transmit data. A station that has the token but does not have any data to transmit passes the token to the next station. Recall that the Ethernet network standard does not include such a mechanism. Ethernet stations rely on detecting collisions while transmitting rather than on avoiding collisions prior to transmission. On a token ring network, collisions cannot occur while transmitting data. A "busy" token (a token marked as in use and carrying the information being transmitted) circulates until it reaches the destination node. That node indicates it has received the data by setting a flag in the token. The token makes its way back to the sending station, which removes the attached message, clears the flag, and releases the now free token onto the ring.

The IBM Token Ring network uses tokens exactly as described above, but as a result of the network's different topology the token travels a different path. Instead of being connected to one another in a physical ring, nodes are connected in star fashion to a central hub called a MultiStation Access Unit (MSAU), also known as a Multistation Access Unit (MAU) or even as a Smart Multistation Access Unit (SMAU). In a one-way, logical (if not physical) circle, the MSAU passes the token from station to station along this star path. Each MSAU can connect up to 8 stations, and up to 33 MSAUs can be connected together, lengthening the logical ring.

Token ring networks have a number of fault-tolerant features. For example, one computer on the network, designated the monitor station, checks for tokens that circulate endlessly because of problems with the sending device and ensures that only one token is circulating the ring at a time. Also, all the computers in the ring help to isolate faults on the network through a process called *beaconing,* in which a computer noticing a fault sends a special signal (called a *beacon*) along the network. That computer continues sending the beacon until it receives a beacon from the next computer upstream. Eventually, the computer immediately downstream from the problem is the computer sending the beacon. Because the beacon identifies the station sending the beacon as well as the identity of the station immediately upstream, stations can use this information to attempt a reconfiguration and remove the damaged portion of the network from the ring. Specifically, MSAUs can use beaconing to detect faulty stations, stations powered off, and faulty portions of the network (including faulty cables) and bypass them.

In both the IEEE 802.5 and the IBM standard, a token consists of 3 bytes:

- A start delimiter byte that signifies the start of the token.

- An access control byte that specifies priority and reservation values for the token. The priority value is used to allow some stations on a token ring network to have a higher priority (and, thus, a greater data transmission capability). Each station has a preassigned priority value, and only stations with a priority value higher than or equal to the priority value in the token can use the token for transmitting data.

- An end delimiter byte that indicates the end of the token.

Token ring LANs are suitable for applications that require a guaranteed minimum rate of data transmission and some fault detection/repair capabilities. Token ring LANs typically provide a data transmission speed of 4 to 16 Mbps (megabits per second).

Fiber Distributed Data Interface

Fiber Distributed Data Interface (FDDI) is a networking technology gaining more and more usage and is typically used as a backbone system to connect multiple LANs. Allowing data transmission at speeds of 100 Mbps, FDDI is also used to provide a high-speed connection between large and/or fast computers.

Defined by ANSI (the American National Standards Institute) as well as by ISO (the International Organization for Standardization), the FDDI standard describes the physical layer (of the ISO/OSI seven-layer communications network model) utilizing fiber-optic cable in a dual-ring LAN. (The ANSI and ISO standards are completely compatible.) The dual rings provide fault tolerance. Each FDDI station is connected to both the rings, dubbed the primary ring and secondary ring. A single failure will isolate a failed station. Multiple failures can cause a ring to be broken up into isolated "ringlets" with no communication possible among the ringlets. FDDI also defines a media access protocol that prescribes a token-passing mechanism. Each FDDI station has a unique 6-byte address.

T1/T3 Lines

Traditionally, T1 and T3 lines were used to connect two widely separated LANs. T1 lines carry data at a rate of up to 1.544 Mbps, whereas T3 lines can operate at 44.763 Mbps. A T1 line consists of twenty-four 64-Kbps channels that can be used for different purposes. For example, a few of the channels might carry voice data, while the rest might carry all other data, including graphics and video. Nowadays, the T1 line is also used to connect an Internet server to an ISP, especially by small organizations providing their own Web site servers.

Integrated Services Digital Network

Widely adopted by public telephone carriers, Integrated Services Digital Network (ISDN) is a family of protocols defined by CCITT and aimed at developing a strictly digital worldwide communications network. Because the line from the subscriber to the local telephone switching station, the trunk line between the switching stations, and the local line to the destination are all digital, ISDN does not require any analog-to-digital conversions and thus provides end-to-end digital connectivity. ISDN also offers greater bandwidth than the plain old (analog) telephone system (POTS again) and can carry voice and other data (computer transmissions, music, and video, for example) simultaneously. Another advantage of ISDN is that it can complete the call setup much faster (by a factor of five or six) than regular analog telephone lines.

ISDN consists of two different protocols, Basic Rate Interface (BRI) and Primary Rate Interface (PRI), one of which needs to be chosen at installation time. PRI can be considered the equivalent of a T1 line. BRI is the more widely implemented standard for ISDN and consists of three separate channels:

- A 16-Kbps D (for *data*) channel that carries ISDN control and signaling data
- A 64-Kbps B (for *bearer*) channel that can carry voice or other data
- Another 64-Kbps B channel that can carry voice or other data

North American telephone companies still have some way to go to completely support ISDN signaling. As a result, sometimes an ISDN line's B channel might support only 56 Kbps and not 64 Kbps. Since no standards for compression on ISDN lines exist yet, ISDN data travels in uncompressed form. The two B channels can be used to simultaneously transmit voice and other data or to transmit the same data to two different locations. The two B channels can also be combined into a single channel to get higher bandwidth to a single location, a procedure known as *inverse multiplexing*.

The defined standard for inverse multiplexing is an extension of the Point-to-Point Protocol (PPP) called *multilink PPP.* (PPP is described in Chapter 3.) However, products (in particular, ISDN modems) implementing this standard are not widely available. Many ISDN modem manufacturers use a proprietary solution for inverse multiplexing. This necessitates that the terminal adapter (the ISDN modem) be the same on both sides of an ISDN connection.

ISDN can be ordered from your local telephone company but is not available everywhere. Still, ISDN can work over existing copper telephone wires. The telephone company tests the copper wire and, if the wire is satisfactory, adds equipment at the customer's premises as well as at the branch exchange. Note that the equipment installed on the customer end provides power and signaling into the network. Thus, when the customer's premises lose power, even voice telephone calls cannot be made unless a separate POTS line is available.

Frame Relay

Frame relay is a packet-switching protocol for use on WANs. Originally specified as a part of ISDN, it was implemented before the ISDN specification was formally adopted. Frame relay can be described as lightweight X.25, without the overhead of the error checking and recovery processes that X.25 uses to make up for the unreliability of analog lines. This is logical, given that X.25 was developed when most telephone lines were still analog, while frame relay began in this era of digital telephone lines (except for the literal last mile to the consumer). Frame relay is typically used to carry data but, with the installation of additional equipment, can also carry voice traffic.

Widely offered by public telephone carriers, frame relay is typically used in conjunction with a leased 56-Kbps, T1, or T3 line. Each subscriber location is assigned a port (consisting of special equipment interfacing between the public carrier and the subscriber). Permanent virtual circuits (PVCs), or permanent logical connections between nodes on the network, are established at subscription time between different frame relay ports. Each port connection is also assigned a committed information rate—the data transfer rate that the carrier guarantees to be available to that port. Although the port may use speeds higher than the committed information rate, in that case the carrier only makes a best attempt to transfer the data at the higher rate.

Frame relay is a connection-oriented protocol. Each call that is set up is identified by a Data Link Call Identifier (DLCI). The DLCI is allocated dynamically unless there are semipermanent virtual circuits, in which case the DLCI is allocated statically at registration time. The DLCI is included in all subsequent data frames. Note that the DLCI has meaning only at a local port. Thus, a PVC that exists between two stations can be identified by different DLCIs, one at each port. Figure 2-3 illustrates this situation.

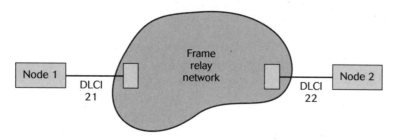

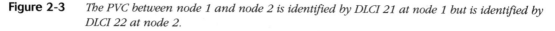

Figure 2-3   *The PVC between node 1 and node 2 is identified by DLCI 21 at node 1 but is identified by DLCI 22 at node 2.*

Frame relay pricing is distance insensitive and depends upon the Committed Information Rate (CIR) offered by the public carrier. The lower the CIR, the lower the price. Some carriers even offer a port with a zero CIR, while other carriers price frame relay service based on the number of PVCs. Compared to Asynchronous Transfer Mode (ATM), frame relay is extremely attractive in price.

One advantage of using frame relay is that a single port can use a number of PVCs and dedicate each one for particular usage. For example, one PVC can be dedicated for users dialing out. This scheme ensures that all available bandwidth is never consumed by only one particular type of traffic—traffic into a site, for example.

Switched Multimegabit Data Service

Switched Multimegabit Data Service (SMDS) is a high-bandwidth packet-switched service that can carry data at a rate from 56 Kbps to 34 Mbps. Like frame relay service, it is also widely offered by public telephone carriers. Unlike ATM and frame relay, which are connection oriented, SMDS is connectionless, meaning that it does not rely on virtual circuits. An SMDS port contacts another SMDS port by dialing a preassigned address, and the route a transmission travels is not predetermined. Public carriers also offer additional services, such as the ability to screen SMDS connections. SMDS charges consist of a fixed monthly cost and a usage cost. The fixed cost depends on the assigned bandwidth. Usage costs don't depend on the geographical separation between SMDS ports but simply on the volume of data exchanged between them.

Asynchronous Transfer Mode

ATM network technology evolved out of a desire to add statistical multiplexing to Synchronous Transfer Mode (STM) technology, currently in widespread use in the telecommunications industry. STM allows a "train" of data units to travel between two nodes of a communications network. Each data unit, called a *bucket,* or *wagon,* pertains to a different connection. (Note that ATM literature also calls the bucket or wagon a *packet* or *cell.*) Within a given time period, the train can travel between the two nodes multiple times. The frequency with which the train repeats the journey, the number of wagons in the train, and the size of each wagon add up to the capacity of the transmission link between the two nodes (ignoring overhead). Before data is transferred between two nodes, multiple connections are set up. A connection setup consists of assigning a particular wagon to a connection. That wagon remains assigned to that connection until the connection is torn down. If no data is traveling over the connection (for example, if both parties of a telephone conversation have stopped talking), the wagon travels "empty."

Obviously, network resources are wasted in the STM scheme. With STM, the wagon number (or position within the train) acts as a connection identifier. ATM modifies this scheme by having the connection identifier travel along with the data in a wagon, any wagon. With the ATM scheme, any time data needs to be sent, it is stuffed along with the connection identifier into the next empty wagon. The connection identifier is called a Virtual Circuit Identifier (VCI). As I said previously, ATM adds statistical multiplexing (which allocates available bandwidth dynamically) to STM. With STM, the number of connections is limited to the number of wagons. ATM has no such limitation. STM cannot dynamically take on more connections by taking advantage of the fact that some of the connections might be idle. ATM can hope that not all the initial connections will need to send data simultaneously and, even if they do, that some of the data is busy and can be buffered for a short while until some empty wagons are encountered.

ATM guarantees delivery of data in the order it is sent but does not guarantee that the data will be delivered. This guarantee of in-order delivery is made possible by the fact that ATM is circuit oriented, and hence all data flows along the same route. ATM is suited to carrying data for a wide variety of applications, including applications that are loss-insensitive but delay-sensitive (for example, real-time audio/video—obviously, the amount of loss must be limited and cannot be extremely large); loss-sensitive but delay-insensitive (for example, file transfer—obviously, the delay must be limited and cannot be extremely large); loss-insensitive and delay-insensitive; loss-sensitive and delay-sensitive.

ATM is by nature a connection oriented service. To provide for "legacy" applications that use a connectionless paradigm, a connectionless service can be implemented on top of ATM. The connectionless service itself is implemented as an ATM application—in other words, it does not constitute an integral part of ATM—that uses the concept of connectionless servers. Connectionless servers utilize routing information contained in the cells and redirect the data to the ultimate destination.

ATM does not fit cleanly into the ISO/OSI model. ATM is most closely related to the data-link layer (layer 2) of the model but also involves flow control, virtual circuits, and other aspects of upper layers. Also, adaptation layers have been defined to carry higher-layer protocols such as IP over ATM. In the end, ATM should be considered not a product but a technology enabling various applications, including backbone service for high-speed networks, LAN emulation, ATM to the desktop, and others.

ATM Standards

As has been said (irreverently), "The nice thing about standards is that there are so many to choose from." The Comité Consultatif International Télégraphique et Téléphonique (CCITT), whose functions have been taken over by the United Nations International Telecommunications Union (ITU) (http://www.itu.ch), defined broadband ISDN based on ATM. The American National Standards Institute (ANSI) (http://www.ansi.org) appointed a working group, T1S1.5, to define ATM standards. A group of communications companies, government agencies, and research groups working to promote ATM started the ATM Forum, which now has a membership of more than 400. The IETF is also involved in defining ATM standards. All these organizations are developing standards that are sometimes complementary and sometimes not quite. An example of these standards is the LAN Emulation Standard, developed by IETF, and RFC 1577, "Classical IP and ARP over ATM," from IETF, which defines how IP may be transmitted over ATM. See the section "LAN Emulation" later in this chapter for more information.

ATM Header Format

An ATM cell consists of a 5-byte header followed by 48 bytes of data. There are two header formats, a UNI header, which is used for user/network interfaces, and an NNI header, which is used for network to network interfaces. Four bits are allocated for Generic Flow Control (GFC) in the UNI header, which controls congestion by limiting the amount of data entering the network. The Virtual Channel Indicator (VCI) identifies an ATM session. The VCI may be permanently or dynamically allocated. The Virtual Path Identifier (VPI) allows a number of VCIs to be grouped together. VPI and VCI values are meaningful only at a particular node, and the values change as the data moves from one link to another. The Payload Type Indicator (PTI) field indicates whether the data within the cell represents user data or control information. This field is also used to show whether congestion has been noted. The Cell Loss Priority (CLP) field is used in a number of ways. One is to hold control information indicating that the user has exceeded a negotiated data transfer rate. For cells carrying user data, this could be set to indicate whether the user is willing to accept loss of data; for example, a database transaction would indicate that the user cannot accept any loss of data. A multimedia application would indicate that the user can accept some loss. The Header Error Check (HEC) field is a CRC check over the ATM cell header only. It does not include a CRC check over the data.

ATM Adaptation Layers

ATM is a connection oriented technology that transfers data in fixed-size cells of 43 bytes. Applications have a wider range of needs. To help meet the needs of applications, ATM defines adaptation layers that provide the various necessary interfaces.

ATM Adaptation Layer 1

Adaptation Layer 1 (AAL1) provides interfacing for applications that are described as constant bit rate. These are applications that generate a predictable pattern of traffic. The data must be transmitted in a sequential fashion with a relatively constant amount of delay.

ATM Adaptation Layer 2

Adaptation Layer 2 (AAL2) provides interfacing for applications that generate traffic in a nondeterministic manner and are termed variable bit rate.

ATM Adaptation Layer 3/4

Adaptation Layer 3/4 (AAL3/4) provides services for applications that work in a connectionless mode (that is, without setting up a circuit or session) and also for applications that generate data of variable size. The applications also expect data transmission errors to be detected. The data might be delayed during transmission without upsetting the application. An application can hand multiple units of data to the ATM layer without waiting for a previous data transmission to be completed.

ATM Adaptation Layer 5

ATM Adaptation Layer 5 (AAL5) is similar to AAL3/4 but has the requirement that applications expect the ATM layer to transfer only one unit of data at a time.

ATM Addresses

The ITU has defined an address format for public ATM networks (that is, ATM networks implemented by commercial data communications carriers). This format is based on telephone system numbering, and the addresses are referred to as E.164 addresses. The ATM Forum has also defined three ATM address formats for private ATM networks. Each of these formats is 20 bytes in length. The first format is based on the ITU E.164 format, the second on an IEEE 802 format, and the third on an ISO specification.

In the United States, ANSI handles registration of ATM addresses. (See http://www.ansi.org/regfact.html for more details.)

LAN Emulation

LAN Emulation (LANE) was a standard developed to let existing Ethernet and token ring applications and protocols work seamlessly over ATM. The idea was to encourage migration to ATM networks by providing an upgrade path that required the fewest changes. LANE provides virtual LANs; that is, workstations and servers that are grouped by function (such as security and application) rather than by the physical port of the bridge that connects them or the LAN segment on which they reside. LANE architecturally consists of four major components: the Broadcast and Unknown Server, the LAN Emulation client, the LAN Emulation Configuration Server, and the LAN Emulation Server.

Broadcast and Unknown Server

The Broadcast and Unknown Server (BUS) is responsible for address resolution. Traditional LANs such as Ethernet and token ring networks depend on broadcast frames for data transmission and address resolution, whereas ATM, as stated previously, is connection oriented. The BUS handles broadcast frames and also unicast frames for which the destination media access control (MAC) address or ATM address remains unresolved. The BUS receives Address Resolution Protocol (ARP) requests and sends these requests to all members of the emulated LAN. The BUS then receives ARP responses and forwards them to the station initiating the address query.

LAN Emulation Client

The LAN Emulation Client (LEC) runs on all nodes on the ATM network, including bridges, routers, switches, workstations, and servers. The LEC initiates connections and data transfer to other LECs. The LEC also requests mapping between MAC addresses and ATM addresses.

LAN Emulation Configuration Server

The LAN Emulation Configuration Server (LECS) is responsible for providing configuration information (such as the ATM address of the LANE server) and for tracking the virtual LAN on which each LAN Emulation client operates.

LAN Emulation Server

The LAN Emulation Server (LES) provides mapping between MAC addresses and ATM addresses. In typical configurations, the LES runs on the same node as the BUS.

To illustrate how all these services interact, consider the case in which a node needs to send data to another node. The steps that accomplish this transaction are:

1. The sending node issues an IP ARP packet.
2. The LANE/Broadcast server broadcasts this ARP packet.
3. The receiving node replies with its MAC address.
4. The sending node issues another ARP packet, requesting the ATM address of the receiving node, which is now identified by its MAC address.
5. The LAN Emulation server responds with the receiving node's ATM address.
6. The sending node can now form an ATM virtual circuit and accomplish the data transfer.

ATM Fault Tolerance

The LES and the BUS constitute a single point of failure that can prove disastrous to an ATM network. Cisco Systems has developed the Simple Server Redundancy Protocol (SSRP) to take care of this situation. SSRP replicates configuration information stored in the LECS and monitors the state of health of the LES and BUS. When an

LEC (the client) attempts to connect (or autoreconnect in the case of LES/BUS failure), the LECS directs the client to a functioning LES (the server). Olicom has extended SSPR with a protocol named Dynamic Connection Redundancy (DCR). DCR provides a way for a client to dynamically locate a functional LES or BUS.

IP Over ATM

On a classical LAN, IP packets are framed as the data part of an Ethernet frame. RFC 1577, "Classical IP and ARP over ATM," defines how IP can be run by using ATM instead of Ethernet or some other technology. This capability is implemented as part of the ATM adaptation layer that runs above the ISO/OSI data-link layer. The advantage of IP over ATM (IPOATM) is that it is more efficient; you do not have to first put IP packets into LAN frames. The disadvantage of IPOATM is that MAC-level broadcast packets are not supported.

Multi-Protocol Over ATM

The Multi-Protocol Over ATM (MPOA) specification is an umbrella of specifications that attempts to unify a number of specifications or standards to achieve ATM internetworking. MPOA is being developed under the auspices of the ATM Forum. MPOA includes:

- IPOATM, a specification developed by IETF and described in RFCs 1577and 1483.
- LANE (a specification developed by the ATM Forum).
- Next Hop Routing Protocol (NHRP), a specification developed by the IETF and described in RFCs 2235, 2233, and 2232. NHRP defines address resolution and routing/queries between different subnets.
- Multicast Address Resolution Server (MARS), a specification developed by the IETF and detailed in RFC 2149. MARS defines how multicast and address resolution can be achieved over ATM.

Integrated Private Network to Network Interface (IPNNI), a specification developed by the ATM Forum. IPPNI defines a routing protocol similar to Routing Information Protocol (RIP) and Open Shortest Path First (OSPF).

ATM at the Desktop

LANE and IPOATM are, strictly speaking, transitional steps in migrating to ATM networks. Both try to hide the fact that the underlying network is an ATM network. However, to take advantage of ATM capabilities such as Quality of Service (QoS), the applications need to be enhanced. The ATM Forum first began defining a new set of APIs to achieve this enhancement. The problem with this approach, however, was that applications written using these APIs could run only on ATM networks. After a while, the ATM Forum changed its tactics; it now defines only how applications can set up, use, and tear down virtual circuits.

The ATM Forum also describes how applications can request QoS parameters and, in detail, the information (and the order of that information) that flows between the various networking layers. The syntax and semantics of APIs are left to the discretion of other standards bodies, such as the Windows Sockets (Winsock) and X/Open groups. The advantage of doing this is that applications written to the Winsock and X/Open APIs run on both ATM and non-ATM networks. Also, existing applications that do not use any QoS parameters run unmodified on ATM networks. Furthermore, because the Microsoft Winsock API is already connection oriented, it is fairly easy to add QoS parameters and still be able to write applications that can run on non-ATM networks.

Gigabit Ethernet

Approximately 100 companies have joined to form the Gigabit Ethernet Alliance, a group that is developing standards for a new generation of Ethernet technology. Prior to the Gigabit Ethernet technology, the two main branches of Ethernet technology were 10 Mbps Ethernet and 100 Mbps Fast Ethernet. Although Gigabit Ethernet is still a technology in progress and has not yet been widely deployed, some proponents of Gigabit Ethernet see it as a viable competitor to ATM. Predicting the outcome of an ATM versus Gigabit Ethernet battle is beyond the scope of this book. Suffice it to say that Gigabit Ethernet will provide data transmission rates on the order of 1 Gbps (gigabits per second) over distances of 300 meters to 10 kilometers. It's fairly clear that initially Gigabit Ethernet will be deployed as a backbone system, either in a LAN or WAN topology, although it's unlikely that Gigabit Ethernet will be deployed on desktops in the near future. In all probability, large configurations will have a three-tiered deployment consisting of Ethernet, Fast Ethernet, and Gigabit Ethernet.

The IEEE has appointed a committee called the 802.3z committee to lay down standards for Gigabit Ethernet. The 802.3z standard calls for Gigabit Ethernet to be delivered over two kinds of physical media, untwisted wire pair (UTP) and fiber-optic cable. As the technology currently stands, Gigabit Ethernet implementations work exclusively over fiber-optic cable. Gigabit Ethernet implementation over UTP remains, at least for now, a technology under development.

Current Gigabit Ethernet implementations are based on a full duplex fiber-optic channel between two stations. In other words, each Ethernet segment consists of only two stations, and each station has its own exclusive transmission channel. Thus, the technology is really based on collision avoidance. Relying instead on collision detection at the very high data transmission rate provided by Gigabit Ethernet would require stations to be extremely close to one another, because at very high speeds, the transmitting station would be able to put multiple data frames on the media before the first data frame arrives at the receiving station. Since the two stations could start transmissions simultaneously, multiple data frames may be lost unless the stations are close to each other. The Ethernet standard requires that at most one data frame transmitted by a station may be garbled and need to be retransmitted.

The 802.3z standard defines two technologies to increase the distance between Gigabit Ethernet stations: carrier extension and packet bursting. Carrier extension is a technique to artificially lengthen short frames (remember that Ethernet frames can be as short as 64 bytes) so that they appear 512 bytes long. This allows workstations to be situated farther apart and still detect collisions. Obviously, this technique wastes network bandwidth because an extra amount of data (which is discarded upon receipt) must be carried. Packet bursting alleviates this problem by allowing a station to transmit multiple frames, unlike on a classical Ethernet network, whereby a station sends a single frame at a time. The first frame is extended to 512 bytes, but the subsequent frames within the burst are not.

Cable Modems

A lot of homes in the U.S. already have access to a high bandwidth communications system in the form of existing cable networks. These networks are capable of carrying data at a rate of up to 30 Mbps. Cable modems allow computers to be connected to the Internet through the cable network, just as classical modems allow computers access through POTS. The cable network speed compares favorably with the 28.8 Kbps (or even 56 Kbps) that regular modems deliver. This higher speed is possible because the underlying media (the cable network) carries signals with a much higher bandwidth (on the order of 6 or 8 Mhz). Thus, cable modems can transmit and receive data using a broader spectrum. Although a regular modem is connected to a computer through a serial port, a serial port could not handle the rate at which cable modems deliver data. So cable modems require computers to have an Ethernet card, with which the cable modem is connected to the Ethernet transceiver. Accordingly, cable modems convert data from Ethernet to analog and vice versa. Because few widely adopted standards exist to govern this type of conversion, the computer and the server the computer is connecting to must both use the same brand of cable modem.

The cable modem's speed of up to 30 Mbps is in fact a theoretical one, and it usually gets watered down significantly for a number of reasons. One problem is that the server at the other end of a cable connection does not have a thick fat pipe to the Internet. Once the server has received the requested data, it can send it to the client quickly, but it may be a while before the server receives this data. Some companies, such as @Home, work around this problem by caching often-requested data at the server (called the head end).

Another problem hindering the cable modem's speed is the cable networks' design for "flooding," or the data flow from the head end to multiple consumers. No provision was made in the design for the consumer to communicate back or for point-to-point communication. Although one solution allows consumers to send requests through a regular modem using the telephone system, this results in an asymmetrical network in that the traffic capacity in one direction is significantly different from that in the other direction. Such a network is useful for applications that seek asymmetrical data flows (for example, Web browsing, through which a small data request possibly returns a large amount of data), but applications such as video conferencing that require high bandwidth in both directions do not work with this kind of system.

The cable networks' cable wiring itself is also a problem; splitters (to allow multiple televisions within a house) and cheap wiring slow transmission speeds. Add the fact that the bandwidth from the home to the cable provider is really shared by multiple consumers, and all of these factors combine to drop the cable modem's actual data transmission rate to the order of 1.5 Mbps, which is, of course, still nothing to sneeze at when compared to 28.8 Kbps or 56 Kbps.

xDSL

Digital Subscriber Line (DSL) technology—the x in the head is a variable and will change with the varieties of DSL—was designed to deliver higher bandwidth over existing copper telephone lines. Strictly speaking, the line is not digital in any way. An xDSL line is a plain copper wire with a digital modem at each end. One advantage of using xDSL technologies is that a plain old telephone will still work on an xDSL line, even when a home or office loses power. That's not true for ISDN.

The existing copper wire is capable of carrying signals with higher bandwidth (in the MHz region), and the limitation of 3.3 kHz on voice lines results from filters at the edge of the telephone network, not from the copper wire line itself. Because the signal on copper wire attenuates rapidly, bandwidth has a direct correlation with line length. For example, a 24-gauge wire is capable of carrying data at a rate of 1.544 Mbps over a distance of 18,000 feet but can carry data at the rate of 51.840 Mbps over 1,000 feet.

All of the technologies described below are similar in one respect: the telephone wire carries a high frequency signal generated by the telephone company. DSL technologies modulate the signal generated by the telephone company.

DS1/T1/E1

DS1/T1/E1 technology, originally developed by Bell Labs, multiplexes twenty 64-Kbps data streams into a single framed data stream. The multiplexed frame is 193 bits long, including the multiplexing/demultiplexing management overhead. Carrying a raw data stream of 1.5444 Mbps, the technology has come to be known as DS1 and, more popularly, as T1. A lot of these lines have been installed, with repeaters required every 6,000 feet or so. In Europe, where twenty 64-Kbps data streams are multiplexed into a single stream carrying data at the rate of 2.048 Mbps, the technology has been dubbed E1.

T1/E1 is used for LAN/WAN access (server access as well as private network access). Current uses also include connecting cellular towers, connecting routers, and so on. T1/E1 is not suited for residential use because of noise—signal crossover routinely limits the use of T1 to one line in a single 50-pair cable. Also, asymmetric systems that deliver more data to a residence and carry less data in the other direction make more sense for residential use than T1/E1 does.

Digital Subscriber Line/Integrated Services Digital Network

DSL/ISDN modems transmit data at a rate of 160 Kbps over copper lines up to 18,000 feet long. As with ISDN, this bandwidth is divided into two B channels that carry data at 64 Kbps and a D channel that can carry 16 Kbps. These are the modems used to provide ISDN Basic Rate Interface service.

High-Data-Rate Digital Subscriber Line

Used to connect cellular antenna stations, PBXs, Internet servers, and private data networks, High-Data-Rate Digital Subscriber Line (HDSL) leverages advances in modulation techniques to deliver data at a faster rate with fewer repeaters. Using two lines, HDSL can provide T1 capability (1.544 Mbps) over distances of up to 12,000 feet. HDSL can also provide E1 capability by using three lines instead of two. HDSL is symmetric; it provides the same data transfer capability in either direction.

Asymmetric Digital Subscriber Line

Asymmetric Digital Subscriber Line (ADSL) was developed after HDSL and is intended for uses that benefit from an asymmetric load capability, including Internet access, remote LAN access, video on demand, and so on. ADSL supports speeds in the range of 1.5 Mbps to 9 Mbps in the downstream direction (that is, from the network to the consumer). Upstream rates can vary from 16 Kbps to 640 Kbps. ADSL has a big advantage over ISDN in that power is fed into the copper cable by the telephone system—in other words, conventional phone service works even when local power is unavailable. ADSL has been standardized by ANSI and ETSI (European Telecommunications Standards Institute).

Some implementations of ADSL use a technique called carrierless amplitude/phase (CAP) modulation to modulate the signal on the line. As the name suggests, CAP modulation suppresses the carrier signal on the line before transmission. Although CAP modulation is simple and relatively inexpensive to implement, it can only carry data at a T1 rate and it is susceptible to interference. CAP modulation is not sanctioned as part of the ADSL standard by either ANSI or ETSI.

Another method of ADSL modulation, discrete multitone (DMT), divides the available frequency into 256 discrete channels and allows different channels to carry different amounts of data since higher frequency channels are more susceptible to noise. Adopted as a standard by both ANSI and ETSI, DMT can achieve higher speeds than CAP but, at least for now, is more expensive to implement.

Rate-Adaptive Digital Subscriber Line

Rate-Adaptive Digital Subscriber Line (RADSL) is simply ADSL with a provision for testing the line quality and length upon startup and adjusting the line speed. RADSL standards are still evolving, so it is unclear whether this adaptive process is a "once-only" or continuous phenomenon.

Very-High-Data-Rate Digital Subscriber Line

This is the fastest DSL technology, delivering data at a rate of 13 Mbps to 52 Mbps downstream and 1.5 Mbps to 2.3 Mbps upstream over a conventional copper wire at distances of 1000 to 4500 feet. Very-High-Data-Rate Digital Subscriber Line (VDSL) is probably the DSL technology furthest from being adopted as a standard.

Single-Line Digital Subscriber Line

Single-Line Digital Subscriber Line (SDSL) is similar to VDSL but has two major differences:

- SDSL is limited to 10,000 feet
- SDSL uses a single line

SDSL standards are still being developed and are at least a year (or more) from being firmed up.

The following table summarizes some of the xDSL information given above.

	Downstream Data Rate (from Network to Consumer)	Upstream Data Rate (from Consumer to Network)	Applications
DSL	160 Kbps	160 Kbps	ISDN service, voice and data communications
HDSL	1.544 Mbps using two twisted-pair cables	1.544 Mbps using two twisted-pair cables	T1, WAN, LAN, server access
HDSL	2.048 Mbps using three twisted-pair cables	2.048 Mbps using three twisted-pair cables	E1, WAN, LAN, server access
ADSL	1.5 Mbps to 9 Mbps	16 Kbps to 640 Kbps	Internet access, video on demand, LAN, RAS
VDSL	13 Mbps to 52 Mbps	1.5 Mbps to 2.3 Mbps	Internet access, video on demand, HDTV, LAN, RAS

Satellite

The quest to provide a fat pipe for access to the Internet has spread, literally from the earth to the sky. Satellite network technology has already progressed from laboratory prototypes to commercially available systems.

Hughes Systems has launched a service called DirecPC. (Recall that DirecTV is a system that provides cable channels for televisions using satellite networks.) The DirecPC system requires the consumer to install a small satellite dish and connect the dish (via cable) to the PC using an ISA card. DirecPC provides a transmission rate of up to 11.7 Mbps downstream. However, this bandwidth is really the capacity of a single transponder shared by multiple consumers. The real bandwidth a particular consumer receives is determined by the popularity of the system—by the ratio of transponders to users. Hughes claims that its system achieves a rate of 400 Kbps per user. Like some cable systems, DirecPC also requires that the consumer have a regular modem to send requests to the DirecPC system. The result is an asymmetrical network—capacity in one direction is significantly different from that in the other direction—useful for asymmetrical applications such as Web browsing. Applications such as video conferencing and basic telephone service, which require high bandwidth in both directions, do not work with such a system. DirecPC charges are based on the amount of data delivered, not on the connect time.

Another satellite/wireless–based system in the making is the Local Multipoint Distribution System (LMDS). One difference with LMDS is that rather than installing a satellite dish, the user installs a small antenna that communicates with a hub station. The hub station then communicates with a central site by using a satellite transponder. The LMDS cable is connected to the PC using an Ethernet card. LMDS divides the available network bandwidth into a number of channels. Although each channel is capable of carrying data at a rate of up to 50 Mbps, actual bandwidth achieved per user depends on a number of factors, including transmission clarity and number of users per channel.

Wireless LANs

With the growing popularity of Personal Digital Assistants, Windows CE machines, and laptop computers, wireless LANs are expected to become increasingly popular. The only question seems to be "when" rather than "if." The IEEE has recently finalized the IEEE 802.11 specification, which describes wireless LANs and a standard for their interoperability. In general, wireless LANs consist of three types of nodes: a client node, a server node, and an access node. The access node provides the same functionality (on a much reduced scale) as a cellular tower, acting as an intermediary between the client node and server node and as a store-and-forward device. The client node is simply the roaming device that initiates a data transfer by making a request, and the server node is the node that the client makes a request to. Wireless LAN technology provides for data transmission speeds of 1 Mbps to 2 Mbps at distances ranging from 200 feet to 1000 feet between the nodes.

Wireless LAN implementation is complicated because a client may send a request through one access device and then move into the vicinity of a different access device. In this scenario, the first access node needs to hand off responsibility to the second access node. Another complication is referred to as the "hidden node" problem. This phenomenon occurs when a wireless node is too far from another node to communicate directly with it, but both nodes are close enough to communicate with an access node. Yet another complication occurs because a wireless node can be expected to power down (to enhance battery life) and periodically wake up and poll the access node. This is another reason why the access nodes need to function as store-and-forward devices.

The IEEE 802.11 specification covers the physical as well as data link layers of the ISO/OSI model. The specification provides one standard for the infrared frequencies and two standards for radio frequencies. The adoption of two standards for radio constitutes a compromise between two camps of companies that are implementing wireless LAN technologies. One camp comprises Lucent Technologies, Digital Equipment, Persoft, and other companies supporting a technology called Direct Sequence, which uses a wide range of frequencies for data transmission. From the meager amount of field data available, it appears that Direct Sequence makes good use of network resources and is suited to installations with relatively fewer nodes. In the other camp, Xircom and a number of other companies employ a competing technology called *frequency hopping*. Frequency hopping provides data transmission utilizing both frequency and time domain variations. Because it can tolerate random noise better than Direct Sequence, this technology is more suited to actual field conditions. Both of these technologies provide for data transmission rates of 1 Mbps or 2 Mbps. The infrared standard also provides for a data transmission rate of 1 Mbps or 2 Mbps and does not require line-of-sight conditions between the two communicating nodes, although infrared signals cannot traverse walls, closed doors, and so on, as radio waves can.

The IEEE 802.11 standard specifies a single MAC layer. This facilitates interoperability and also allows for the possibility of a future MAC implementation in silicon that might have widespread usage and drive the costs of IEEE 802.11 LANs down. This MAC layer is a carrier sense, multiple access, collision avoidance scheme. (Recall that Ethernet technology uses the CSMA/CD [collision detection] protocol.) The standard specifies two algorithms to accomplish collision avoidance.

The first algorithm is the point coordination function (PCF), which is optional according to the IEEE 802.11 specification. The PCF is nondistributed in nature, in that the collision-avoidance intelligence resides in a single node. This node polls the various nodes, and this polling may give some nodes a higher priority than others. The PCF operates for a limited amount of time; it is periodically replaced with a distributed intelligence media access algorithm called the distributed coordination function (DCF). The DCF is the IEEE 802.11 specification's primary means of collision avoidance. The IEEE 802.11 MAC specification requires that Unicast frames be acknowledged by the receiver. Frame collisions can also be avoided by means of a handshake process whereby the sender first sends a request-to-send indication and awaits the receipt of a clear-to-send indication. Obviously, this scheme guarantees collision avoidance at the cost of optimal network utilization.

References

http://www.itu.ch

http://www.standards.ieee.org

http://www.ansi.org

http://www.adsl.com (ADSL Forum home page)

http://www.gigabit-ethernet.org

http://www.iol.unh.edu/consortiums/ge/index.html (Gigabit Ethernet Consortium)

RFC 2333, "NHRP Protocol Applicability Statement"

RFC 2332, "NBMA Next Hop Resolution Protocol"

RFC 2331, "ATM Signaling Support for IP over ATM—UNI Signaling 4.0 Update"

RFC 2226, "IP Broadcast over ATM Networks"

RFC 2225, "Classical IP and ARP over ATM"

RFC 2149, "Multicast Server Architectures for MARS-Based ATM Multicasting"

RFC 2022, "Support for Multicast over UNI 3.0/3.1–Based ATM Networks"

RFC 1932, "IP over ATM: A Framework Document"

RFC 1755, "ATM Signaling Support for IP over ATM"

RFC 1626, "Default IP MTU for Use over ATM AAL5"

RFC 1577, "Classical IP and ARP over ATM"

RFC 1483, "Multiprotocol Encapsulation over ATM Adaptation Layer 5"

3

More About Transports

THIS CHAPTER PRIMARILY COVERS THE PROTOCOLS that are at the network and transport layers (layers 3 and 4) of the International Organization for Standardization Open Systems Interconnection (ISO/OSI) seven-layer model.

Internet Protocol

The Internet consists of a number of host computers, as well as devices called *routers*. Several host computers are connected to form networks, with some of the networks forming islands. The islands of networks are connected by the routers. Each individual host computer and router must have a unique address so that data packets can be sent to and from that device. Internet Protocol (IP) defines a format for assigning addresses and also defines a mechanism for transferring unreliable data called a *datagram*. IP datagrams are encapsulated as the data portion of lower-level protocols such as Ethernet, token ring, Asynchronous Transfer Mode (ATM), and Point-to-Point Protocol (PPP).

IP Addressing

IP version 4 (IPv4) defines network addresses as 32 bits long. IP addresses are assigned by Internet Assigned Numbers Authority (IANA), whose Web site can be found at http://www.iana.org. IP addresses are divided into a number of categories called *classes*. These classes are summarized in Table 3-1 on the following page.

Table 3-1 IP Address Classes

Class	Most Significant Bits of Address	Network Mask Value	Number of Addresses Available	Number of Hosts Available
Class A	0000	255.0.0.0	128	16,777,214
Class B	1000	255.255.0.0	16,384	16,382
Class C	1100	255.255.255.0	2.1 million	253
Class D (multicast)	1110	N/A	N/A	N/A

IP addresses are often represented in *dotted decimal* notation. Each byte (with a value between 0 and 255) is separated from other bytes by a dot, or period. An example is the IP address 225.25.25.25. Each IP address has an associated 32-bit *mask value*. The mask, when ANDed with the address, divides the address into two parts. One part is a network address that uniquely identifies the network, and the other is a host address that uniquely identifies the host within a given network.

An organization that receives a class B address might not have 16,000-odd computers, but it is likely to have a couple of hundred computers at each of a number of sites. The organization can simply redefine the network mask value, extending the number of bits that constitute the mask. This process is called *subnetting;* it reduces the number of addresses available for host computers and routers but increases the number of available networks.

Some IP addresses have a special meaning and cannot be assigned to a computer or router. An address of all 0s or all 1s has special meaning, as do some others. Examples include those shown in the following table.

Network Mask Value	Meaning
255.255.255.255	Broadcast on this net only
<net>.255.255.255	Broadcast on class A network
<net>.255.255	Broadcast on class B network
<net>.255	Broadcast on class C network
<127>.any	Internal host loopback (address)

Multicast Addressing

Class D IP addresses are reserved for use as multicast addresses. IP addresses from 224.0.0.0 through 239.255.255.255 are multicast addresses. A multicast address represents a group of IP nodes that form a logical group. The IP nodes (which might be a collection of routers and host computers) can be widely distributed geographically. Just as in nonmulticast addressing, some multicast addresses are reserved and have special meaning. For example, 224.0.0.1 represents all subsystems on a given subnet, 224.0.0.2 represents all routers on the subnet, and so forth. Full details can be found in RFC 1918, RFC 1519, RFC 1518, and RFC 1466.

IP Datagrams

An IP datagram consists of an IP header followed by data that is often called the *payload*. The IP header is of variable length. Figure 3-1 shows an IP header.

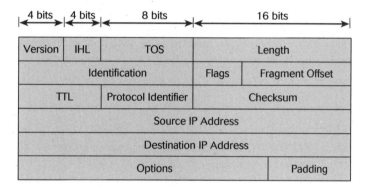

Figure 3-1   *An IP header.*

The Version field of an IP header consists of 4 bits and is usually set to 4, denoting the IP protocol version. As use of IP version 6 (IPv6) becomes more widespread, the usual value will change to 6. IP version 5 was an experimental implementation.

The Internet Header Length (IHL) field consists of 4 bits and specifies the length of the IP header in number of 32-bit words. IP headers contain a minimum of 20 bytes.

The Type Of Service (TOS) field consists of 8 bits and represents special processing requests for the packet—low delay, high throughput, and so forth. See RFC 791 for full details. A wide range of routers on the Internet currently ignore this field.

The Length field consists of 16 bits and represents the total length of the IP packet in number of bytes. This implies that an IP packet cannot be longer than 65,535 bytes, and since the IP header itself consumes a minimum of 20 bytes, the payload can be 65,515 bytes at most. All hosts and routers are required to support an IP packet with a minimum size of 576 bytes (20 bytes for the IP header, 512 bytes for the payload, and 44 bytes for options or the protocol header of lower layers). This requirement ensures that IP packets of this size will be transmitted unfragmented. (Fragmentation is explained later in this section.)

IP datagrams are themselves encapsulated within frames, such as an Ethernet or token ring frame. IP can flow over a number of different lower-layer protocols, and an IP datagram can also traverse multiple networks, each of which might have a different implementation of the lower-layer protocol. Thus it is extremely difficult to set an IP datagram size that can be encapsulated within the lower-layer protocol.

IP solves this problem by letting the IP datagram size be independent of the frame size. The IP implementation breaks the IP datagram into multiple fragments. Each fragment has the IP header but carries different data. The More Fragments (MF) bit in the Flags field is set in all but the last IP header. Note that a single source computer might send multiple IP datagrams that are being fragmented. So the source IP address will not suffice. A port number will work, but port numbers exist only for higher-level protocols such as UDP and TCP.

This is where the Identification field in the IP header is used. All the siblings that comprise a single IP datagram will have the same protocol identifier. The Identification field is assigned by the sending IP. The 13-bit Fragment Offset field indicates the position of the payload for purposes of reassembling the original data stream. The first fragment has an offset value of 0. Note that each fragment travels as a separate IP packet, and different IP packets can take different routes. Hence the reassembly can only be accomplished at the destination and not by an intermediate router. RFC 815 and RFC 791 discuss fragment reassembly techniques.

The Flags field consists of 3 bits. The highest-order bit is always set to 0. The next bit is called a Don't Fragment bit and, when set, indicates that fragmentation is unacceptable. The last bit is called a More Fragments bit and is cleared in the last fragment but set in all other fragments.

Because of increasing network speeds, problems might arise with fragmentation. Consider the following calculation. Let's assume that IP packets of the maximum size are being sent and that these are getting fragmented. That means a total of $2^{16} - 1$ packets of $2^{16} - 1$ bytes will be sent before an identifier is reused. This calculation ignores protocol overhead for lower layers as well as the IP protocol overhead. The total number of bits is thus approximately $2^3 \times 2^{16} \times 2^{16}$, or 2^{35}, which is approximately 32 gigabits. With speeds of 1 gigabit per second, the identifier will be reused in about 32 seconds. (The actual time will be less, since the calculation presented involves an artificial, best-case scenario.)

The Time To Live (TTL) field is used differently than originally intended. The original intent was that this quantity would represent a number of seconds for the packet to live, and 255 seconds seemed a reasonably long time. The problem is that it is extremely difficult to estimate a meaningful value to set. Another problem is that a router that sees the packet for milliseconds still has to take a full second off the counter. Effectively, this field is used as a counter indicating the number of nodes (host computers, routers, and so forth) that a packet has visited—that is, a *hop count*. Each node decrements the count, and a packet is discarded when the counter hits 0. The default value is 32, but this field can be set to any value by the source IP.

The Protocol Identifier field consists of 8 bits and indicates the upper-level protocol embedded within the payload of the IP packet. Table 3-2 shows some typical values.

Table 3-2   Typical Values of the Protocol Identifier Field

Value	Protocol
1	Internet Control Message Protocol
2	Internet Group Management Protocol
6	Transmission Control Protocol
7	Reserved
8	Exterior Gateway Protocol

See RFC 1700 for the latest and complete details on the protocol identifier. The protocol identifier is used by IP to decide which upper layer the packet should be handed to—for example, User Datagram Protocol (UDP) or Transmission Control Protocol (TCP).

The Checksum field provides a means of verifying that the IP packet was not distorted during transmission. The checksum is a 16-bit one's complement of the 16-bit sum of the header contents. Note that the checksum has to be recomputed at each node, including the intermediate nodes because the header will change (for example, in the TTL field).

The Options field is of variable length and might be absent. (A length of 0 is permissible.) The field has two defined formats:

- A single byte containing the option type
- A variable number of bytes containing the option type, length, and value

The option type consists of three subfields:

- A COPIED flag. A value of 1 indicates that the option should be copied to all other fragments of the datagram. A value of 0 indicates that the option should not be copied to the other fragments.
- An option class that consists of 2 bits. A value of 0 is used for control, and a value of 2 is used for debugging. Values 1 and 3 are reserved.
- An option number consisting of 5 bits.

Table 3-3 summarizes IP option types. Note that the numerical value of the option type can be computed from the information provided. See RFC 791 for complete details.

Table 3-3   IP Options

Option Class	Option Number	Length in Bytes	COPIED Flag	Description
0	0	1	0 or 1	Indicates end of option list.
0	1	1	0 or 1	Used for padding within the option list.
0	2	Variable	1	Specifies security options. Not used on the Internet; replaced by IP security.
0	3	Variable	1	Used to specify loose source routing and to record the route taken by a datagram. With source routing the source IP stack specifies the exact route for the benefit of intermediate routers.
0	7	Variable	0	Used simply to record the route. Each router records its address in the space provided and updates a pointer indicating where the next router should record its address.
0	8	4	1	A stream identifier introduced for benefit of the now defunct Atlantic Satellite network. Not used; allowed only in IP version 5.
0	9	Variable	1	Used for strict source routing and to record the route. Strict routing differs from loose routing in that intermediate routers have less flexibility in routing the packet.
2	4	Variable	0	Used to record the time at which the datagram was processed.

The Padding field is an extra space that is used to guarantee that the IP header ends on a 32-byte boundary. For example, if the Options field ends at 30 bytes, the Padding field would consist of 2 bytes. If the Options field ends at 50 bytes, the Padding field would consist of 14 bytes.

Ports

Applications must be able to identify with whom or what they want to communicate. An IP address is not enough, since multiple applications will probably be running simultaneously on a given computer, and these might be communicating with different applications on different or even the same remote computer. For example, assume that application A running on computer 1 wishes to communicate with application B running on computer 2. At the same time, application C running on computer 3 needs to communicate with application D running on computer 2. One could assign multiple IP addresses to computer 2 and have application B use one IP address and application D use another IP address. But this would be wasteful of IP addresses. Instead, the communication is accomplished with the use of ports. As described later, UDP and TCP both use ports to identify the sending and receiving application. The source and destination IP address identify the computers on which the applications are running. Thus a pipe, or data stream, is uniquely identified by a set of four values:

- A source IP address
- A source port value
- A destination IP address
- A destination port value

Some important and well-known applications are assigned port values. These pre-assigned values are only used for the server. The port values at the client are dynamically allocated. A single port at the server might have multiple streams since a number of clients might be connecting to it. This is acceptable because the combination of the four values noted above is still unique. These port values are gaining in importance because firewalls, described later in this chapter, sometimes filter based on port values.

User Datagram Protocol

UDP provides an extremely thin wrapper around IP. It provides a datagram service (a connectionless, unreliable delivery service), but uses IP to do the actual work. It adds functionality to IP in the following ways:

- It provides multiplexing and demultiplexing (via UDP ports) so that multiple applications on a client or server or both can have their own streams of datagrams.
- It provides a means of calculating a checksum and verifying the validity of the datagram received. Recall that IP provides a checksum that validates only the IP header, not the IP data. UDP checksums are generated over the entire UDP packet, including the UDP data.

UDP does not provide more reliability than that offered by the underlying IP implementation. Applications using UDP must provide for retransmission of lost datagrams, detection of duplicate datagrams, reassembly (datagrams might arrive in a different order than the order in which they were sent), flow control, and so forth.

A UDP packet consists of a UDP header and UDP data encapsulated as the data portion of an IP packet. The format of the UDP header is shown in Figure 3-2.

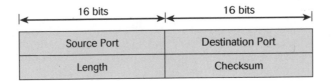

Figure 3-2   *A UDP header.*

The fields in the UDP header consist of 16 bits each. The source and destination ports are used to multiplex and demultiplex datagram streams so that they are delivered to the correct application. The Length field denotes the length of the UDP data packet, including the header, in number of bytes. This length does not include the IP header or options. The UDP checksum is computed by (logically, not physically) prepending a pseudoheader to the UDP packet and then calculating the checksum over the pseudoheader plus the UDP packet. The format of a UDP pseudoheader is shown in Figure 3-3.

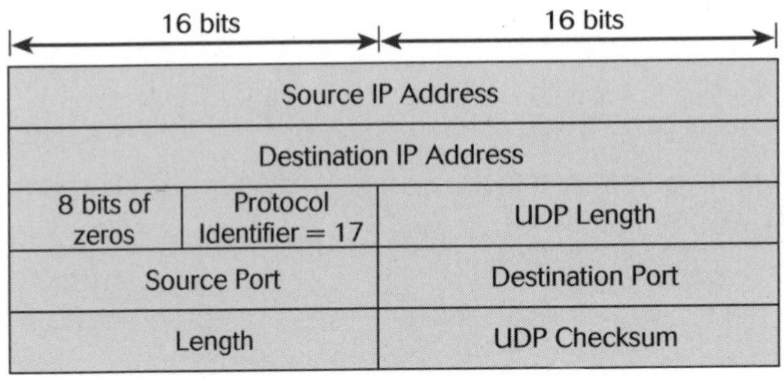

16 bits		16 bits	
Source IP Address			
Destination IP Address			
8 bits of zeros	Protocol Identifier = 17	UDP Length	
Source Port		Destination Port	
Length		UDP Checksum	

Figure 3-3   *A UDP pseudoheader.*

The checksum is generated by first computing the 16-bit one's complement of the bytes in the UDP pseudoheader, UDP header, and UDP data. (In other words, the one's complement of that sum is the checksum.) If the checksum is not generated, a value of 0 is transmitted for the checksum. If the actual calculation yields a checksum of 0, a checksum with all bits set to 1 is sent instead. A detailed description of the UDP pseudoheader can be found in RFC 768, "User Datagram Protocol."

Transmission Control Protocol

IP provides an unreliable mechanism for transferring data between two computers. This is referred to as a "send-and-pray" mechanism. TCP provides a reliable, error-free, full-duplex channel between two computers. TCP uses IP to transfer the data but also provides mechanisms (internal to TCP) that take care of lost and duplicated IP datagrams. TCP also takes care to rearrange IP datagrams that arrive at the destination out of order. In other words, TCP provides a reliable stream of data that is in the exact sequence generated by the source.

TCP accomplishes all this by breaking the stream of data into packets small enough to fit inside IP datagrams. These are called *segments*. The IP datagrams are numbered and sent using an acknowledgment-with-retransmission paradigm. The receiver sends an explicit or implicit acknowledgment for each IP datagram. The sender waits for some time and then retransmits the IP datagram if it does not receive an acknowledgment.

Sliding Window Protocols

A sliding window protocol defines a window in terms of the number of data packets that a sender is allowed to transmit simultaneously. This is the maximum number of packets that the sender can transmit without receiving any acknowledgment. Figure 3-4 on the following page shows an example of a sliding window protocol.

In the figure, the size of the sliding window is set to 4. The upper part of the figure shows the sender with a window of 4 indicating that the first four data packets, numbered 1 through 4, can be sent. If the receiver acknowledges packets 1 and 2, the window then advances to cover packets 3 through 6.

Sliding window protocols make efficient use of the network. Most networks are full duplex, which means that data can be carried both to and from a computer simultaneously. Without a sliding window protocol, a computer must transmit one data packet, wait for the acknowledgment, transmit the next packet, and so forth. This method of transmission uses the network in only one direction at a time, and is called a *stop-and-wait* protocol. In its simplest form, a sliding window protocol has a window size of 1 and in effect reduces to a stop-and-wait protocol. Note that the window size need not be defined statically. TCP is an example of a sliding window protocol that dynamically changes the window size to suit network conditions.

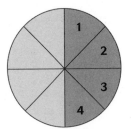

Sender sliding window = packets 1,2,3,4

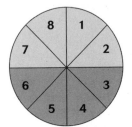

Sender sliding window = packets 3,4,5,6

Figure 3-4   *A sliding window protocol.*

TCP Segment Header

Figure 3-5 shows a TCP segment header, also commonly referred to as simply a "TCP header." TCP segment headers are of variable length, with a minimum size of 20 bytes.

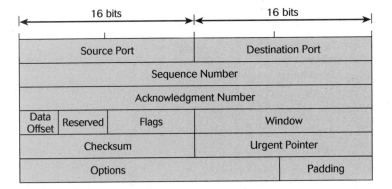

Figure 3-5   *A TCP segment header.*

Before I discuss the individual fields in the header, it is worthwhile to point out that the header does not contain any information on the number of data bytes within the TCP segment. The TCP segment is carried as the payload of an IP datagram, and the length of the TCP data is computed as the length of the IP payload minus the size of the TCP header.

As mentioned earlier, TCP provides a reliable stream mechanism between two processes. The end points of the reliable data stream are uniquely identified by:

- The Source IP Address field in the IP datagram header
- The Destination IP Address field in the IP datagram header
- The Source Port field in the TCP segment header
- The Destination Port field in the TCP segment header

The sequence number and the acknowledgment number identify the position of the data within the data stream being sent and the position of the data within the data stream being acknowledged as having been received safely. The sequence number identifies the position of the first data byte within the data stream. The acknowledgments are cumulative—that is, the Acknowledgment Number field identifies the largest sequence number that has been safely received. The receiver might wait for a while before sending an acknowledgment, in the hope that more TCP segments will be received and a single acknowledgment can be sent. Also, the sender might delay sending data for a short time in the hope the application will soon have more data to send and the data can be sent as a single segment. In general, it is more efficient to send a larger single segment than to send multiple smaller segments.

Applications such as terminal emulators that echo for the far end of a TCP connection typically echo a few characters at a time and expect data to be sent immediately. Thus such applications do not work well when the sender buffers the data for a while. To account for this possibility, TCP provides a push option. The push option is indicated within the Flags field, a 6-bit field that consists of the values listed in Table 3-4.

Table 3-4 Flags Field Values

Value	Description
32	URG: urgent data present
16	ACK: acknowledgment of receipt of data
8	PSH: push the data to the application as soon as possible
4	RST: reset the TCP connection
2	SYN: synchronize the connection; note the sequence number within the TCP segment header
1	FIN: end of transmission; this end is ready to terminate the connection

The Data Offset field consists of 4 bits and indicates the number of 32-bit words within the TCP header. This field is required because the TCP header is variable in length. If necessary, the header is padded with bytes set to 0.

The Reserved field is set to 0 and consists of 6 bits.

The Window field is related to the sliding window concept explained earlier. The value indicates the number of bytes the sender is willing to accept (the new size of the receiver window). The position of the data the receiver is willing to accept is indicated by the sequence number.

The Checksum field is used to detect data transmission problems. The value is the 16-bit one's complement of the one's complement sum of all 16-bit words in the TCP segment, pseudoheader, header, and data.

Figure 3-6 illustrates the TCP pseudoheader.

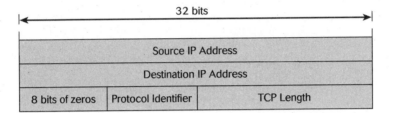

Figure 3-6   *The TCP pseudoheader.*

The Urgent Pointer field of the TCP segment header is a 16-bit value. The sum of the urgent pointer plus the sequence number represents the sequence number of the last byte of urgent data. TCP protocol implementations allow a higher-level application to be informed of the existence of urgent data and to recognize that all urgent data has been read.

The Options field is of variable length. There are a number of different options, and more than one might be present in a TCP header. The options have two different formats:

- A single byte containing the option type
- A variable number of bytes containing the option type, length, and value

The various option types are explained below. These descriptions are not exhaustive—for full details, see RFCs 1323, 1185, and 1072, among others.

End Of Option List

The End Of Option List option is indicated by an option type of 0, a length of 1, and no value. This option indicates the end of the option list.

No Operation

The No Operation option is indicated by an option type of 1, an option length of 1, and no value. This option is used for padding to align the next option on a 32-bit boundary.

Maximum Receive Segment Size

The Maximum Receive Segment Size option is indicated by an option type of 2, a length of 4, and a value that is the maximum receive segment size. This option is used by the sender to indicate the size of the largest TCP segment it is prepared to receive; it can be set only when the TCP connection is being set up (when the SYN flag bit is set). In the absence of this option, the default receive segment size is set to 536 bytes. This is the default IP datagram size (576 bytes) minus the minimum size of the IP datagram header (20 bytes) and the minimum size of the TCP header (20 bytes). This option is useful because it allows the TCP connection to send data using the largest possible segment size.

Window Scale

The Window Scale option is indicated by an option type of 3, a length of 3, and a value that indicates the amount by which the receive window should be scaled.

This option is extremely useful on WANs, which are characterized by high latency and high throughput. The maximum window size with TCP is normally 65,535 bytes (the most bytes a 16-bit number can hold). Consider a cross-country connection. The round-trip time can easily be 30 milliseconds. At 4 MB/sec, it would take the sending TCP 16.4 milliseconds to transmit the window size. This is not an efficient usage of resources, and the problem is only likely to get worse as transmission speeds increase. The Window Scale option provides a means of increasing the maximum window size beyond 65,535 bytes. A Window Scale value of n indicates that the actual window size should be treated as (window size) $\times$ (2^n). Since the scaling is a power of 2, which is the same as doing a bitwise shift, this option is sometimes also known as the Window Shift option. Obviously, this option can only be used when both ends of a TCP connection agree.

SACK Permitted

The SACK Permitted option is indicated by an option type of 3 and a length of 2. This option indicates that the sender is willing to receive selective acknowledgments. This option can be sent only when the TCP connection is being initiated. Please see the next section for an explanation of Selective Acknowledgement (SACK).

SACK

The SACK option is indicated by an option type of 5 and a variable length. This option indicates that some data blocks have been received but some intermediate data blocks are missing. This option allows some efficiency. Consider the case in which 1000 blocks of data are transmitted and every block except block number 500 is received. If the SACK option is used, only one block (number 500) needs to be retransmitted.

TCP Echo and TCP Echo Reply

The TCP Echo and TCP Echo Reply options are used together to estimate the round-trip time for the TCP connection. The TCP Echo option is indicated by an option type of 6. This option can be sent only when initiating a TCP connection. The TCP station that receives the TCP Echo option responds with the TCP Echo Reply option. (The TCP Echo Reply option has a type value of 7 and a length of 6.) The round-trip time estimate is important since too low an estimate results in unnecessary re-transmissions whereas too high an estimate results in the sender wasting time waiting for an acknowledgment that may never arrive.

As with the IP header, the Padding field in the TCP segment header is an extra space that is used to guarantee the TCP header ends on a 32-byte boundary.

Zero Window Probe

TCP provides a mechanism called the Zero Window Probe. Once the sending node has transmitted a full window of data, the sender waits for the receiver to send an acknowledgment. If that acknowledgment is lost, a deadlock occurs and no more data is transmitted. To prevent this from happening, the sending node is allowed to send a single byte of data, called a Zero Window Probe, beyond the end of the sliding window. The receiving TCP node is expected to respond to the Zero Window Probe. The response might indicate that the receiving node is indeed unable to accept more data (perhaps because the application above the TCP protocol stack has yet to process the previous data). Thus a Zero Window Probe might result in a situation in which no more data can be sent, but that does not mean the TCP connection should be shut down. The first Zero Window Probe is sent after the normal timeout interval has elapsed. Should the receiver not respond, more probes are sent in a timeout interval that increases exponentially.

Silly Window Syndrome

RFC 1122 describes a TCP phenomenon called Silly Window Syndrome. Silly Window Syndrome can lead to significant performance problems and inefficient network use. Silly Window Syndrome occurs when the receiving TCP window is very small. This might be because the receiving window is indeed very small. It might also be because of a combination of circumstances involving outstanding data that has not been acknowledged and a small amount of data that needs to be sent.

Consider a case in which the receiving window size is 1024 bytes and the sending TCP sends two 512-byte segments. The receiving TCP acknowledges the first segment. When this acknowledgment arrives, the sending TCP computes the window as 512 bytes. Let's assume that the TCP application asks for a 64-byte segment to be sent urgently and for another 512-byte segment. The sending TCP sends the 64 bytes and also 448 (512 – 64) bytes. If the receiving TCP acknowledges the urgent data, the window is computed by the sender as only 64 bytes. The effect is that small TCP segments are sent, which causes inefficient use of resources.

RFC 1122 provides a detailed explanation of how to avoid Silly Window Syndrome. The major points of the solution involve both the sending and receiving node. The sending TCP should delay sending when the segment to be sent is obviously too small, unless the data has the push option set. The delay must be related to the round-trip time. The receiving TCP should not advance the window by small amounts. The receiving TCP should also wait for a while before sending acknowledgments, in the hope that more data will arrive and a single acknowledgment can be sent. Again, the delay must be related to the round-trip time and should not be so long that the sending TCP retransmits the data.

Efficient operation of TCP depends on properly adjusting the various operational parameters and is a challenge in itself, even when a transmission network with known characteristics (such as a LAN) is considered. When one considers other networks, such as WANs and wireless networks (which are more prone to data loss and disconnection), efficient TCP operation is even more of a challenge, and an entire book could be written on this subject alone. Some of the parameters that can significantly affect TCP operation include:

- Adjusting the receive window size
- Correctly estimating the round-trip time
- Deciding when to measure the round-trip time
- Deciding when acknowledgments are sent

Internet Control Message Protocol

Internet Control Message Protocol (ICMP) is used by hosts and routers to exchange control information, such as errors and bootstrapping information. Logically, ICMP is an application protocol that sits above IP. Figure 3-7 on the following page shows the ICMP message format and how the ICMP message is encapsulated within an IP packet.

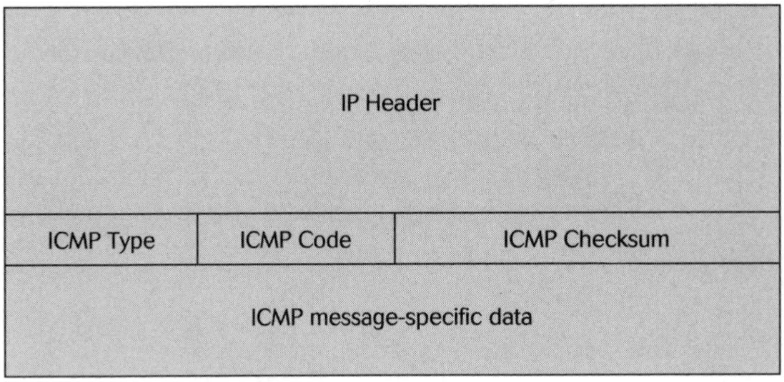

IP Header		
ICMP Type	ICMP Code	ICMP Checksum
ICMP message-specific data		

Figure 3-7   *The ICMP message format.*

The ICMP message-specific bits are the payload of the IP packet. The protocol identifier within the IP header is set to 1. Note that even though logically ICMP is an application protocol, ICMP is considered an integral part of any IP implementation because ICMP affects IP operations.

Certain ICMP messages are generated only by routers, while some ICMP messages are generated by both routers and host computers. An ICMP message should never be generated in response to an ICMP message. This prevents infinite recursion of ICMP messages. In particular, ICMP messages are not generated in the following cases:

- When an ICMP error message is received
- When a datagram addressed to a loopback, broadcast, or multicast address is received
- When a noninitial IP fragment is received

Two classes of ICMP messages are defined: ICMP error messages and ICMP query messages. RFC 1256, RFC 1122, RFC 792, and others provide details about ICMP messages, including their complete formats. Some of the ICMP messages that are important enough to have been named are described later in this section.

In general, a router sends an ICMP message to report an error. If a router discards a datagram because of a lack of resources (such as memory), it sends an ICMP message named *source quench* to the originator of the datagram. A router sends an ICMP message named *destination unreachable* when it receives a data packet for a destination that it does not know how to reach. A router sends a host an ICMP message named *redirect* to advise it that a different router is more appropriate for sending data packets to a particular destination. ICMP error messages include the header of the IP datagram that caused the error. This allows the originator to figure out which destination is causing problems, since multiple conversations could be going on at the same time. Hosts generally send ICMP messages to test network connectivity. They do this using an ICMP message named *echo*. A host that receives an echo message responds with an ICMP *echo reply* message. These messages are used to test network connectivity and also to estimate the round-trip time.

Address Resolution Protocol and Reverse Address Resolution Protocol

IPv4 assigns a logical address to every computer, router, and so forth. With advances such as a video on demand, every TV is a potential candidate for an IP address—not to mention every lightbulb, air conditioner, heater, toaster, and microwave. Since IP addresses are only logical addresses, some association must be made between IP addresses and physical device addresses, such as Ethernet and token ring network card addresses. Address Resolution Protocol (ARP) provides a means of locating a physical device address when an IP address is known. This functionality is called *address resolution*. ARP is defined in RFC 826.

With the advent of IP running over media such as ATM, RFC 2320 and RFC 1390 have defined an ARP-like mechanism for address resolution for a network that uses ATM instead of Ethernet. Reverse Address Resolution Protocol (RARP) also defines a way to obtain an IP address when a physical device address is known. One case in which this would be useful is when a diskless computer boots up. RARP is defined in RFC 1931 and RFC 903.

Figure 3-8 shows the format of the ARP/RARP message.

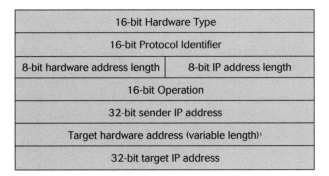

| 16-bit Hardware Type |
| 16-bit Protocol Identifier |
| 8-bit hardware address length | 8-bit IP address length |
| 16-bit Operation |
| 32-bit sender IP address |
| Target hardware address (variable length)[1] |
| 32-bit target IP address |

[1] The target hardware address length is specific to the ISO second layer protocol being used. For Ethernet the length is 48 bits.

Figure 3-8   *The ARP/RARP message format.*

The Hardware Type field identifies the type of hardware involved. For example, a value of 1 indicates an Ethernet LAN. The Protocol Identifier field defines the protocol that the message contains. The only defined values correspond to ARP and RARP. In the case of ARP, the sender fills out its own hardware address along with its own IP address and the target IP address. The ARP message is either broadcast or sent as a directed packet to a default gateway.

The Operation field identifies the nature of the message. The defined values are shown in the following table.

Operation Value	Description
1	ARP request
2	ARP response
3	RARP request
4	RARP response

Internet Group Management Protocol

A node with a normal IP address (a nonmulticast address) can dynamically join and leave a multicast group. Internet Group Management Protocol (IGMP) provides a means of joining and leaving multicast groups. When a router receives an IP datagram with a multicast address, the router must know whether members of that multicast group exist on the local net in order to forward the IP datagram. Routers gain this knowledge using IGMP.

A router periodically sends an IGMP query message that is effectively a poll message. This query message is sent with an IP TTL value of 1, thus limiting the message to the local subnet. Every node that receives the query starts a random timer. When the timer expires, the node sends a report that is itself addressed to the multicast group. Each node that has not yet sent a report simply cancels its timer and desists from sending a report. This reduces unnecessary traffic. If a router receives no responses, it assumes that no members of the multicast group exist on the local network. Nodes that join a multicast group immediately transmit a report for that group, and that report is usually repeated once or twice. RFC 1112 provides complete details of the IGMP query and response messages.

IGMP is similar to ICMP in that it is a logically higher protocol that uses the services of IP. In practice, since IGMP affects IP protocol behavior, IGMP is considered and implemented as part of IP. To avoid network traffic problems, no ICMP error messages are generated when a message addressed to a multicast address is received.

Figure 3-9 shows an IGMP message. The IGMP-specific bits are the payload of an IP packet.

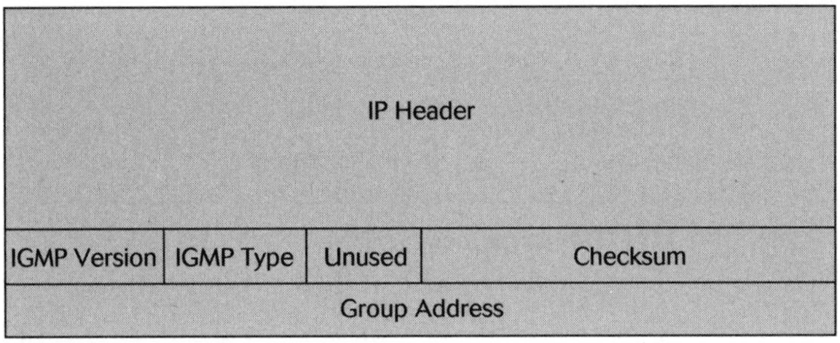

IP Header			
IGMP Version	IGMP Type	Unused	Checksum
Group Address			

Figure 3-9   *An IGMP message.*

The IGMP Version field consists of 4 bits and represents the IGMP protocol version number. RFC 1112 defines this value as 1.

The IGMP Type field consists of 4 bits and represents the type of IGMP message. A value of 1 denotes a host membership query report; a value of 2 denotes a host membership report.

The Unused field consists of 8 bits and is reserved for future use. It must be set to 0 when sending and must be ignored upon receipt.

The Checksum field contains the one's complement of the sum of the message. The Checksum field is set to 0 while the checksum is computed.

The Group Address field is meaningless for IGMP query messages. This field is set to 0 when sending query messages and is ignored upon receipt. In an IGMP report message, the Group Address field is set to the IP multicast group address for which the report is being sent.

Network Time Protocol

Network Time Protocol (NTP) is used for synchronizing the clocks on various computers that are connected in a network. NTP provides a mechanism to achieve and maintain clock synchronization within a millisecond. The time transmitted using NTP is in Universal Time Coordinate (UTC; essentially the same as Greenwich Mean Time), and the receiving computer is expected to adjust for time zone, daylight saving time, and so on. NTP assigns each computer to one of sixteen levels. A level-one computer has access to a very precise time signal or clock. Computers at a higher level query a server at a lower level to retrieve the time. A client can access more than one server at a lower level, thus providing for redundancy and robustness. A version of NTP called Simplified NTP (SNTP, defined in RFC 1769) was developed in 1995 for personal computers. Prior to that, three different versions of NTP were developed: NTP version 3 (1995, defined in RFC 1305), NTP version 2 (1989, defined in RFC 1119), and NTP version 1 (1988, defined in RFC 1059). Versions of NTP have been developed for UNIX and Windows operating systems.

Routing and Routing Protocols

Routers are devices that are used to connect various networks that would otherwise remain separate. Figure 3-10 shows a simple example of router use.

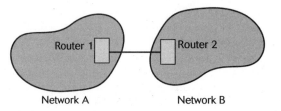
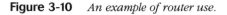

Figure 3-10   *An example of router use.*

In this example, the router pair R1/R2 connects two LANs that are geographically separate. Note that routers always operate in pairs. This does not mean that a network always consists of an even number of routers. Figure 3-11 shows a network that consists of three routers.

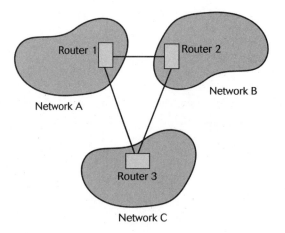
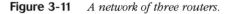

Figure 3-11   *A network of three routers.*

Routers connect networks using a variety of methods. The connection between the routers might be a dial-up connection or a leased line connection. The line can be an XDSL, ATM, Frame Relay, ISDN, X.25, or any other type of line. A router operates at the network layer (layer 3) of the ISO/OSI seven-layer model. Actions performed by a router include:

- Verifying the validity of the data packet. This includes performing checksum calculations and verifying data in fields in the packet header such as number of hops (the number of routers that have forwarded the packet).
- Consulting a data structure called a *routing table* to see where the data packet should go next. A routing table can quickly identify a port over which a data packet should be sent if a destination address is known.
- Queuing the packet for delivery.
- Actually forwarding the packet.
- Exchanging routing information with other routers.

Routing algorithms have been devised to update the routing table to reflect changes in network topology. The goal of a routing algorithm is to be simple, fast, easy to implement, robust—that is, to make few errors while sending a data packet to its next destination—and also to be resilient to network changes. In the face of such changes, the routing tables at various routers should be updated in a timely and synchronized manner so that all routers have a consistent view of the network.

Routing protocols implement routing algorithms. Routing protocols operate on network protocols such as IP and Internet Packet Xchange (IPX). These are sometimes referred to as *routed protocols*. In other words, a routed protocol is the entity upon which a routing protocol operates. Based on functionality and algorithms, there are several different ways to classify routing algorithms. Note that a particular routing algorithm might fall into several of these classes. The classes include:

- Static routing
- Dynamic routing
- Intradomain routing
- Interdomain routing
- Flat routing
- Hierarchial routing
- Centralized routing
- Distributed routing
- Single path routing
- Multipath routing
- Host-intelligent routing

- Router-intelligent routing
- Link state routing
- Distance vector routing
- Policy routing

These classes are described in the following sections.

Static Routing and Dynamic Routing

With *static routing*, each router has a routing table configured at installation time, and no changes are made dynamically. Periodically, the network administrator might manually reconfigure the routing table. Obviously, static routing cannot respond at all to network topology changes; hence this routing algorithm is rarely used.

Dynamic routing algorithms attempt to adapt to changing network configurations. These algorithms are widely used. Of course, different routing algorithms analyze different pieces of data and exchange routing information.

Intradomain Routing and Interdomain Routing

The networks of large companies are typically organized into smaller domains. An Internet Service Provider (ISP) can also organize its clients into a number of sub-domains. With this organization, some routers are designated as intradomain routers and have knowledge only of routers within the domain. One router in the domain acts as a conduit to the world outside the domain. This is the only router within the domain that requires knowledge of routing outside the domain. Figure 3-12 illustrates this concept.

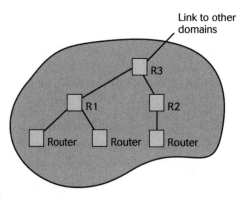

Figure 3-12   *Intradomain and interdomain routing.*

In the figure, routers R1 and R2 are intradomain routers; router R3 is the interdomain router. The combination of the three subdomains serviced by R1, R2, and R3 appears as a single domain to the outside world. All messages to and from the external world are transmitted through router R3.

Flat Routing and Hierarchical Routing

In a *flat routing* scheme, all routers operate as equals, or peers. In a *hierarchical routing* scheme, some routers act as peers, but the only way for these routers to reach other nodes is through another router at a higher level. The routers at the higher level of the hierarchy effectively form a backbone. Intradomain routing is therefore flat, while routing for a packet that originates in a subdomain, travels to a backbone router, and then travels out of the domain is hierarchical. Referring back to Figure 3-11, a packet originating in the subdomain serviced by router R1 or R2 and leaving the domain via a hop through router R3 is routed hierarchically.

Centralized Routing and Distributed Routing

With *centralized routing*, all routing tables are calculated at a central site (usually called the *routing control center*) and distributed to the routers. An advantage of centralized routing is that the routers have a consistent view of the network because all routers have the same routing tables. Another advantage is that the computational effort is concentrated at a single point. The disadvantage is that the routing control center is a single point of failure that can bring the whole network down. Also, the hub-and-spoke topography of this system, with the routing control center forming the hub, puts a burden of higher bandwidth on lines leading to the hub. The advantage of all routers having the same table is somewhat marred by the fact that in large networks, routers closer to the routing control center receive their updated tables earlier than routers that are farther away. So the potential for a router to have an inconsistent view of the network still exists.

Distributed routing algorithms perform routing calculations at a number of nodes. The routing update messages are distributed and do not tend to cause higher bandwidth usage in certain directions, as occurs with the hub-and-spoke topography of centralized routing. Distributed routing is more fault tolerant, but the network might take some time before all nodes have a consistent view, which can result in routing loops.

Single Path Routing and Multipath Routing

Single path routing algorithms provide only a single path, or route, to each destination. The advantage is that the routing table size is reduced. *Multipath routing* algorithms define multiple paths to the same destination. This can provide better use of line capacity and higher overall throughput. Another advantage of multipath routing is that the network is more fault tolerant because it has an element of redundancy. The disadvantage is that multipath routing tables are usually larger and the algorithms are more complex.

Host-Intelligent Routing and Router-Intelligent Routing

In *host-intelligent routing,* the host generates a data packet that contains not just the destination address, but also a complete list of nodes that the data packet will traverse. The nodes are listed in the order in which the data packet traverses them. The router simply acts as store-and-forward device. This routing scheme is also known as *source routing*. The host generates a special data packet that floods all paths it encounters. Each router sends the packet along all the paths it is aware of and adds its identity to the packet while doing so. Multiple packets can reach the destination with this scheme. The destination then sends the packet back to the host, which can examine the packet to determine which nodes the packet visited. The host now has a route that it can use. The advantage of source routing is that the packet is usually routed optimally. The disadvantage is that the routing discovery mechanism floods the network with packets. Source routing is not widely used.

In *router-intelligent routing*, the host simply generates a data packet with a destination address. The routers perform their own calculations (periodically, not on a per-packet basis) and use these calculations to determine where the data packet should go next. Obviously, the intelligence is built into the router in this scheme.

Link State, Distance Vector, and Policy Routing

Link state and *distance vector* are two of the major families of routing algorithms. *Policy routing* is a type of distance vector routing.

A link state router broadcasts a list of nodes to which it is connected. This list is called the *link state*. In link state routing, the routers send a relatively small amount of link state data to a large number of nodes. This information is transmitted on an as-needed basis (when the link state changes). Link state algorithms involve more computation than distance vector routing. However, link state routing is less likely to result in routing loops. Examples of link state routing include:

- ISO Intermediate System to Intermediate System
- Netware Link Services Protocol
- Open Shortest Path First (OSPF)

A router operating with a *distance vector* algorithm sends its entire routing table (all the information it has) to just its neighbors; it sends a large amount of information to a small number of nodes. Distance vector routing attempts to minimize the number of hops each data packet has to travel (the number of nodes a data packet traverses). It works best in small networks with few redundant connections. Distance vector routing is simpler and requires less memory than link state routing. A distance vector router must be configured to know its neighbors and the cost of the link to each neighbor in terms of time and resources.

Distance vector algorithms, also called Bellman-Ford algorithms or Ford-Fulkerson algorithms, converge more slowly than do link state protocols. In other words, the routing state tables at each node have settled down to steady state value, and the collective picture presented by the unification of all routing tables reflects network reality. An extreme example of this slower convergence is the *count-to-infinity problem*. Consider Figure 3-13. Assuming that the cost of each link is 1, Node X decides it can reach Y with a cost of 1. Node Z decides it can reach Y with a cost of 2 (1 to reach X, and then X has a cost of 1 to reach Y). Let's say that the link between X and Y goes down. X decides to send data packets intended for Y to Z (because Z has a cost of 2). X reports that it has a cost of 3 to reach Z (1 to reach Y, and then Y has a cost of 2). Y updates its tables to show a cost of 4. This sequence continues until the routers reach a maximum assigned value.

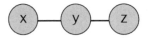

Figure 3-13   *A simple three-node network with two routers.*

One solution to the count-to-infinity problem is called the split horizon rule, which states that the distance to a destination should not be reported on the link that is used to reach that destination. In our example, Y would not report a cost of 2 to reach Z to X. However, the split horizon rule does not work for all topologies. If the network topology is complex enough the count-to-infinity problem still occurs even with the split horizon rule in effect. For example, a network such as the one shown in Figure 3-14, with three routers involved instead of two, would still have the count-to-infinity problem.

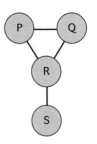

Figure 3-14   *A network with three routers.*

Examples of distance vector routing include:

- Routing Information Protocol (RIP)
- AppleTalk Routing Table Management Protocol (RTMP)
- Interior Gateway Routing Protocol (IGRP)

Policy routing protocols result from the modification of distance vector routing protocols. The algorithm is modified to take into account factors such as business agreements rather than just physical factors such as number of hops. Policy routing algorithms are used fairly often.

Border Gateway Protocol

Border Gateway Protocol (BGP) is a dynamic, interdomain, distributed, flat, multipath, router-intelligent routing protocol. It was designed to address the deficiencies of Exterior Gateway Protocol (EGP) and is considered a successor to EGP. BGP might very well completely replace EGP on the Internet. BGP is designed to detect routing loops and to use some metrics (hop count, link bandwidth, and so forth) while making routing decisions.

BGP routers initially exchange their entire routing tables. Updates are sent when information changes. These updates are incremental, representing only the changes. BGP tables contain multiple paths to the same destination, but only the most optimal path is conveyed to other routers. Obviously, some metric is required to decide which path is more optimal than another. BGP considers metrics while making routing decisions. These metrics consist simply of a number assigned by a network administrator. While assigning this number, the network administrator takes into account factors such as hop count, link speed, and link stability.

BGP update messages are sent using TCP. The update messages convey information about domains that can be reached from a particular node. BGP can detect failures on hosts and routers by means of the "keep-alive" messages that are generated every 30 seconds or so. At times, BGP is also referred to as a protocol that supports Classless Interdomain Routing (CIDR). This simply means that a routing table used by BGP consists of a 32-bit IP address and mask and that the routing decision treats an IP address as a "flat" value.

BGP has been revised, and the new revision is called Border Gateway Protocol–4 (BGP-4). Among other features, BGP-4 takes into account the fact that network masks are of variable length.

Exterior Gateway Protocol

Exterior Gateway Protocol (EGP) is a dynamic, interdomain, distributed, flat, single path, router-intelligent routing protocol. EGP is used extensively on the Internet. It attempts to convey information about node reachability via updates. The updates contain information along the lines of "where you can go from node X" or "you can get there from here"—that is, which hosts and routers are reachable from which routers. EGP updates are sent on a regular basis to all neighboring nodes. Each update contains information about the neighbors of the router sending the update. Each router collects these updates and assembles a routing table from that information.

Interior Gateway Routing Protocol

Interior Gateway Routing Protocol (IGRP) is a dynamic, intradomain, distributed, flat, multipath, distance vector routing protocol. It was developed by Cisco Systems for use in complex networks. IGRP takes into account a variety of factors such as network bandwidth, reliability, network load, and message size in order to arrive at a routing decision. The weight that each factor has on the routing decision is configurable by a network administrator. In the absence of such configuration, the protocol works with default settings. IGRP features include split horizon (explained earlier).

Open Shortest Path First

Open Shortest Path First (OSPF) is a dynamic, intradomain, distributed, hierarchical, multipath, link state routing protocol. OSPF routers send updates when the link state changes, and they also send "keep-alive" messages to indicate that a particular router is still healthy and functional. OSPF supports "quality of service" requests, which occur when an application indicates that some data is urgent. In this case, OSPF can use links at its disposal to dispatch the data as soon as possible.

Routing Information Protocol

Routing Information Protocol (RIP) is a dynamic, intradomain, distributed, flat, single path, distance vector routing protocol. RIP was developed by Xerox and subsequently adopted by other vendors such as 3Com, Apple, Banyan, Novell, and Ungermann Bass. RIP is best suited for small to medium-sized networks. It is not suitable for large networks because it places a hop limit of 16. RIP does not adapt well to changes in network conditions such as delays or changes in network load. The trend has been to replace RIP with modern routing protocols.

Windows Sockets

Windows Sockets is more popularly known as *Winsock*. The current version of Winsock, version 2, was released in early 1993. Winsock is similar to the Berkeley sockets for UNIX and provides an abstraction for writing network-aware applications.

The primary purpose for inventing Winsock was to enable development of network-aware applications that could work with any vendor's TCP/IP protocol stack. Doing so was necessary because each vendor had a proprietary interface to its TCP/IP implementation. With the first version of Winsock (version 1.1), the underlying transport mechanism was limited to TCP/IP. Winsock version 2 works with other transport protocols, such as ATM and Internet Packet Exchange/Sequenced Package Exchange (IPX/SPX). These different transport mechanisms can be used simultaneously by a number of applications. Winsock version 2 is backward compatible, allowing Winsock 1.1 applications to run without requiring any modifications. Figure 3-15 shows the Winsock architecture.

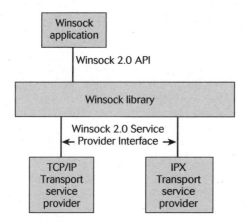

Figure 3-15   *The Winsock architecture.*

Microsoft and Intel provide software known generally as the Winsock dynamic-link library (DLL). In actual practice, different versions of DLL exist for different versions of Windows, and each version is named differently. The Winsock DLL exports two different application programming interfaces (APIs). At the top, it exposes the Winsock 2.0 API for the benefit of applications. At the bottom, it exposes a Winsock Service. These APIs benefit system software developers who want to extend Winsock by adding another underlying transport mechanism.

WinInet

WinInet (also known as Win 32 Internet API) is a programming interface and software library provided by Microsoft for the Windows operating system. It enables rapid and easy development of Internet-aware applications that can utilize Hypertext Transfer Protocol (HTTP), File Transfer Protocol (FTP), and Gopher. WinInet provides functionality that allows applications to use a consistent paradigm that is similar to reading and writing files. Using WinInet, applications can be developed without dealing with the intricacies and knowledge of Winsock, TCP/IP, or higher protocols such as FTP and HTTP. WinInet also provides secure connections to an Internet server using Secure Sockets Layer (SSL) or Kerberos. (For more information about SSL and Kerberos, see Chapter 5, "Cryptography and Security Basics.")

Bridge Routing Protocols

Bridges are typically used to connect LANs when the communication does not have a network layer protocol. There are two types of routing protocols for bridges: *transparent bridging* and *source routing bridging*. Note that some bridges might implement both of these routing protocols; this combination is called source routing transparent (SRT). SRT bridges normally behave as transparent bridges, but if they encounter a data packet with source routing information embedded within it, the bridge will recognize that effect and behave like a source routing bridge.

Transparent Bridging

A *transparent bridge* is so named because the bridge is invisible, or transparent, to the nodes that are communicating with each other. A transparent bridge listens to all packets that arrive at its two ports. As it listens, the bridge builds a database of the node addresses on each side, or link, of the bridge. When a packet arrives, the bridge looks at the destination address and ignores the packet if the address is on the same link. If the address is on the other link, the bridge forwards the packet. If the bridge finds that the destination address does not exist within its database, which means that the bridge does not know what side the node is on, the bridge forwards the packet.

All of this works well as long as the network the bridge is connected to does not have routing loops. Routing loops can be disastrous at the data link layer, since there is no TTL field, as there is in the network layer.

The *spanning tree* algorithm allows bridges to be introduced into networks that have an arbitrary topology (including loops) without the fear of loops unnecessarily flooding the network with multiple copies of a packet. The spanning tree algorithm is similar to the distance vector algorithm but does not suffer from the count-to-infinity problem. It attempts to build a tree that covers each node within the network. A bridge with the lowest identifier is designated as the *root bridge* and is placed at the root of the tree being built. This root bridge is dynamically elected. Each bridge then computes the cost to reach the root bridge. While computing the cost, the bridge takes into account the rate of transmission on each link. At this stage, the algorithm is refined to take advantage of the fact that each bridge cares only about the path to the root and not the path to more distant bridges.

A single bridge on each LAN segment is chosen to send the control messages. This bridge, called the *designated bridge,* is the bridge that has the least cost to reach the root. If more than one bridge has the same minimal cost, the bridge with the lower identifier is chosen. Designated bridges send control messages that include three pieces of information:

- The identity of the bridge sending the packet
- The identity of the bridge that the sending bridge assumes is the root
- The routing cost to the root

These control messages are not forwarded by bridges. At this stage, each bridge knows which port to use to reach the root. This port is called the *designated port.* The spanning tree can now be constructed, consisting of links for which the bridge is a designated bridge plus the designated port. Data packets received on the spanning tree are forwarded. Data packets received on other links are dropped.

Note that a lot of the finer details of the spanning tree algorithm (timers, for instance) have been omitted here. For details consult IEEE Standard 802.1d which is the authoritative source for spanning tree algorithms.

Source Routing Bridging

The idea behind *source routing bridging* is that the source node inserts into the data packet a complete path that the data packet should traverse. Obviously, a source node must determine the route (and cache it for reuse) before it can send the packet. The route is discovered by means of an initial explorer packet. This packet gets copied by bridges onto all possible links, with each bridge putting its identity into space provided within the packet. The destination node can then choose the best route (as it sees fit) and send that back to the source node. The destination node can also send all the control packets back and let the source node select the route.

Firewalls

As more and more corporations host Web sites and connect to the Internet, security requirements for their networks increase. Firewalls provide the required security by allowing a corporation to isolate its internal network and computers from the Internet while allowing Internet users access to a limited amount of data and services. Firewalls can be broadly divided into three categories:

- Stateless or packet-level filters
- Circuit filters
- Application-level filters

Stateless or Packet-Level Filters

Packet-level filters are set up to forward or block a packet solely on the merits of the packet, without taking into account any past history or state. They do consider the source address or port as well as the destination address or port. The network layer protocol header might also be examined by such filters. This type of firewall is the simplest to implement and operate without any noticeable effect on network through-put. Unfortunately, the quality of security is not high. For example, you can use tunneling to bypass the filtering rules. In other words, if the rules forbid forwarding HTTP traffic but allow Telnet, the HTTP traffic can be tunneled within the Telnet session.

Circuit Filters

A *circuit filter* is a type of firewall somewhere between a stateless filter and an application-level filter. A circuit filter "remembers" a limited amount of history about a packet, and the decision to route a packet is made on the basis of its history as well as its contents. Obviously this method is more complicated than stateless filters because the state of the packet must be updated and consulted and inspection of the packet is also required. Filtering takes into account the source and destination addresses as well as the type of service. Circuit filters are actually implemented as a gateway: a client communicates with the filter, which then contacts the server on the client's behalf. These filters are used more often for outgoing packets than for incoming packets (for example, for Telnet).

Application-Level Filters

Application-level filters provide a high degree of security but at the cost of lower speed and higher complexity. These filters are deployed on a firewall server. The actual application server is on a private network behind the firewall server. Clients connect to the firewall server, which also behaves like the application server. A client, in fact, cannot detect that it is communicating with a firewall server (in this instance, also called a *proxy application server*). The firewall in turn pretends to be a client and sends the client request it has received to the actual application server. Before it does this, the firewall applies some logic to decide whether the request is valid and whether the client is authorized to do what is requested. This implies that the firewall has an intimate knowledge of the application and the protocol involved. One potential disadvantage is that the application proxy server can become a performance bottleneck.

IP Next Generation and IP Version 6

The current IP (IPv4) is rapidly proving to be inadequate for today's needs. The recent explosive growth of the Internet will only exacerbate the problem. The main problems with IPv4 are as follows:

- It provides only 32 bits for IP addressing. In a world where almost every company and home PC owner is getting onto the Internet, and where every toaster, TV, fridge, microwave, and lightbulb is a potential candidate for an IP address, there simply are not enough IPv4 addresses to go around.

- It is running out of network addresses as well. A Class A address can provide up to 16 million nodes, a Class B address can provide up to 64,000 nodes, and a Class C address can provide up to 256 nodes. A node can be a computer, a router, or simply a networked peripheral such as a printer. Class B addresses are the most popular, since few companies are big enough to have 16 million nodes and a lot of companies need more than 256 nodes. However, there are only 16,384 Class B addresses.

- The routing tables on the core Internet routers are getting huge, and the problem will only get worse. Routers will either take more time to handle each packet, or they will have the silicon and smarts to handle huge routing tables and still handle each packet quickly but will become very expensive devices. Neither alternative is attractive.

- It does not lend itself well to applications that require quality of service such as multimedia applications that need to transfer vast amounts of time-critical data.

- It does not lend itself well to new applications that require a higher level of security and authentication.

To address all these concerns, the IETF started an initiative in the early 1990s. The first concrete result was the publication of RFC 1752 in 1995. RFC 1752 described the requirements for what it called *IP Next Generation* (IPng) and, in some assisting documents, described the header, routing, addressing, and security aspects of the new protocol. More RFCs have followed, such as RFC 1883, and the protocol has been officially renamed *Internet Protocol version 6* (IPv6).

The notable enhancements in IPv6 include the following:

- It provides for a much bigger address space. IPv6 addresses are 128 bits long, which provides approximately 2^{96} more addresses than IPv4.

- It provides faster processing of IPv6 headers by routers. Even though the header is now longer (40 bytes for IPv6 compared to the minimum 20 bytes for IPv4), it has fewer fields (8 for IPv6 compared with 12 for IPv4). In addition, most of the options that aren't processed by routers have been moved into separate extension headers.

- It defines mechanisms that provide authentication, confidentiality, and integrity for the IP packet.

- It provides a way for applications to label IP packets that need special handling. Typical applications that use this include multimedia and real-time applications.

IPv6 Addresses

IPv6 addresses are 128 bits long. IPv6 assigns IP addresses to interfaces (which exist on nodes) rather than to the nodes themselves. A node can have multiple interfaces and hence multiple IP addresses. A single interface can also have multiple IP addresses.

IPv6 provides three kinds of addresses: unicast, multicast, and anycast, described in the following sections. IPv6 also provides a couple of mechanisms for dynamically assigning IP addresses. The first is similar to Dynamic Host Configuration Protocol (DHCP), described later in this chapter, in which a client makes a request to a configuration server. The server assigns an address from a pool of preconfigured values. This is sometimes described as *configuration with state*. The server maintains state information and leases the address to the client for a finite time. The client can renew the lease. If enough addresses are available, a client will be assigned the same address it received for the previous request.

The second mechanism for dynamically obtaining an IP address is a *stateless* mechanism. With this mechanism the client generates an IP address by concatenating the link-local-address with a local identifier such as an Ethernet card address. An IPv6 host computer might have no code that can distinguish the type of address. On the other hand, an IPv6 router might completely understand the different address types and take different actions based on the type of address.

Unicast Addresses

Figure 3-16 shows the different kinds of unicast addresses defined by IPv6. Each unicast address consists of 128 bits.

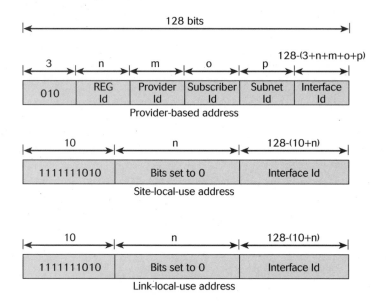

Figure 3-16   *Unicast addresses defined by IPv6.*

ISPs are assigned a pool of provider-based addresses, and they in turn assign these globally unique addresses to their subscribers.

Site-local-use addresses are for the benefit of organizations that want to use Internet standard protocols for communication within the organization without having Internet connectivity to begin with. These addresses can be easily upgraded to globally unique addresses if the organization decides to provide Internet connectivity. This upgrade can be done by an administrator without going to each node and changing the IP address, as would be required with IPv4.

The last type of unicast address is a link-local-use address, used most often by computers that connect primarily through a single line, such as an ISDN telephone line.

Multicast Addresses

IPv6 provides a much larger number of multicast addresses than IPv4 provides. Figure 3-17 shows an IPv6 multicast address, which consists of 128 bits.

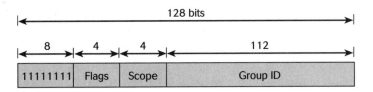

Figure 3-17 *An IPv6 multicast address.*

An IPv6 multicast address has the first 8 bits set to 1s. The Flags field consist of 4 bits, with the 3 higher-order bits reserved and set to 0. The last bit is set to 0 to indicate a permanent multicast group assigned by an Internet authority. This denotes a multicast group that is widely known and that has widespread interest.

The Scope field is a 4-bit field that identifies the nature and scope of the multicast address. The possible values are shown in Table 3-5.

Table 3-5 Scope Field Values

Value	Description
0	Reserved
1	Node-local-scope
2	Link-local-scope
3–4	Unassigned
5	Site-local-scope
6–7	Unassigned
8	Organization-local-scope
9–E	Unassigned
F	Reserved

Anycast Addresses

IPv6 introduces the concept of the anycast address, which is similar to a multicast address in the sense that it is assigned to more than one interface (the interfaces typically being on different nodes). A packet sent to an anycast address is sent to any one of the member interfaces. The choice of which one is left to the delivering node.

Anycast addresses are indistinguishable from multicast addresses. An anycast address is assigned from the range of available multicast addresses. Nodes that use a multicast address as an anycast address must be informed of that use via a configuration file or some other means.

IPv6 Header

IPv6 headers have a fixed length, unlike IPv4 headers. Figure 3-18 shows an IPv6 header.

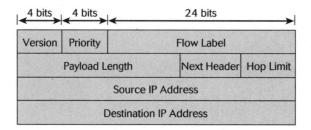

Figure 3-18   *An IPv6 header.*

In an IPv6 header the Version field consists of 4 bits and is set to 6, denoting the IP version number.

The Priority field consists of 4 bits and allows a source to specify the priority of IP packets relative to other IP packets the source might be generating. Values 0 through 7 denote applications that implement some form of congestion control in response to changing network conditions. Recommended values are shown in Table 3-6.

Table 3-6   Priority Field Values

Value	Description
0	Uncharacterized
1	Idle time or filler traffic (such as netnews)
2	Unattended data transfer (such as e-mail)
3	Reserved
4	Attended data transfer (such as HTTP and FTP)
5	Reserved
6	Interactive traffic (such as Telnet)
7	Internet control traffic (such as routing protocol–related packets)

Values 8 through 15 are used for traffic that is not adaptive to network conditions—for example, conditions in which the application does not lend itself well to congestion control. The lower values are recommended for traffic that the sender is more willing to lose—for example, the application should assign a priority value of 8 to video traffic and 15 to audio traffic, assuming that it is willing to lose video data before it loses audio data.

The Flow Label field consists of 24 bits and is used by the source to request special handling by routers. The name for this field comes from the fact that a flow is considered a sequence of packets between a source and a destination. The expectation is that special needs applications, such as multimedia and real-time applications, will use this field.

The Payload Length field consists of 16 bits and contains the length of the IP packet that follows the fixed-length header. This includes the length of all extension headers plus the length of the payload.

The Next Header field consists of 8 bits and identifies the type of header immediately following the IPv6 header. This identifies the upper-layer protocol data embedded within the IPv6 datagram. The values are the same as those defined for IPv4 and are found in RFC 1700.

The Hop Limit field consists of 8 bits and indicates the remaining number of hops the IP packet can make. This is analogous to the TTL field of an IPv4 header.

The final two fields are the 128-bit Source IP Address and the 128-bit Destination IP Address.

IPv6 Extension Headers

IPv6 provides a way to place a number of optional extension headers between the IPv6 header and the IPv6 payload. This is illustrated in Figure 3-19. This scheme allows routers to rapidly process the header, especially when no extensions are present. This scheme also lends itself well to future enhancements.

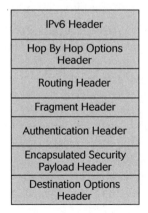

Figure 3-19   *Optional IPv6 extension headers.*

The variable-length Hop By Hop Options header must be examined by every node (including routers) that the packet traverses. Currently the only defined use for this header is to transmit IP packets with payloads greater than 64K bytes. This is called the Jumbo Payload option.

The variable-length Routing header provides capabilities similar to IPv4 source routing (described earlier in this chapter). This header contains a list of nodes that the IP packet must traverse to reach its destination.

IPv4 provides fragmentation and reassembly at the source node as well as at intermediate nodes. IPv6 provides fragmentation only at the source node and reassembly at only the destination node. The 8-bit Fragment header provides the information needed for reassembly.

The IETF IP Security working group has defined two security extension headers. These can be used in conjunction with the new IPv6 header, but they can also be used with the IPv4 header. (IPv4 nodes can provide optional support for these two mechanisms.) The two extension headers, the Authentication header and the Encapsulated Security Payload, are jointly known as IPSec. IPSec is a distinct protocol from IPv6 that has been implemented in conjunction with IPv4.

Authentication Header

The variable-length Authentication header (AH) provides authentication, confirming that the IP packet is indeed from who it claims to be from; and integrity, confirming that the IP packet contents have not been modified en route. Note that the AH does not provide confidentiality—the payload or data within the IP packet is readable by applications and processes other than the intended recipient.

The AH requires the use of MD5, which is a message digest algorithm. MD5 is discussed in more detail in Chapter 5, "Cryptography and Security Basics." The AH should be free from export restrictions since it does not provide confidentiality or data encryption. The AH can eliminate unwarranted IP datagrams from clients that are "attacking" an IP host. Via AH, IP provides a mechanism whereby an IPv6 client is required to establish credentials before the host will accept any further datagrams.

Encapsulated Security Payload

Encapsulated Security Payload (ESP) is intended primarily to provide confidentiality. It renders data meaningless to anyone other than the intended recipient. Depending on the algorithm used, ESP can provide authentication and data integrity as well. ESP is likely to run into problems with export restrictions. It allows use of different encryption algorithms, although DES CBC is preferable because it provides interoperability. The data and part of the variable-length ESP header are encrypted.

ESP can operate in two modes. In tunneling mode, the ESP data is a complete IP datagram. In transport mode, the ESP data begins with a transport-layer header, such as TCP.

Destination Options Header

The Destination Options header information is optional. If included, it contains information that should be examined (and acted on) by the destination IPv6 protocol stack. Routers that are handling the IPv6 packet need not examine this field.

IPv6 Interoperability

One of the design goals for IPv6 was a smooth transition between IPv4 and IPv6. A single host or router can run both IPv4 and IPv6 protocol stacks at the same time. The IPv6 addressing mechanism makes allowances to provide for IPv4 interoperability. Figure 3-20 illustrates this compatibility.

Figure 3-20 *An IPv4-compatible IPv6 address.*

The IPv4-compatible address is used for tunneling, a technique whereby one protocol datagram (the data plus the header) is encapsulated as the data portion of a different protocol datagram. In this instance, the complete IPv6 datagram is encapsulated within the payload of an IPv4 datagram. The expectation is that special routers will be used to connect two IPv6 "clouds" over a link that supports only IPv4. Each router will be assigned a unique IPv4-compatible unicast address.

The second type of address is called an IPv4-mapped IPv6 address. This type of address is assigned to nodes that support only IPv4.

Multicast Transmission and Multicast Routing

Multicast transmission is a transmission from a single station to a group of stations that have expressed some interest in receiving transmissions of a particular nature. Note that this is a "one-to-many" transmission and is different from a broadcast transmission which is "one-to-all." The most famous implementation of multicast transmission is multicast backbone (Mbone) described in Chapter 7, "Discovery and Management." A number of companies have joined under the auspices of a body called IP Multicast Initiative (IPMI) to promote IP multicast technology. Details of IPMI may be found at http://www.ipmulticast.com.

There are two basic approaches to multicast routing—dense mode and sparse mode—described in the sections below. Note that multicast routing technology is still undergoing development and standardization.

Dense Mode Multicast Routing

Dense mode multicast routing assumes that the multicast group stations to which the data transmission is directed are densely distributed across the network, and it also assumes that plenty of bandwidth is available. Examples of dense mode protocols include Distance Vector Multicast Routing Protocol (DVMRP), Multicast Open Shortest Path First (MOSPF), and Protocol Independent Multicast/Dense Mode (PIM/DM). All of these protocols generate a lot of transmissions and involve building a routing path from each source of transmission to the multicast group. DVMRP is described in RFC 1075 and requires the use of a unicast routing protocol as well. MOSPF is described in RFC 1584 and requires the use of Open Shortest Path First (OSPF), a unicast routing protocol. PIM/DM, as the name implies, is independent of an underlying unicast routing protocol, but at the cost of more data transmission and even possible duplication of data transmission.

Sparse Mode Multicast Routing

Sparse mode multicast routing assumes that the various nodes having membership in a multicast group are widely distributed and that transmission capacity is a precious commodity. PIM/SM is an example of this kind of routing. All data for a multicast group is transmitted in the same manner by PIM/SM, irrespective of where the data came from (as compared with dense mode multicast routing, which routes traffic differently based on the source of the data). PIM/SM does rely on underlying unicast routing protocols, but it does not dictate the use of any particular unicast routing protocol.

Serial Line Internet Protocol

Serial Line Internet Protocol (SLIP) was once fairly widely used, but it has been replaced by PPP. SLIP provides framing for IP packets over point-to-point serial lines. You can think of SLIP as somewhat analogous to Ethernet or token ring. On a LAN, IP datagrams are encapsulated within Ethernet frames. On a serial line, IP datagrams are encapsulated within SLIP (or PPP) frames. Thus SLIP can encapsulate only IP packets and cannot handle other network protocols such as DECNet or IPX (by Novell).

SLIP designates the end of a data frame by a special character called an END character. An END character contained within user data is transmitted as 2 bytes—an ESC byte followed by an END byte. SLIP does not provide any error detection or retransmission. It requires that both ends of the serial line connection be completely preconfigured because it does not have any provisions for the configuration to be negotiated.

SLIP does not have a standard way of dynamically assigning IP addresses to a client. Vendors have made private extensions to SLIP to accomplish this. With the growing popularity of PPP, which defines a standard way of accomplishing the same objective, this is fast becoming a moot point. SLIP is described in RFC 1055.

Point-to-Point Protocol

Point-to-Point (PPP) provides a standard means of encapsulating higher-level network protocols for transmission over point-to-point serial lines. Thus PPP provides the same functionality as SLIP. As with SLIP, you can think of PPP as somewhat analogous to Ethernet or token ring. On a LAN, IP datagrams are encapsulated within Ethernet frames. On a serial line, IP datagrams are encapsulated within PPP frames.

PPP differs from SLIP in that PPP offers a lot more functionality. For example, PPP has the ability to encapsulate other network protocols such as DECNet, IPX, and Appletalk in addition to IP datagrams. PPP is also more flexible; it provides link configuration capabilities as well as the ability to let the two ends of the serial line connection negotiate capabilities, and it provides error detection.

PPP can easily be extended to encapsulate more network protocols. It provides compression techniques for data transmission, and the ability to dynamically assign an IP address to a remote node by using a protocol called IP Control Protocol (IPCP). With IPCP, the IP address is assigned by the dial-in server from a preconfigured pool of addresses. The address is returned to the pool when the remote session ends.

PPP comprises three main components:

- A High Level Data Link Control (HDLC) protocol that is used for the data encoding on the wire.
- A Link Control Protocol (LCP) that provides functionality to configure, establish, and test the link. LCP frames are sent before user data is transmitted.
- A Network Control Protocol (NCP) that provides functionality to configure the various network protocols that PPP can encapsulate.

PPP does require slightly more overhead to provide this extra functionality. SLIP requires just one extra byte per packet, while PPP requires a minimum of 8 extra bytes per packet. PPP also requires that some LCP and NCP packets be exchanged before data transmission can begin. The users have obviously voted that the extra overhead requirements are well worth it for the additional functionality.

PPP has two mechanisms for providing security over PPP connections. These are described in RFC 1334. The first is called *Password Authentication Protocol* (PAP), which is enjoying decreasing popularity in an increasingly security conscious world. The main reason for this decrease is the fact that with PAP, passwords are transmitted in plain text. The second mechanism is called *Challenge Handshake Authentication Protocol* (CHAP). With CHAP, the server sends a challenge to the user. The challenge is unique for each new PPP session. The client computes a response to the challenge using a secret value that is known to both the client and the server. Meanwhile, the server independently computes the same response and then compares the expected response with the response received from the client. PAP and CHAP do not obviate the need for further security, since they both provide identification of the device that is dialing in, not of the user or the phone number.

PPP is described in RFC 1171. The PPP security extensions PAP and CHAP are described in RFC 1334.

PPP enables two computers to communicate with each other in a somewhat secure manner. It provides a number of methods by which one computer communicating through PPP can verify the identity of who or what it is communicating with. These methods are described in the following sections.

Password Authentication Protocol

Password Authentication Protocol (PAP) defines a simple two-step method by which one entity can identify itself to another. The host initiating the connection is referred to as the client or peer. The client sends a request to the server (also called the authenticator) and includes a user ID as well as a password. The authenticator evaluates the user identity and password and then responds with a simple answer indicating whether the credentials are acceptable or not. The user identity and password are sent in plain text, which is a major drawback to PAP. PAP is described in RFC 1334.

Challenge Handshake Authentication Protocol

Challenge Handshake Authentication Protocol (CHAP) provides a more secure means of authentication than PAP. CHAP is a three-stage protocol that is driven by the authenticator (rather than the client, as in PAP). The authenticator issues a challenge to the client. The client calculates a value using a one-way hash function with MD5 and sends it back to the authenticator. (For more information about hash functions and MD5, see Chapter 5, "Cryptography and Security Basics.") This computation uses the client user identity, a plain text password, and the challenge (among other elements). The authenticator also computes the same value independently and compares the value with the value returned by the client. CHAP is described in RFC 1994.

Microsoft Challenge Handshake Authentication Protocol

Microsoft Challenge Handshake Authentication Protocol (MS-CHAP) is closely related to CHAP. The authenticator sends a challenge, and the client computes a response based on the challenge and an MD4 hash of the client's user identity and password. (See Chapter 5, "Cryptography and Security Basics," for details about MD4.) The major difference between MS-CHAP and CHAP is that with MS-CHAP the authenticator need not have access to the plain text user identity and password of the client. This provides a higher level of security.

Virtual Private Network

A virtual private network (VPN) allows an exchange of data between two computers in a secure manner even when the data flows across a public network. The name *virtual private network* derives from the fact that the data exchange happens almost as if the two computers were exchanging data using a private network.

VPNs are implemented using a technique called *tunneling*. Tunneling (also sometimes referred to as *encapsulation*) encloses the data and protocol envelope generated by one protocol stack and treats it as the data for another protocol. The second protocol and its envelope provide routing and data encryption so that the data can be routed correctly to the destination and decrypted. Tunnels can be established at the data-link layer or the network layer of the ISO/OSI seven-layer model. Point-to-Point Tunneling Protocol (PPTP), Layer 2 Forwarding (L2F), and Layer 2 Tunneling Protocol (L2TP) are examples of data-link layer tunneling. IPSec Tunneling mode is an example of network layer tunneling. (These protocols are described in more detail in the following sections.) Each of these protocols uses slightly different techniques to set up and maintain the tunnel. Data is typically transmitted through the tunnel using datagrams. Encryption methods (if any) and data compression techniques are negotiated when the tunnel is created. In some cases the tunnel client might also be assigned an IP address. PPTP, L2F, and L2TP all embed the data in a PPP frame for transmission across the connecting network.

Point-to-Point Tunneling Protocol

Point-to-Point Tunneling Protocol (PPTP) is based on a specification developed by a consortium of companies that includes Microsoft, 3Com, Ascend Communications, and others. PPTP encapsulates IP, IPX, or NetBEUI packets within an IP packet. PPTP uses TCP to exchange messages for tunnel maintenance, and uses PPP for encapsulating the data carried within the tunnel. The data carried within the tunnel can be compressed or encrypted. The encryption method used is RSA RC4 (described in Chapter 5).

PPTP can operate when the protocol is supported only on the client and on the end server the client is communicating with. No support is required from any of the routers or servers within the network the two computers are communicating across. Figure 3-21 illustrates this situation.

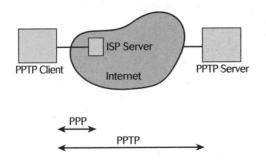

Figure 3-21   *The PPTP protocol, scenario one.*

The client first establishes a PPP session with the ISP. The client then establishes another PPP session directly with the PPTP-enabled server.

PPTP can also work in a situation in which no PPTP software is available on the client and only the ISP server (the server the client dials into) and the server the client is communicating with support PPTP. This scenario is illustrated in Figure 3-22.

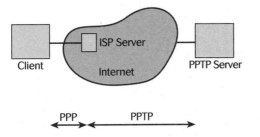

Figure 3-22   *The PPTP protocol, scenario two.*

In this scenario, the client establishes a PPP session with the ISP server. The ISP server is responsible for setting up and maintaining the PPTP tunnel between itself and the server the client wants to communicate with.

Figure 3-23 shows a simplified version of the various packets involved in PPTP transmissions over dial-up connections. (PPTP can also operate over a LAN, in which case the configuration would be slightly different.)

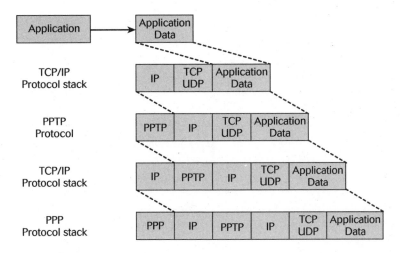

Figure 3-23 *The packets in PPTP transmissions over dial-up connections.*

Layer 2 Forwarding

Layer 2 Forwarding (L2F) is a tunneling protocol defined by Cisco Systems that accomplishes tunneling using data-link layer protocols such as ATM and Frame Relay. L2F requires that all routers and servers (including the ISP) through which the data flows support L2F.

Layer 2 Tunneling Protocol

Layer 2 Tunneling Protocol (L2TP) is the outcome of an attempt to have a single IETF-blessed data-link–layer tunneling protocol. It combines the best features of PPTP and L2F.

L2TP encapsulates PPP frames for transmission over IP, X.25, Frame Relay, or ATM. L2TP uses User Datagram Protocol (UDP) for tunnel maintenance and UDP/PPP for transmitting data through the tunnel. The data carried through the tunnel can be compressed or encrypted. The encryption can be performed by any encryption method used with PPP, for example CHAP, MS-CHAP, or PAP. (See the section on PPP earlier in this chapter for details.) Future versions of L2TP are also expected to support IPSec. L2TP is documented in an RFC draft proposal.

IPSec Tunneling

IPSec (discussed earlier in this chapter) is a standard used to transmit data securely across a network. IPSec specifies how a complete IP packet (including the IP header) is encrypted and then placed into another IP packet as its data. IPSec tunneling is a process by which the IP stack at the receiving end discards the outer IP header and decrypts the data, which is itself an IP packet. This IP packet is treated as any normal IP packet would be.

Terminal Access Controller Access Controller System

Terminal Access Controller Access Controller System (TACACS) is a protocol developed by Cisco Systems to provide security services for dial-in users and devices. When a client dials in, the server that the client is connecting to obtains credentials (username and password) from the client. TACACS defines a protocol in which the dial-in server can forward the credentials to an authentication server. The authentication server verifies the credentials and tells the dial-in server whether access should be permitted.

The XTACACS protocol is an extension to TACACS that permits multiple authentication servers to be present. XTACACS also provides mechanisms for tracking the user connect time, which can be used for accounting purposes.

Both XTACACS and TACACS use UDP as a transport mechanism. The code for TACACS and XTACACS is available for free from Cisco. Cisco does not provide any further support. TACACS transmits passwords in clear text. TACACS+ (derived from TACACS) supports PAP and CHAP (described earlier in this chapter). See RFC 1492 for more details.

Remote Authentication Dial-In User Service

Remote Authentication Dial-In User Service (RADIUS) is a protocol that provides security services for dial-in users and devices. Dial-in servers receive calls from users and forward the user credentials to RADIUS servers. A RADIUS server verifies the credentials (perhaps by contacting yet another server) and tells the dial-in server whether access should be permitted. RADIUS not only determines whether the user credentials are valid (whether the user is a known user and is indeed who he or she claims to be), but also provides information about what services the user is allowed to access. RADIUS also provides accounting information such as the user connect time. RADIUS is a competitor of XTACACS. RADIUS code is freely available; no other support is provided. See RFCs 2138 and 2139 for more details.

Dynamic Host Configuration Protocol

Dynamic Host Configuration Protocol (DHCP) allows individual computers to obtain configuration information from the DHCP server. The configuration information consists of an IP address, IP subnet mask, default router address, default DNS server address, IP packet TTL value, and so forth. The advantage of using DHCP is that administrative overhead is vastly reduced. Prior to widespread use of DHCP, network administrators had to run around to each computer and manually configure it. Another advantage is that mobile users will find it much easier to go to an office located in a different city and log in to the corporate network. For example, a statically allocated IP address assigned in New York might not work in the company's Seattle LAN. A RAS server can also use a DHCP server to obtain an IP address to hand out to a client that is dialing into the RAS server.

DHCPInform is a feature within DHCP that allows clients to obtain all information other than an IP address (IP TTL, default router address, and so forth) without providing an IP address. This is for the benefit of clients that already have an IP address but need the rest of the information.

DHCP is based on the old BOOTP protocol and depends on routers allowing BOOTP messages to pass through. DHCP provides leasing of configuration information and can reclaim the resources once the lease is terminated. This functionality is missing from BOOTP. Note that DHCP clients will not function with a BOOTP server (and vice versa) without special provisions being made in the client and server software.

Multiple DHCP servers can exist within a network or LAN segment. The servers must be configured properly, since DHCP is strictly a client/server protocol and makes no provisions (not yet, at least) to provide server-to-server communication. A client broadcasts a request to a DHCP server, and more than one DHCP server might respond, offering resources such as an IP address. The client then broadcasts its acceptance of a particular server's offer. This allows the other DHCP servers to realize that the client will not be using their offered resources, so they can return these resources back into the pool for future use.

DHCP servers can have multiple scopes. Each scope can have a set of different resources associated with it, such as a pool of IP addresses. Some addresses might be marked as reserved. The addresses marked as reserved are typically those belonging to entities that do not behave as DHCP clients—routers and DNS servers, for instance. This allows the DHCP server to act as a single repository of information on IP addresses for DHCP as well as non-DHCP clients.

A DHCP server need not be present for each LAN segment. Routers can forward the DHCP requests and responses if they are properly configured. Routers must be configured to forward DHCP requests, which are also identical to BOOTP requests. A BOOTP request contains the physical address (such as an Ethernet address) of the requesting client.

The DHCP address also contains the Gateway IP address (Giaddr) field. A router can be connected to multiple network segments and can distinguish which network the packet arrived on by identifying the card/network connection that received the packet. (See Figure 3-24.) Routers fill the Giaddr field to indicate which network segment the DHCP request is from. DHCP requests that do not go through routers will reach the DHCP server with the Giaddr field set to 0. When a DHCP server receives a request with the Giaddr field set to 0, the DHCP server satisfies the request using a default scope.

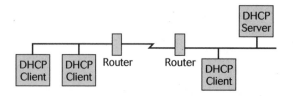

Figure 3-24 *A DHCP server servicing multiple network segments.*

DHCP servers can have different sets of parameters for each scope. This allows the DHCP server to reserve a pool of addresses for a particular network segment. This scheme has a limitation because some companies are handed Class C addresses due to the lack of IP addresses. A company that further subdivides the Class C address needs multiple DHCP servers or routers to connect the subnets.

DHCP is officially defined in RFC 1541. DHCP is defined by the Dynamic Host Configuration Working Group of IETF.

References

IP Multicast and Multicast Routing

http://www.ipmulticast.com

http://www.stardust.com

RFC 1584, "Multicast Extensions to OSPF"

RFC 1112, "Host Extensions for IP Multicasting"

RFC 1075, "Distance Vector Multicast Routing Protocol"

PPP

RFC 1764, "The PPP XNS IDP Control Protocol"

RFC 1763, "The PPP Banyan Vines Protocol"

RFC 1762, "The PPP DecNET Phase IV Protocol"

RFC 1717, "The PPP Multilink Protocol"

RFC 1663, "PPP Reliable Transmission"

RFC 1662, "PPP in HDLC-like Framing"

RFC 1661, "The Point-to-Point Protocol"

RFC 1638, "PPP Bridging Control Protocol"

RFC 1619, "PPP Over SONET/SDH"

RFC 1618, "PPP Over ISDN"

RFC 1598, "PPP in X.25"

RFC 1570, "PPP LCP Extensions"

RFC 1552, "The PPP Internetwork Packet Exchange Control Protocol"

RFC 1548, "The Point-to-Point Protocol"

RFC 1547, "Requirements for an Internet Standard Point-to-Point Protocol"

RFC 1378, "The PPP AppleTalk Control Protocol"

RFC 1377, "The PPP OSI Network Layer Control Protocol"

RFC 1334, "PPP Authentication Protocols"

RFC 1333, "PPP Link Quality Monitoring"

RFC 1332, "The PPP Internet Control Protocol"

TCP

RFC 1739, "A Primer on Internet and TCP/IP Tools"

RFC 1693, "An Extension to TCP: Partial Order Service"

RFC 1644, "T/TCP – TCP Extensions for Transactions Functional Specification"

RFC 1470, "Tools for Monitoring and Debugging TCP/IP Internets and Interconnected Devices"

RFC 1347, "TCP and UDP with Bigger Addresses, A Simple Proposal for Internet Addressing and Routing"

RFC 1337, "TIME-WAIT Assassination Hazards in TCP"

RFC 1323, "TCP Extensions for High Performance"

RFC 1273, "A Measurement Study of Changes in Service-Level Reachability in the Global TCP/IP Internet: Goals, Experimental Design, Implementation, and Policy Considerations"

RFC 1263, "TCP Extensions Considered Harmful"

RFC 1185, "TCP Extension for High-Speed Paths"

RFC 1180, "A TCP/IP Tutorial"

RFC 1146, "TCP Alternate Checksum Options"

RFC 1144, "Compressing TCP/IP Headers for Low-Speed Serial Links"

RFC 1110, "A Problem with the TCP Big Window Option"

RFC 1106, "TCP Big Window and Nak Options"

RFC 1072, "TCP Extensions for Long-Delay Paths"

RFC 1025, "TCP and IP Bake Off"

RFC 962, "TCP-4 Prime"

RFC 896, "Congestion Control in IP/TCP Internetworks"

RFC 879, "The TCP Maximum Segment Size and Related Topics"

RFC 872, "TCP on a LAN"

RFC 813, "Window and Acknowledgement Strategy in TCP"

RFC 793, "Transmission Control Protocol"

Routing

RFC 1787, "Routing in a Multiprovider Internet"

RFC 1786, "Representation of IP Routing Policies in a Routing Registry"

RFC 1723, "RIP Version 2 Carrying Additional Information"

RFC 1716, "Towards Requirements for Routers"

RFC 1702, "Generic Routing Encapsulation over IPv4 Networks"

RFC 1701, "Generic Routing Encapsulation"

RFC 1520, "Exchanging Routing Information Across Provider Boundaries in the CIDR Environment"

RFC 1519, "Classless Inter-Domain Routing: An Address Assignment and Aggregation Strategy"

RFC 1517, "Applicability Statement for the Implementation of Classless Inter-Domain Routing"

RFC 1479, "Inter-Domain Policy Routing Protocol Specification: Version 1"

RFC 1478, "An Architecture for Inter-Domain Policy Routing"

RFC 1397, "Default Route Advertisement In BGP2 and BGP3 Versions of the Border Gateway Protocol"

RFC 1388, "RIP Version 2 Carrying Additional Information"

RFC 1380, "IESG Deliberations on Routing and Addressing"

RFC 1364, "BGP OSPF Interaction"

RFC 1267, "Border Gateway Protocol Version 3"

RFC 1264, "Internet Routing Protocol Standardization Criteria"

RFC 1195, "Use of OSI IS-IS for Routing in TCP/IP and Dual Environments"

RFC 1136, "Administrative Domains and Routing Domains"

RFC 1104, "Models of Policy Based Routing"

RFC 1075, "Distance Vector Multicast Routing Protocol"

RFC 904, "Exterior Gateway Protocol"

IPv6

RFC 1972, "A Method for the Transmission of IPv6 Packets over Ethernet Networks"

RFC 1971, "IPv6 Stateless Address Autoconfiguration"

RFC 1970, "Neighbor Discovery for IPv6"

RFC 1933, "Translation Mechanisms for IPv6 Hosts and Routers"

RFC 1897, "IPv6 Testing Address Allocation"

RFC 1887, "An Architecture for IPv6 Unicast Address Allocation"

RFC 1886, "DNS Extensions to Support IPv6"

RFC 1885, "Internet Control Message Protocol for IPv6"

RFC 1884, "IPv6 Addressing Architecture"

RFC 1883, "IPv6 Specification"

RFC 1809, "Using the Flow Label Field in IPv6"

IPSec

RFC 1829, "The ESP DES-CBC Transform"

RFC 1828, "IP Authentication Using Keyed MD5"

RFC 1827, "IP Encapsulating Security Payload"

RFC 1826, "IP Authentication Header"

RFC 1825, "Security Architecture for the Internet Protocol"

General References

http://www.intel.com/IAL/winsock2

http://www.microsoft.com/intdev/pptp/pptp-f.htm

http://www.microsoft.com/win32dev/netwrk/winsock2/ws295sdk.html

RFC 2139, "RADIUS Accounting"

RFC 2138, "Remote Authentication Dial-In User Service (RADIUS)"

RFC 1753, "IPng Technical Requirements of the Nimrod Routing and Addressing Architecture"

RFC 1752, "The Recommendation for the IPng Protocol"

RFC 1492, "An Access Control Protocol, Sometimes Called TACACS"

RFC 1392, "Internet User's Glossary"

RFC 1390, "Transmission of IP and ARP over FDDI Networks"

RFC 1386, "The U.S. Domain"

RFC 1256, "ICMP Router Discovery Messages"

RFC 1122, "Requirements for Internet Hosts – Communications Layers"

RFC 950, "Internet Standard Subnetting Procedure"

RFC 815, "IP Datagram Reassembly Algorithms"

RFC 792, "Internet Control Message Protocol"

RFC 791, "Internet Protocol"

RFC 768, "User Datagram Protocol"

RFC 719, "Discussion on RCTE"

4

Encoding Standards

THIS CHAPTER DISCUSSES A VARIETY OF encoding standards, although only some of the protocols described have been adopted by a standards body. I'll cover standards for characters, files, and data structures. I'll also cover the part of Multipurpose Internet Mail Extensions (MIME) pertaining to encoding of characters. The part of MIME pertaining to encoding of electronic mail messages is described in Chapter 9, "Electronic Mail Messaging."

Character Encoding

Character encoding defines how characters are represented within data items that a computer processes. Character encoding is usually specified as a table in which each character is assigned a name and a numeric value. The numeric value can be used as an index into the encoding table and is often called a *code point*. An example of an encoding table is the US-ASCII table shown on the next page in Table 4-1. Note that character encoding specifies the value assigned to each character but not necessarily any order of precedence based on these values. For example, the values cannot be used for sorting text strings, so a different table, called a *sorting table*, is usually employed. The sections that follow describe various character encoding schemes.

7-Bit ASCII/US-ASCII

Strictly speaking, the 7-bit ASCII encoding scheme uses 8 bits, with the most significant bit always set to zero. In terms of storage, each character occupies 8 bits (one byte). This encoding scheme is also referred to as US-ASCII and is specified by the International Organization for Standardization (ISO) in its ISO 646 standard. A vast majority of computers support the US-ASCII encoding scheme. Various other encoding schemes can be considered extensions of the US-ASCII scheme in that they are capable of representing a wider range of characters, with the first 128 character representations the same as those in US-ASCII. English, Swahili, and Latin languages can be accommodated using ISO 646. Table 4-1 presents the 7-bit US-ASCII table.

Table 4-1 The 7-Bit US-ASCII Table

Character	Decimal Value	Hexadecimal Value
NUL	0	0
SOH	1	1
STX	2	2
ETX	3	3
EOT	4	4
ENQ	5	5
ACK	6	6
BEL	7	7
BS	8	8
HT	9	9
NL	10	a
VT	11	b
NP	12	c
CR	13	d
SO	14	e
SI	15	f
DLE	16	10
DC1	17	11
DC2	18	12
DC3	19	13
DC4	20	14
NAK	21	15
SYN	22	16
ETB	23	17

Table 4-1   The 7-Bit US-ASCII Table

Character	Decimal Value	Hexadecimal Value
CAN	24	18
EM	25	19
SUB	26	1a
ESC	27	1b
FS	28	1c
GS	29	1d
RS	30	1e
US	31	1f
SP	32	20
!	33	21
"	34	22
#	35	23
$	36	24
%	37	25
&	38	26
'	39	27
(	40	28
)	41	29
*	42	2a
+	43	2b
,	44	2c
-	45	2d
.	46	2e
/	47	2f
0	48	30
1	49	31
2	50	32
3	51	33
4	52	34
5	53	35
6	54	36
7	55	37
8	56	38
9	57	39

Table 4-1   The 7-Bit US-ASCII Table

Character	Decimal Value	Hexadecimal Value
:	58	3a
;	59	3b
<	60	3c
=	61	3d
>	62	3e
?	63	3f
@	64	40
A	65	41
B	66	42
C	67	43
D	68	44
E	69	45
F	70	46
G	71	47
H	72	48
I	73	49
J	74	4a
K	75	4b
L	76	4c
M	77	4d
N	78	4e
O	79	4f
P	80	50
Q	81	51
R	82	52
S	83	53
T	84	54
U	85	55
V	86	56
W	87	57
X	88	58
Y	89	59
Z	90	5a
[	91	5b

Table 4-1   The 7-Bit US-ASCII Table

Character	Decimal Value	Hexadecimal Value
\	92	5c
]	93	5d
^	94	5e
_	95	5f
`	96	60
a	97	61
b	98	62
c	99	63
d	100	64
e	101	65
f	102	66
g	103	67
h	104	68
i	105	69
j	106	6a
k	107	6b
l	108	6c
m	109	6d
n	110	6e
o	111	6f
p	112	70
q	113	71
r	114	72
s	115	73
t	116	74
u	117	75
v	118	76
w	119	77
x	120	78
y	121	79
z	122	7a
{	123	7b
|	124	7c
}	125	7d
~	126	7e
DEL	127	7f

8-Bit Encoding

The 7-bit encoding defined by ISO 646 was inadequate for a wide variety of human languages. As a result, ISO defined a series of encoding standards known as the 8859 series. The 8859 series of encoding standards uses 8 bits instead of 7 bits, allowing the most significant bit of the byte to be set to 1 instead of 0. The first 128 characters in all of the 8859 series encoding standards are identical to those in ISO 646. Table 4-2 lists some of the 8859 character sets and the languages they can represent. Full details can be found at http://www.w3.org/International.

Table 4-2   Some of the ISO 8859 Character Sets

Character Set	Language
8859-1	Afrikaans, Albanian, Basque, Catalan, Danish, Dutch, English, Faroese, Finnish, French, Galician, German, Icelandic, Irish, Italian
8859-2	Croatian, Czech, Hungarian
8859-3	Esperanto, Maltese
8859-5	Bulgarian, Byellorussian, Macedonian
8859-6	Arabic
8859-7	Greek
8859-8	Hebrew
8859-9	Turkish
8859-10	Lapp, Latvian, Lithuanian

ISO 8859-1 is widely implemented. Sadly, the other character sets were implemented rather loosely, and a lot of vendors did not completely follow the specifications. Only time will tell, but Unicode, which we'll cover in the next section, seems rather more promising than the ISO 8859 standards.

Unicode (16-Bit Encoding)

Unicode is a character encoding scheme that is growing in importance. The Unicode standard is published by the Unicode Consortium. Unicode attempts to unify the various standards into a single standard, allowing the possibility of generating software that can easily serve a number of languages and users. Products such as Microsoft Windows NT and Novell Netware version 4 now ship with Unicode support.

Unicode represents each character with two bytes; that is, as a 16-bit value. The first 128 code points in Unicode have the same values as in US-ASCII, and the first 256 code points have the same value as in ISO 8859-1.

The major goals for the Unicode Standard are as follows:

- Universal: The specification should be broad in scope such that it accommodates computer languages and spoken languages. The Unicode Standard defines encoding for almost all spoken languages in the world, including Latin, Greek, Indic, Hangul, Chinese, Japanese, and Sanskrit.

- Efficient: The specification should result in efficient software. With a fixed-width character, software need not search forward or backward for escape sequences, and text processing software can be efficient as well as simple to write.

- Unambiguous: The specification should provide that a given 16-bit value always results in the same character.

The Unicode Consortium publishes a number of items besides the Unicode Standard. The consortium publishes Unicode Technical Reports, which are not (yet) considered part of the Unicode Standard. Usually, the contents of technical reports is incorporated into a subsequent version of the Unicode Standard. Technical reports also serve as a vehicle to deliver minor updates to the Unicode Standard. The latest Unicode specification is labeled Unicode 2.1. Notable differences between Unicode 2.0 and Unicode 2.1 include the following:

- Addition of an object replacement character
- Addition of the Euro sign
- Additional math property characters
- Errata for various categories, including letter property, identifier, bidirectional behavior, and others
- UTF-7 sample code correction
- Unicode character database changes

The Unicode Consortium also publishes draft Unicode Technical Reports. These have been edited for content and are posted to the Unicode Consortium Web site (http://www.unicode.org) to invite public and internal feedback.

Unicode provides for a single code point for each character. Unlike US-ASCII, Unicode distinguishes between special characters such as the minus sign and the hyphen, providing distinct encodings for each. However, Unicode does not provide different code points for, say, an "a" and an "*a*" (italic a). This is a font issue, rather than an encoding issue. Unicode is also capable of handling languages that do not flow left to right, and it provides a unified definition for the Chinese/Japanese/Korean (CJK) ideographs.

The Unicode Standard divides the range of available codes into linguistic and functional categories, depicted on the next page in Figure 4-1.

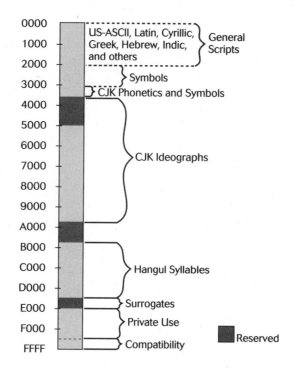

Figure 4-1 *The Unicode Standard space allocation.*

The categories describe the following information:

- The General Scripts area is allocated for scripts that have relatively small character sets. These include Latin, Cyrillic, Greek, Hebrew, Indic, among others. Of course, the first 128 characters have values that are numerically the same as those in US-ASCII.

- The Symbols area is allocated for punctuation, scientific and mathematical symbols, and other special characters.

- The CJK Phonetics and Symbols area defines miscellaneous phonetics, symbols, and punctuation for CJK.

- The CJK Ideographs area defines 20,902 CJK ideographs.

- The Hangul Syllables area defines 11,712 Hangul syllables.

- The Surrogates area reserves 2024 code points for future extensibility.

- The Private Use area reserves 6400 code points for user and vendor definitions.

- The Compatibility area defines some characters that have other Unicode definitions but that need a second definition for compatibility purposes.

Some code points are reserved. The values 0xFFFF and 0xFFFE are special and should not be used.

Note that Unicode does not imply a sorting order. Unicode simply assigns a numeric value to each character and symbol. Another table (which is outside the scope of this book) is required for sorting strings; for example, to decide that "but" sorts ahead of "cat." This sorting table is language dependent. Unicode also does not deal with fonts.

Unicode and ISO 10646

In the early 1990s, both the ISO and the Unicode Consortium were engaged in defining a character code standard. The two bodies cooperated to define a single standard. Each body still publishes its own specification (after extensive consultation with the other body); however, when one body publishes its specification, the other body publishes its own, new specification to match. Thus, ISO 10646-1:1993 is a standard from ISO that is matched by the Unicode Standard. ISO has made some modifications for the Korean language (and has also added more character definitions). The Unicode Standard version 2.0 matches the ammendments to 10646.

ISO 10646 has two forms:

- A 4-byte, 31-bit encoding form. The 2^{31} code positions are conceptually subdivided into 128 groups. Each group consists of 256 planes. Each plane consists of 256 rows of 256 cells. This encoding is referred to as UCS-4 (Universal Character Set, 4-byte form).
- A 2-byte, 16-bit encoding form. Sometimes referred to as the Basic Multilingual Plane, this encoding is also referred to as UCS-2 (Universal Character Set, 2-byte form).

The Unicode Standard version 1.1 is identical to UCS-2, provided the correct ISO 10646 specification is considered. Details of ISO 10646 may be found at http://www.iso.ch.

UTF-7

UTF-7 stands for Universal Transformation Format, 7-bit form. Unicode represents a character as a 16-bit value. Current network infrastructure does not permit the transmission of 8-bit data, let alone 16-bit data. UTF-7 is a conversion scheme that transforms Unicode characters to ASCII characters. Unicode characters that are outside the ASCII range are represented using Shift sequences. UTF-7 thus allows transmission of Unicode data through networks that deal well with 7-bit data. UTF-7 is also reversible, meaning that the original Unicode data can be obtained by doing a reverse transformation.

UTF-7 is detailed in RFC 1642; further details can be found at http://www.unicode.org. UTF-7 is not part of the ISO 10646 specification. The Unicode Standard Version 2.0 book from the Unicode Consortium includes sample C code that converts characters from Unicode to UTF-7 and vice versa.

UTF-8

Universal Transformation Format, 8-bit form (UTF-8) converts a 16-bit Unicode character into a series of from 2 to 5 bytes, with the lead byte detailing how many bytes follow. The number of bytes depends on the value of the particular Unicode character, and all characters with ASCII values (from 0 through 127) are represented in a single byte following the lead byte. UTF-8 is considered fairly efficient, but when searching for a particular character in the middle of a byte stream, one might have to parse backward up to 4 bytes in order to find the start of a character. UTF-8 is also reversible (just like UTF-7); the original Unicode data can be obtained by doing a reverse transformation.

UTF-8 was originally developed by the X/Open Consortium and is now part of the ISO 10646 specification. Complete details can be obtained from the Unicode Consortium Web page at http://www.unicode.org. The Unicode Standard Version 2.0 book also includes C code for a sample application that converts Unicode characters to UTF-8 and vice versa.

MIME Character Encoding Techniques

MIME is primarily a protocol for transmitting and sending e-mail messages, but a portion of MIME specifies how characters are encoded. MIME has two ways of encoding characters, Quoted-Printable and Base64. MIME encoding techniques are used to transform data from a form in which all 8 bits are in use to a form in which the data is represented using 7-bit ASCII. This ensures that the data can be successfully transferred through the Internet, where a lot of the mail transport can handle only ASCII data. Prior to MIME, this was accomplished using Uuencode to encode the data and Uudecode to decode the data. (I'll cover Uuencode and Uudecode later in this chapter).

A field called Content-Transfer-Encoding is defined in the MIME header with six possible values. These are Quoted-Printable, Base64, Binary, 7Bit, 8Bit, and X-Token.

Quoted Printable

Quoted Printable encoding is used for data in which the majority of the characters are already 7-bit ASCII characters. The intent with this encoding technique is to leave the ASCII characters alone and to encode only the characters that have the high bit (of an 8-bit byte) turned on. Quoted-Printable transforms non-ASCII characters into a sequence of two characters, with the first character being an equal sign (=). The result is that most of the message is readable, even when it has not been decoded. Quoted-Printable encoding is decribed in RFC 1521.

Base64

The Base64 encoding technique renders data unreadable without decoding it and results in the message being expanded by a factor of one third. The encoding algorithm converts every group of three characters (24 bits) into four ASCII characters (32 bits) in the following way: each 6-bit group is used as an index into an array of 64 printable characters, and the character referenced by the index is placed into the output string. A 65th character, the equal sign (=), is used to specify a special processing function. These 65 characters, which are common among US-ASCII, Extended Binary Coded Decimal Interchange Code (EBCDIC), and ISO 646, are known as the Base64 alphabet, which is shown in Table 4-3.

Table 4-3 The Base64 Alphabet

6-Bit Value	Encoding	6-Bit Value	Encoding	6-Bit Value	Encoding	6-Bit Value	Encoding
0	A	17	R	34	i	51	z
1	B	18	S	35	j	52	0
2	C	19	T	36	k	53	1
3	D	20	U	37	l	54	2
4	E	21	V	38	m	55	3
5	F	22	W	39	n	56	4
6	G	23	X	40	o	57	5
7	H	24	Y	41	p	58	6
8	I	25	Z	42	q	59	7
9	J	26	a	43	r	60	8
10	K	27	b	44	s	61	9
11	L	28	c	45	t	62	+
12	M	29	d	46	u	63	/
13	N	30	e	47	v	(pad)	=
14	O	31	f	48	w		
15	P	32	g	49	x		
16	Q	33	h	50	y		

Characters in the encoded stream that are not part of the Base64 alphabet are ignored. This permits the insertion of extra carriage return and linefeed characters into the data stream to ensure that the message can pass through intermediate e-mail gateways. These characters are simply ignored when the message is decoded.

Binary, 7Bit, 8Bit, and X-Token

Binary encoding indicates there is no encoding, non-ASCII characters may be present, and the lines may be too long for Simple Mail Transfer Protocol (SMTP) to be able to successfully transport the message.

7Bit encoding indicates there is no encoding, the characters are all ASCII, and the lines are short enough for SMTP to be able to successfully transport the message.

8Bit encoding indicates there is no encoding, the lines are short, and non-ASCII characters may be present.

X-Token encoding indicates the encoding technique is privately negotiated between the sender and receiver SMTP.

The intent with explicitly defining Binary, 7Bit, and 8Bit encoding is to provide for future features in the sense that all of these indicate no encoding is used, but future implementations may leverage knowledge provided by these encoding techniques.

Uuencode/Uudecode

Uuencode is a method of encoding files to make them suitable for transmission. A lot of the network infrastructure supports transmission of 7-bit characters only. Uuencode is a method of transforming files that have bytes with the most significant bit set into files in which the bytes do not have the most signifcant bit set. Uuencoded files are often referred to as ASCII files, since the contents of the file are ASCII characters. Uudecode accomplishes the reverse transformation of Uuencode. Uuencoded files typically have an extension .uu_, for example filefoo.uu_.

Abstract Syntax Notation One

Abstract Syntax Notation One (ASN.1) is a protocol that is at the Presentation layer (layer six) of the ISO seven-layer model. ASN.1 is in widespread use in telecommunications, cellular phones, aviation information exchange, as well as the Internet. ASN.1 provides specification notation for the purposes of describing a standard and also provides a means of specifying rules for encoding data structures while the data is being transported between two systems that are running a well-defined protocol. An example of this usage is ASN.1 notation used for specifying details of the Lightweight Directory Access Protocol (LDAP).

ASN.1 is defined in two ISO draft standards: ISO 8824, titled "Specification of Abstract Syntax Notation One," and ISO 8825, titled "Specification of Basic Encoding Rules for Abstract Syntax Notation One." This section emphasizes a description of ASN.1 for the purpose of encoding data structures.

ASN.1 encoding lends itself well to automation in terms of having compilers and routines do the parsing for the encoding and decoding. ASN.1 defines various types of encoding rules, described in the following sections.

Basic Encoding Rules

Basic Encoding Rules (BER) starts with some predefined data types that are commonly used. These are called primitive data types. Using primitive data types, an application can construct complex data structures called *constructed types*. BER encodes each data item as a tag, length, and value.

The tag consists of three parts—a class, a form, and a value:

- A tag class can be either Universal, Application, Private, or Context Specific. Universal tags apply to the data types defined by the ASN.1 specification. Application tags are defined by a particular application. Private tags are defined by a vendor. Context Specific tags have meaning only within the context of a data structure.

- A tag form can be either Primitive or Constructed.

- A tag value can be any of those listed in the table below.

Data Type	Tag Value
Boolean	1
Integer	2
Bit String	3
Octet String	4
NULL	5
Object Identifier	6
Object Descriptor	7
EXTERNAL	8
Real	9
Enumerated	10
Sequence	16
Set	17
NumericString	18
PrintableString	19
TeletextString	20
VideoTextString	21
IA5String	22
UTCTime	23

Data Type	Tag Value
GeneralizedTime	24
GraphicString	25
VisibleString	26
GeneralString	27

If the data item being encoded is a Constructed type, the length might not be known. In this case, the value would be a nested structure of tag/length/value constructs.

Canonical Encoding Rules

Canonical Encoding Rules (CER) is a variation of BER that can operate on huge amounts of data using less memory. BER requires the message to be completely available, whereas CER can start encoding a message that is still being constructed.

Distinguished Encoding Rules

Distinguished Encoding Rules (DER) is a variation of BER that adds data privacy. (See Chapter 5, "Cryptography and Security Basics," for details.) With the growing emphasis on electronic commerce, usage of DER is likely to increase.

Packed Encoding Rules

Packed Encoding Rules (PER) is a variation of BER that emphasizes efficiency by generating a more compact encoding using less processing power. PER is used when CPU capacity and transmission bandwidth are precious commodities (for example, in the aviation industry).

References

CCITT Recommendation X-288, "Specification of Abstract Syntax Notation.One"

CCITT Recommendation X-209, "Specification of Basic Encoding Rules for ASN.1"

http://www.iso.ch

http://www.unicode.org

http://www.w3.org/International

RFC 2279, "UTF-8: A Transformation of ISO 1064E"

RFC 2152, "UTF-7: A Mail-Safe Transformation of Unicode"

RFC 2049, "Multipurpose Internet Mail Extensions (MIME) Part Five: Conformance Criteria and Examples"

RFC 2048, "Multipurpose Internet Mail Extensions (MIME) Part Four: Registration Procedures"

RFC 2047, "MIME (Multipurpose Internet Mail Extensions) Part Three: Message Header Extensions for Non-ASCII Text"

RFC 2046, "Multipurpose Internet Mail Extensions (MIME) Part Two: Media Types"

RFC 2045, "Multipurpose Internet Mail Extensions (MIME) Part One: Format of Internet Message Bodies"

RFC 1698, "Octet Sequences for Upper Layer OSI"

RFC 1642, "UTF-7: A Mail-Safe Transformation Format of Unicode"

RFC 1521, "MIME (Multipurpose Internet Mail Extensions) Part One: Mechanisms for Specifying and Describing the Format of Internet Message Bodies"

5

Cryptography and Security Basics

CRYPTOGRAPHY IS THE SCIENCE OF SCRAMBLING data into a form that is unintelligible to everyone but an intended audience. This is accomplished by means of an encryption algorithm, or *cipher*. The scrambled data is called cipher text. The original data is called plain text. *Cryptanalysis* is the art of breaking ciphers. *Authentication* is the means of being sure of the identity of the person or process that one is communicating with. Authentication can be one-way, where either party is sure about the identity of the other, or two-way, where both parties are sure of the identity of the other.

In this chapter, I'll review encryption standards and other security basics. Figure 5-1 provides an overview of material covered in this chapter.

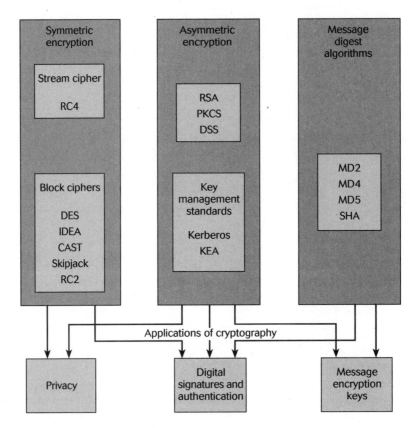

Figure 5-1 *An overview of cryptography and encryption.*

Encryption Methods

In general there are two types of encryption methods. These are *symmetric encryption* (also called convention encryption) and *asymmetric encryption* (also called public key encryption).

Symmetric Encryption

Think of symmetric encryption as a mathematical formula of the form

Encrypted Data = Function (Data, Key)

with an inverse function existing of the form

Plain Text Data = Inverse Function (Encrypted Data, Key)

Figure 5-2 shows the flow of data in symmetric encryption.

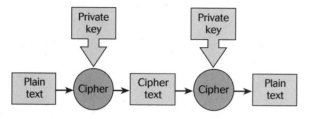

Figure 5-2   *Symmetric encryption.*

The trick here is to arrange things in such a way that even when the function and inverse function are publicly known, recovering the plain text data without knowledge of the key is impossible.

Symmetric encryption is also referred to as secret key encryption because the secret key must be shared between the sender and receiver of data. In the next few sections, I'll discuss some important symmetric encryption algorithms, or ciphers. In general, there are two types of ciphers. A *block cipher* takes a given length of data as input and produces a different given length of encrypted data. A *stream cipher* converts plain text to encrypted text one bit at a time.

Data Encryption Standard

Data Encryption Standard (DES) is a block cipher that operates on 64-bit blocks of data by using a 56-bit key. DES has been extensively analyzed and tested and is considered a very secure system. DES can be operated in two different modes, Electronic Code Book (ECB) mode and Cipher Block Chaining (CBC) mode. In ECB mode, DES operates on 64 bits of data at a time using the same 56-bit key. Thus, each 64-bit set of data is encrypted independently of the rest of the data. In CBC mode, each 64-bit block of data is XORed with the previous 64-bit block before being encrypted. This ensures that the same 64-bit block of data will encrypt to different values when it occurs at different places in the message being sent.

DES is designed to be extremely fast and lends itself well to being implemented in hardware. Exporting products that use DES is prohibited by the United States government. DES is approved by ANSI.

For situations in which DES is considered to be insecure, a variation of DES called Triple-DES is used. Strictly speaking, there are a number of variations in the way Triple-DES has been used. The most basic variation is to encrypt the data using a DES key. The resulting data is then encrypted using a second key, and the data from the second encryption is then encrypted using yet a third key. The three keys are unrelated to each other.

International Data Encryption Algorithm

International Data Encryption Algorithm (IDEA) is another block cipher. It uses a key length of 128 bits. IDEA is a European standard (from ETH, Zurich) that was proposed in 1990. IDEA is considered secure and compares favorably with DES in speed of implementation and security of the encryption against cryptanalysis.

CAST

CAST is a block cipher that uses 128-bit keys in the United States, but a 40-bit version also exists for export. CAST is used by Northern Telecom (NORTEL).

Skipjack/Capstone

Skipjack is a cipher developed by the National Security Agency (NSA) that uses 80-bit keys. Skipjack is part of the initiative called Capstone, a plan by the U.S. government to develop publicly available cryptography standards that are to the government's liking. Capstone has four major components:

- A cipher, called Skipjack.
- A digital signature algorithm that follows the Digital Signature Standard (DSS).
- A hash function that follows the Secure Hash Algorithm (SHA).
- A chip that implements all of the above. Fortezza is a PCMCIA based upon this chip.

Skipjack is implemented using the proprietary Capstone chip, and the algorithm is secret. Controversy has arisen over the fact that Skipjack would leave the keys with "escrow agencies," which would be able to decrypt messages when ordered to do so by a court.

RC2 and RC4

RC2 and RC4 are ciphers designed by Ron Rivest, a cofounder of RSA Data Security. These use variable-length private keys and are designed as replacements for DES to help in exporting a product. RC2 is a block cipher with a block length of 64 bits; RC4 is a stream cipher. RC2 and RC4 are designed to be as fast, or faster, than DES. With a 40-bit (or less) key length, the export process has been streamlined. RC2 and RC4 are proprietary to RSA Data Securities.

Asymmetric Encryption

Asymmetric encryption was first developed in the 1970s. The idea behind asymmetric key encryption is that two keys are involved. The first key (the public key) is published and is used by entities intending to send data securely to the key owner. The second key (the private key) is known only to the owner. What makes asymmetric encryption interesting is that the two keys are often reversible. This means that the private key can be used to encrypt data that can be decrypted only by using the public key and vice versa. This capability leads directly to the concept of digital signatures, discussed in the sections that follow. The concept of asymmetric encryption rests on the assumption that it is extremely difficult to find the factors of a very large number that is the product of two primes. No mathematical proof exists for this assumption, and it is a case of proof by demonstration in real life. Figure 5-3 illustrates the basics of public key cryptography.

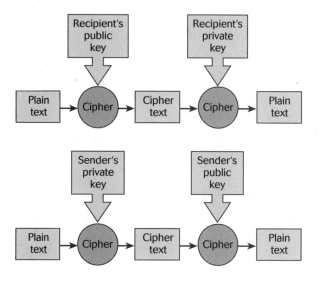

Figure 5-3   *Asymmetric encryption.*

The upper part of the figure illustrates encrypting plain text data using the recipient's public key. The recipient then decrypts the cipher text using his or her private key. This ensures that only the intended recipient (who is presumably the only person in possession of the recipient's private key) can decipher the message.

The lower part of the figure shows another method of asymmetric encryption. Here the text is encrypted using the sender's private key and deciphered by using the sender's public key. If the expected plain text is known in advance, this method provides a basis for digital signatures. Here the message could have come only from the particular sender because only that person is in possession of the sender's private key.

RSA

RSA is named after its inventors: Ron Rivest, Adi Shamir, and Leonard Adleman, founding members of RSA Data Security. RSA might be not only the most famous asymmetric encryption cipher, but the most famous cipher, period. The mathematical assumption behind RSA is that it is extremely difficult to find the factors of a very large number that is the product of two primes. Also, given the public key, it is relatively hard to deduce the private key. RSA has been extensively analyzed, and it is considered secure, provided a sufficiently long key is used. Although 512 bits is considered too short for security, 1024 bits is considered good. Some have argued recently that increases in processor speed have made RSA vulnerable to a brute attack. However, the very same increases in processor speed also allow longer keys for encryption or double encryption, thus increasing security.

Public Key Cryptography Standards

The Public Key Cryptography Standards (PKCS) have been proposed by RSA Laboratories and a consortium of companies that includes Microsoft, Apple, Digital Equipment, Sun Microsystems, and Lotus. There are actually a number of different standards (and more are likely to be added as PKCS continues to evolve) in the PKCS family, each of which covers a different area. Table 5-1 lists the various standards. (Note that PKCS 2 and PKCS 4 have been merged into PKCS 1.)

Table 5-1   Public Key Cryptography Standards

Name	Description
PKCS 1	Describes how data may be encrypted and decrypted using RSA public keys
PKCS 3	Describes the Diffe-Hellman protocol (for key exchange and agreement)
PKCS 5	Covers encryption using a secret key
PKCS 6	Describes a format for certificates that are a superset of X.509 certificates
PKCS 7	Defines message syntax for messages that include encrypted data and signatures
PKCS 8	Defines a format for private keys
PKCS 9	Defines data items used by other PKCS standards
PKCS 10	Defines syntax for certification requests
PKCS 11	Defines an application programming interface (API) for devices such as smartcards that implement cryptographic functionality

Digital Signature Standard

Digital Signature Standard (DSS) is a cipher endorsed by the U.S. government. The key length can vary between 512 and 1024 bits. DSS is meant for producing digital signatures (see the section on digital signatures later in this chapter) and not for data privacy. Some security holes have been found with the DSS standard and it is not yet in widespread use.

Message Digest Algorithms

Before we go on to discuss applications of ciphers, such as authentication and digital signatures, it's helpful to consider message digest algorithms. Message digest algorithms, together with asymmetric encryption, provide the means for digital signatures.

First consider a hash function. A hash function takes a variable number of bits as input and produces a fixed-length string—the hash value. If the hash function is extremely hard to invert, it is referred to as a message digest. A message digest algorithm practically ensures that the hash value is unique.

MD2, MD4, and MD5

MD2, MD4, and MD5 are message digest algorithms that were invented by Rivest. Each produces a 128-bit hash value. MD2 is the slowest, whereas MD4 is the fastest. MD5 could be described as a variant of MD4 that sacrifices speed for some security. For detailed information, see RFC 1321 (MD2), RFC 1320 (MD4), and RFC 1319 (MD5).

Secure Hash Algorithm

Secure Hash Algorithm (SHA) is a message digest algorithm that produces a 160-bit hash value. SHA has been approved as a standard by the U.S. government (as part of the Capstone project). SHA is a little more secure than MD4 or MD5 because it produces a longer hash function. The longer hash function reduces the chance that two different inputs will hash to the same value.

Applications of Ciphers

Using the techniques described above, a number of interesting applications have been developed. Some of these are described in the following sections.

Data Privacy and Secure Communications Channel

An obvious use of security is to ensure that data is kept private and secure while it is transported by means of a communications channel. Netscape's Secure Sockets Layer versions 2 and 3, as well as Microsoft's Private Communications Technology are examples of transport level security that guarantees privacy. Obviously, both Secure Sockets Layer and Private Communications Technology are not just cryptography applications. They are also APIs for programmers writing to a transport-level interface. SSL and PCT are described in more detail later in this chapter.

Digital Signatures

Digital signatures provide a means for the contents of a message and the identity of the sender to be verified. A digital signature is implemented using an asymmetric encryption cipher and a hash function. Digital signatures depend on the fact that asymmetric encryption ciphers are reversible. Digital signatures also depend on the fact that the original message, the signature, and the key pair are related so that changing any one of them will result in a failure to verify the signature. Figure 5-4 on the next page shows in detail how digital signatures work.

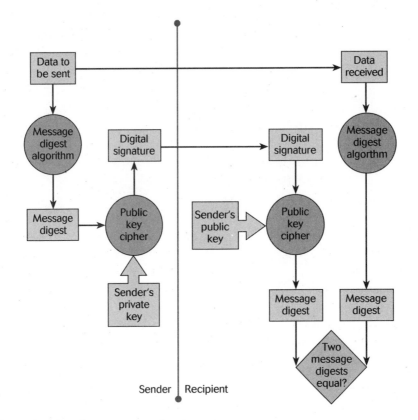

Figure 5-4 *How digital signatures work.*

The sender prepares a message digest (depicted in the upper left corner of the figure). This message digest is then encrypted using the sender's private key. The recipient receives the message and decrypts the message digest using the sender's public key. The recipient also computes the message digest, which should match the decrypted message digest. If it does, the signatures verify. If it doesn't, either the message contents have been meddled with or the signature is a forgery.

RSA and Digital Signatures

RSA can be used for generating and verifying digital signatures. To sign a message, the sender encrypts the message using his or her private key. The sender transmits the message and the signature. The recipient decrypts the message using the sender's public key and compares the result with the message already received. If the message was in fact signed by the sender, the two should match.

Note that when RSA is used for ensuring data privacy, the sender encrypts the message using the recipient's public key (instead of the sender's private key, as is done for signing).

Digital Signature Standard

Digital Signature Standard (DSS) is an asymmetric encryption cipher endorsed by the U.S. government. The key length can vary between 512 and 1024 bits. DSS is used for producing digital signatures and not for data privacy. It is based on the digital signature algorithm (DSA) adopted by the National Institute of Standards and Technology (NIST).

Whether DSA/DSS will replace the more widely adopted RSA digital signature scheme is a question only time will answer. DSA/DSS have been criticized for a number of shortcomings, some of which have been addressed. One issue that remains is that DSA is more processor intensive (and time intensive) for signature verification than for signature generation. This is contrary to the belief that signature verification is done more often than signature generation.

Time Stamping Services

When a digital signature is stamped by a trusted authority, the trusted authority can add a time stamp to the signature, leading to the concept of time stamping services. The trusted authority can thus attest to the fact that the given party signed the document at a given date and time.

Authentication

Authentication is the process by which you know for certain that the person or process with which you are carrying on a conversation is indeed the party they claim to be. Authentication can be accomplished by a number of different means. It can be based on a unique property possessed by the person or process. One example is fingerprints. Authentication can also be based on knowledge possessed by the person or process. An example here is digital signatures, where the unique knowledge is the sender's private key. SSL and PCT provide authentication services (in addition to data privacy).

Another general method of authentication is the Microsoft NTLM Challenge/Response protocol. The Microsoft NTLM Challenge/Response protocol has its roots in the first version of LAN Manager that shipped for the OS/2 operating system. This authentication mechanism is based on what a person or process possesses; in this case, a secret password. A client connects to the server, and the server sends a challenge to the client. The client then generates a challenge response by using a hash of the user password. This challenge response is then sent to the server. The Microsoft Windows NT server will know the user's password, so it can independently compute the challenge response and verify that the client's response is correct. (Strictly speaking, the server could be in another domain, and in that case, the server uses a feature of Windows NT called *pass through validation* to validate the client response.) There are well documented APIs that a programmer can use to implement Microsoft NTLM Challenge/Response protocol so that the programmer (at the server or the client end) doesn't need to bother with details of the cryptographic algorithm. The main point here is that the user's password is never sent over the wire. For more information, see "Windows NT Security Service Provider Interface" later in this chapter.

Authenticode

Authenticode is a new Microsoft technology that first shipped with Microsoft Internet Explorer version 3. Authenticode is actually two things: it's a technology that clients can use to verify the nature of code they download, and it's also an API that developers can use to sign their code.

The technology enables code that is downloaded over the Internet to be verified as to sender identification and whether or not the code has been altered. This is a direct application of asymmetric encryption. Microsoft has engaged the services of Verisign to act as a certificate authority. Clients and application developers can request and be issued certificates. Internet Explorer then allows the client to choose a security level that applies to any code downloaded over the Internet. By means of asymmetric encryption, the client can verify the authenticity of any code it has downloaded. A piece of code called the Windows Trust Verification Service allows the client to choose the level of security. For example, a client can choose to deem all code from a particular company as safe or unsafe.

Message Encryption Keys

So which encryption method—symmetric or asymmetric—should an application use? In practice, both are used simultaneously! One reason is that asymmetric encryption is much slower than symmetric encryption, so a randomly generated private key is used to encrypt the data. The encrypted data is then sent along with the private key. But the private key is encrypted using the recipient's public key. This randomly generated private key is called a *message encryption key*.

Another situation in which to use both symmetric and asymmetric encryption is when a message is being sent to multiple recipients. If only asymmetric encryption were used, the message would have to be repeatedly encrypted using each recipient's public key. This would be very time consuming. Instead, the message is encrypted once using a randomly generated private key. Then the message encryption key is repeatedly encrypted using each recipient's public key.

Secure Electronic Transaction

Secure Electronic Transaction (SET) is one protocol aimed at improving the scope and breadth of commerce on the Internet. SET is a specification developed by Visa and MasterCard. Other companies, including Microsoft, Netscape, IBM, and GTE, have also contributed. The latest SET specification consists of three volumes: a business description, a protocol description, and a programmer's guide. SET is a technology used to securely transfer credit card information over the Internet, and also an API for developers to use in developing Internet commercial applications. SET uses DES for encrypting the data as well as RSA for encrypting the symmetric encryption key and credit card number.

Secure Sockets Layer

Sockets was described in Chapter 3, "More About Transports." Secure Sockets Layer (SSL) adds to Sockets and allows a client communicating with a server to negotiate security and authentication levels. Upon session initiation, SSL requires a symmetric session key and encryption algorithm to be negotiated. The symmetric key is used for encrypting and decrypting data. Authentication of the client/server might also be performed while the session is being established. Once the negotiation is completed, the client and server can transmit data to each other in a secure manner by encrypting the data. SSL includes support for RSA public key (during the negotiation), RC2 and RC4 (encryption cipher), IDEA (encryption cipher), DES and Triple-DES (encryption cipher), and MD5 (message digest algorithm).

The latest version of SSL is version 3, which is supported by both Microsoft and Netscape browsers.

Private Communications Technology

Private Communications Technology (PCT) provides security for client/server applications. The intention is to make the contents of the client/server interaction messages private to the two parties involved. The server is always authenticated, whereas the client is optionally authenticated.

Functionally, PCT is similar to SSL. Just like SSL, PCT negotiates a symmetric key and encryption algorithm when a session is established. (The symmetric key is used for encrypting and decrypting data.) The major difference between PCT and SSL is that PCT separates authentication from encryption. Thus, one can have a strong authentication mechanism and still meet U.S. government export regulations. (Recall that government regulations prohibit technologies with greater than 40-bit encryption from being exported.) Other differences exist as well. PCT is more efficient because it requires fewer and shorter messages as compared to SSL. PCT supports RSA, Diffe-Hellman, and Fortezza for key management; DES, Triple-DES, RC2, and RC4 (encryption algorithms); and DSA and RSA (for digital signatures).

PCT is implemented in Internet Explorer version 3 or later as well as in Microsoft Internet Information Server (IIS) version 2 or later. Other parties, such as Spyglass and Open Market, have announced support for PCT.

Transport Layer Security

The Internet Engineering Task Force (IETF) has set up a working group called Transport Layer Security (TLS) that is attempting to define a single transport layer security interface that builds on SSL, PCT, and Secure Shell Remote Login. Microsoft has submitted a discussion draft that attempts to combine the best features of SSL version 3 and PCT version 2.

Certificates

Asymmetric encryption leads to the requirement that the private key should indeed be kept private. Another requirement is that there needs to be a trusted way to associate a public key with a person, process, or entity. How does one know that a public key really belongs to John Doe? (If Jane Doe publishes a key but declares it to be John's public key, data sent to John is now readable by Jane, instead of only by John.) This leads to the concept of *certificates*. A certificate is an object that securely binds a user to a key. Certificates also contain some other data, such as date of validity. A certificate is issued and signed by a certificate authority (CA), but note that all we did by introducing a CA is move the burden of certificate validation from one entity to another.

So how do we validate the public key of the CA? This problem is solved by adding another CA (and another, and another, if need be) until we reach a universally trusted CA. A possible arrangement would be a company CA that is trusted by all people within the company, a higher level regional CA, a CA for a country, and so on.

Certificate Servers

Certificates may be stored in directory service objects or in servers dedicated for that task. Two examples of certificate servers are those from Microsoft and Netscape. Certificates might also need to be revoked from time to time. This is accomplished when the CA issues a certificate revocation list (CRL). (Obtaining CRLs securely raises some issues that are beyond the scope of this book.)

X.509

X.509 is a standard that specifies a format and syntax for certificates. Strictly speaking, X.509 also concerns itself with the specification of authentication services (the standard does not specify a cryptographic algorithm for accomplishing this), but X.509 is more closely associated with the certificate syntax. Various standards having to do with data confidentiality and authentication—for example SSL, Secure HTTP (S-HTTP, described in Chapter 14, "Electronic Commerce"), and Privacy Enhanced Mail (PEM, described in Chapter 9, "Electronic Mail Messaging")—use X.509 certificates. X.509 certificates are expected to be more widely used in the area of electronic commerce. The first version of X.509 was published in 1988. X.509 is now in its third version.

The primary purpose of a certificate is to bind a user to a public key, uniquely associating a particular user with that user's public key. Some of the fields in an X.509 certificate include the following. (Note that the list is not exhaustive.)

- X.509 version number
- Authentication service algorithm identifier
- Name of the certificate issuer
- Certificate validity period
- Public key information

Key Management

As mentioned earlier, private keys need to be kept private. Certificates need to be managed. When symmetric encryption is used, symmetric keys need to be established and communicated between the two parties in a secure manner. Kerberos is one example of an application that accomplishes these objectives.

Kerberos

Kerberos, a protocol developed by the Massachusetts Institute of Technology, provides a number of services. One service is to store private keys securely in a database. These keys are known only to Kerberos and the key owner. Another is to act as a trusted third party when two parties need to exchange a private key. Kerberos is a trusted system in the sense that each of the two parties trusts Kerberos's judgment. Kerberos also provides a means of authentication and key exchange. It uses the DES encryption method.

Kerberos provides three levels of protection. It is up to the consumer of Kerberos to decide which level is appropriate. Kerberos provides an authentication service when a network connection is initiated, and the clients then assume that future messages from a given network address originate from the authenticated party. Other consumers (or applications) of Kerberos require each message to be authenticated but do not care about encrypting the contents of the message. This is referred to as *safe messages* in the Kerberos world. The highest security level, where each message is authenticated and encrypted, is for private messages.

Kerberos works with the concept of tickets and a ticket granting service. Consider a user walking up to a client and logging on. The user is prompted for a username. When the username is entered, a request is sent to a Kerberos authentication server. The authentication server checks that the user is known and, if so, generates a random key. It then creates a ticket containing the current time, the lifetime of the ticket, the client's IP address, and the random session key just generated. This information is then encrypted using a key known only to the authentication server. The same ticket is also encrypted using the user's private key and sent to the client. The client workstation then prompts the user for a password. The password is converted to a DES key, and that DES key is used to decrypt the ticket. The ticket is saved away. The ticket can be used to prove the user's identity to the authentication server.

Diffe-Hellman

Diffe-Hellman is a commonly used algorithm for key agreement. The algorithm allows two entities to independently compute an identical key by exchanging information across public (that is, insecure) channels. When properly used (with an appropriate length key), Diffe-Hellman is considered secure. Diffe-Hellman is patented in the United States, but the patent expired in 1997.

Key Exchange Algorithm

The Key Exchange Algorithm (KEA) is suitable for key exchange but not for data privacy. KEA is based on a modified version of the Diffe-Hellman algorithm and uses a 1024-bit key.

Simple Key Management for Internet Protocols

Simple Key Management for Internet Protocols (SKIP) is a key management protocol developed by Sun Microsystems. SKIP is easy to implement. It specifies how to compute a key on the basis of the public key certificates. However, using SKIP means less flexibility in negotiating the encryption algorithm or hash algorithm. SKIP is specified as an optional algorithm for implemention in Internet Protocol Security (IPSec). See Chapter 3, "More About Transports," for details about IPSec.

Internet Security Association and Key Management Protocol

Internet Security Association and Key Management Protocol (ISAKMP) is mandatory for supporting IPSec. Compared to SKIP, ISAKMP provides more flexibility in negotiating an encryption algorithm or hash algorithm.

Cryptanalysis and Attacks

Cryptanalysis is the science of converting cipher text into plain text without knowledge of the key involved. A cipher is only as good as its weakest point, whether key generation or key distribution.

Most encryption algorithms are based on assumptions that are considered to be true, but no rigorous proof exists. As stated earlier, one assumption is that it is extremely difficult to find the factors of a very large number that is the product of two primes.

With the advent of greater and greater computing power, even brute force attacks (described in the following section) are increasingly feasible. This seems to necessitate that larger keys be used to encrypt messages. But here one runs into problems with the U.S. government in general and the Federal Bureau of Investigation (FBI) and National Security Agency (NSA) in particular. Both of these agencies want the capability to decrypt any given data at any time. They've decreed the maximum key length to be one that, presumably, they feel comfortable they can decrypt. However, with increased computing power, people besides the FBI and the NSA are in the same position.

Brute Force

A brute force attack is an approach in which every possible key is tried. The problem is that the required number of computations increases exponentially with the length of the key. Some people argue that increases in computation speed have rendered encryption algorithms vulnerable. The other side of the coin is that increased computing power makes it easier to increase key lengths, and that increases exponentially the required computing power for brute force attacks.

Cipher-Text-Only Attack

A cipher-text-only attack describes a situation in which all the attacker has is cipher text. In practice the attacker can make some guesses about possible contents and go from there.

Chosen-Plain-Text Attack

In a chosen-plain-text attack, the attacker is able to generate cipher text from plain text of his or her choice. From this the attacker tries to compute the key. RSA is vulnerable to this type of attack.

Known-Plain-Text Attack

In this approach, the attacker knows part or all of the plain text that generated the cipher text. Again, the attacker's objective is to compute the key.

Timing Attack

A timing attack is a recent development in which the attacker measures the amount of time required to perform modular exponentiation operations and tries to leverage that. RSA and Diffe-Hellman are vulnerable to this sort of attack.

Interloper Attack

In an interloper attack, the attacker manages to insert himself between the two parties exchanging data. If this is achieved while the two parties are exchanging keys, the attacker can decrypt all the messages. The attacker can keep up the masquerade by properly encrypting the messages and sending them on to the intended party. A simple way to avoid this is by using digital signatures.

Guessing-the-Key Attack

No matter how secure the algorithm, the person implementing the algorithm might leave a hole whereby the whole key or a significant portion of the key can be guessed. One example is Netscape's implementation of security in a beta version of Netscape Navigator. A part of the key used for encryption was based on the current time rather than being unknowable.

Another example comes from Microsoft Windows for Workgroups version 3.11. This operating system uses a password list file. A user logs on to the computer just once, and anytime the user accesses a resource on another computer that requires a different password, that password and the resource name are stored in the password list file. This password list file is encrypted with a presumed random (and unknowable) key. The problem with the first version of Windows for Workgroups was that it used the user name as part of the key. Hence an attacker could guess at a significant portion of the key. That permitted attackers to decrypt the contents of the password list file. This password scheme has since been strengthened.

Cryptography and Application Programming Interfaces

This section describes APIs that help a programmer add security to the applications he or she is developing. At times, it is hard to distinguish between an application and an API. The differences depend on the point of view. To repeat an example from earlier in the chapter, the SSL protocol is an API for somebody writing to a transport level interface, but it is an application (ensuring privacy) at a higher level.

Data Privacy and Secure Communications Channel

An obvious use of security is to ensure that data is kept private and secure while it is transported by means of a communications channel. SSL versions 2 and 3 as well as PCT are examples of applications transporting data between a client and a server in a manner that guarantees privacy. Obviously, both SSL and PCT are not just cryptography applications but also APIs from the view of programmers writing to a transport level interface.

Windows NT Security Service Provider Interface

NT Security Service Provider Interface (NT SSPI) is an API that first shipped with Windows NT version 3.5. The API provides a layer between applications and the security scheme being used. This allows the underlying security scheme to be modified more easily and also makes the job of the application developer simpler. The application can ask for an authenticated connection without any knowledge of the authentication scheme being used. The application can also ask for data to be signed on a per message basis. SSPI started with LAN Manager and an MSN dialect of NTLM, but more vendors are working on other providers.

Microsoft Cryptographic API

Where SSPI allows basic cryptographic operations, the Microsoft Cryptographic API (CryptoAPI) allows a broader range of cryptographic control. CryptoAPI allows an application to encrypt and/or sign data using a number of different cryptography methods as well as decrypt data and verify signatures. Different cryptography methods are implemented by cryptography service providers (CSPs) that plug into the CryptoAPI. The advantage is that applications using CryptoAPI require only minor modifications to add support for new CSPs as they become available.

CryptoAPI version 1 ships with a base RSA provider as the default CSP. This default CSP supports the following:

- 40-bit RC2 and RC4
- 512-bit RSA
- MD2 and MD5
- 160-bit Secure Hash Algorithm (SHA)

CryptoAPI version 2 adds support for certificates. This includes support for X.509 version 3 certificates as well as PKCS 7 and PKCS 10.

Microsoft intends to make CryptoAPI a cross platform API and not just an API limited to the world of Windows. With that goal in mind, Microsoft has licensed CryptoAPI to RSA, allowing RSA to ship CryptoAPI as part of its products.

Microsoft Wallet and Personal Information Exchange

Microsoft Wallet is designed to securely store personal information, whereas Personal Information Exchange (PFX) is designed to securely transport the information stored in the digital wallet. Wallet is designed to store private information such as a social security number, credit card numbers, and certificates. The first version of Wallet shipped in 1996, and version 2.1 is currently shipping with Internet Explorer version 4. The wallet is stored on a user's computer (on a hard disk or smartcard). Obviously, access to the wallet needs to be controlled, and this is accomplished by PFX. PFX is a draft that describes how information is retrieved from and stored in the wallet. Applications of PFX include making the wallet portable—a person should be able to carry the wallet from a computer at work to a computer at home. Obviously, Wallet is an encryption application, whereas PFX is an API. The APIs have been designed to protect passwords so that instead of allowing an application to retrieve a password, the API allows an application only to query whether a supplied password is correct. PFX has been submitted to the World Wide Web Consortium (W3C) as a draft for a standard.

Authenticode

Authenticode uses run time technology that allows a client to check the identity of the person or organization that has issued a piece of code and an API set that allows a person or organization writing code to sign the code. Authenticode also allows the client to verify that the code has not been tampered with.

Authenticode is based on asymmetric encryption and depends on Verisign to issue and manage public keys for the persons or organizations signing the code using Authenticode. Authenticode is based on PKCS 10 (certificate requests), X.509 (certificate specification), and SHA and MD5 (hash algorithms).

Java APIs

This is a family of APIs that is still evolving. Java enterprise APIs support database connectivity and legacy applications. Java Database Connectivity (JDBC) provides standard SQL database connectivity. Java IDL provides an object-oriented interface. Java RMI provides a means of distributed processing between Java objects. Java Management API provides a means for developing Java applets for enterprise network management. Java Server API provides an API for access to the server and for developing applets, called servlets, that extend the server. Java Media API is for developers of multimedia applications. Java Security API provides cryptography, security, digital signatures, and authentication. JavaBeans API provides a means of plugging into existing object models such as COM, CORBA, OpenDOC, and OLE.

References

http://home.netscape.com/assist/security/ssl/index.html (for information on Secure Sockets Layer)

http://www.microsoft.com/security

http://www.rsa.com/rsalabs/pubs/PKCS

RFC 2315, "PKCS 7: Cryptographic Message Syntax Version 1–5"

RFC 2314, "PKCS 10: Certification Request Syntax Version 1–5"

RFC 2313, "PKCS 1: RSA Encryption Version 1–5"

RFC 2268, "A Description of the RC2(r) Encryption Algorithm"

RFC 2144, "The CAST-128 Encryption Algorithm"

RFC 1984, "IAB and IESG Statement on Cryptographic Technology and the Internet"

RFC 1848, "Mime Object Security Services"

RFC 1704, "On Internet Authentication"

RFC 1511, "Common Authentication Technology Overview"

RFC 1411, "Telnet Authentication: Kerberos Version 4"

RFC 1321, "The MD5 Message-Digest Algorithm"

RFC 1320, "The MD4 Message-Digest Algorithm"

RFC 1319, "The MD2 Message-Digest Algorithm"

Locating Information

P
A
R
T

II

6

Directory Services

DIRECTORY SERVICES ARE SIMILAR TO the telephone book's white and yellow pages. Using a telephone book, one can search for an entity, such as an East Indian restaurant, within a known context, such as a city. Or one can search for a particular restaurant by name. Using directory services, a computer program searches for attributes of a different sort, such as access control, domain/group membership, authentication, network addresses, and port addresses. To manage the vast volume of data that it has to deal with, a directory service is typically implemented using a database stored on a server.

Figure 6-1 shows a typical directory service implementation. Clients connect to the directory service to query and update the directory service database. Some directory services can communicate information to and from other directory services.

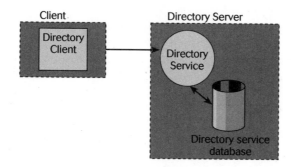

Figure 6-1   *A typical directory service implementation.*

Directory services often provide a mapping between a human-friendly name and an address that a human would have trouble remembering. This is called a *name service,* and is one of many services that a directory service provides. Domain Name System (DNS) is an example of an extremely popular name service.

Domain Name System

Domain Name System (DNS) is a hierarchical name service that is designed to efficiently cover a large name space. A *name space* is simply a collection of all the names a name service makes available. A name space also defines the conventions and syntax for naming objects.

DNS is a mechanism primarily meant to provide a mapping between names and Internet Protocol (IP) addresses. While this is the most popular use of DNS, it also provides other functionality such as storing and providing information about users and mailing lists, and facilitating mail exchange.

Among other things, DNS defines a name space, a distributed database, and a protocol for exchanging information. Each of these is described in the following sections. It is important to note that, although the term *DNS* typically refers to a server, the DNS mapping mechanism provides a client/server solution. A client typically wishes to connect to another computer to exchange electronic mail or download a file. The client may know the name of the computer but not its IP address. DNS provides the mapping by means of software running on the client that contacts the DNS server and retrieves the desired information. A single computer can act as both a DNS server and a DNS client.

A directory or name service can typically be represented as a tree, and this is true for DNS as well. Each entry in a DNS tree is called a *node.* Each node has a name. The node at the top of the tree is called the *root.* Each node can also be described by a *domain name,* also known as a *fully qualified domain name.* A domain name is constructed by using the name of the node, and then appending the name of the parent of that node and all remaining parent nodes in respective order to the root of the tree. In a domain name, a dot separates the node names. The root, which is also represented as a dot, is always omitted from a DNS domain name. Each component of the domain name can be up to 63 bytes long, and the total length of the name is limited to 256 bytes. These components are usually printable ASCII characters but need not be so. DNS treats the domain name as case insensitive. Figure 6-2 shows a partial DNS tree.

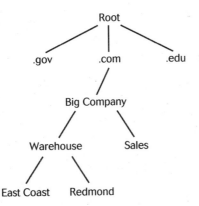

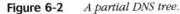

Figure 6-2   *A partial DNS tree.*

In this figure, *Redmond.Warehouse.BigCompany.com* is an example of a DNS domain name. Notice that such names are syntactically the opposite of the full path of a filename. Consider the filename:

\\Server\Share\Directory1\File1

In this example, the components farthest away from the root directory appear at the end of the path, rather than at the beginning, as in a DNS domain name.

DNS second-level names, or domains, are currently limited to the following:

- .mil, used by the U.S. military
- .gov, reserved for government agencies
- .com, for commercial entities
- .net, for network providers
- .edu, for educational institutions
- .org, for organizations, such as the Public Broadcasting System
- a dot followed by two letters, to identify a country; for example, .us for the United States and .ca for Canada

As of this writing, seven more second-level names have been proposed for addition to DNS:

- .firm, for businesses or firms
- .store, for businesses selling goods or services
- .web, for entities engaged in activity on the World Wide Web

- .arts, for entities engaged in cultural activities
- .rec, for organizations engaged in recreational activities
- .info, for entities dealing in information services
- .nom, for individuals

As stated earlier, the DNS name space is simply the collection, or tree, of DNS domain names along with the rules for creating those names. Each node within a DNS domain name represents an entity such as a computer or an e-mail alias. Each domain has an assigned DNS server where administration of the domain is performed. A company or large site may subdivide the domain into a number of subdomains for administrative purposes and convenience. In that case, each subdomain would have a DNS server that owns the database for that subdomain. All changes to a database are made by its server, and this server is interrogated by other DNS servers and clients as needed. A server that owns the database for a domain or subdomain is said to be the authoritative server for that domain or subdomain.

Resource Records

As stated above, DNS defines a distributed database, among other things. The database resides on servers that administer various domains and subdomains. This database is organized into *resource records*. A resource record contains an IP address, the name of a host willing to accept mail for this domain, and other information. Each DNS node is described by one or more resource records. RFC 1183 and RFC 1035 define the format for DNS resource records.

Figure 6-3 shows the components of a resource record.

Name
Type
Class
TTL
RDLength
RData

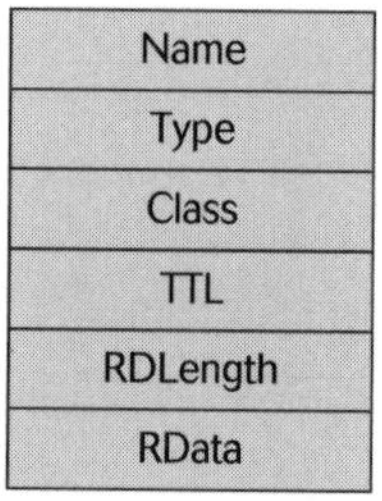

Figure 6-3   *The components of a resource record.*

The Name field is a string that identifies the domain that owns this resource record. The Type field is a 16-bit value that identifies the type of resource record—for example, a type A resource record contains an IP address, a type MX resource record contains the name of a mail server, and so on. The table on the facing page lists some of the values that can be included in the Type field.

Type	Description
A	IP address
NS	Authoritative name server
MD	Mail destination (obsolete, replaced by MX)
MF	Mail forwarder (obsolete, replaced by MX)
CNAME	Canonical name for an alias
SOA	Indicator of start of authority over a zone
MB	Mailbox domain name (experimental)
MG	Mail group member (experimental)
WKS	Well-known service description
PTR	Domain name pointer
HINFO	Host information
MINFO	Mailbox or mail list information
MX	Mail exchanger
TXT	Text string

The Class field is 16 bits long and identifies the protocol family of the resource record type—for example, IN for Internet, CH for Chaos, and so on. In practice, only the IN value is used. The Time To Live (TTL) field contains a signed 32-bit value that indicates the time in seconds that the resource record should be retained in a cache. The RDLength field specifies the length of the RData field in bytes. The RData field is of variable size, depending on the type of the resource record. (For example, the RData field contains a 32-bit IP address for a type A resource record.)

For efficiency, DNS servers typically cache resource records obtained from other DNS servers. The TTL field describes the TTL value in number of seconds—that is, the time in seconds after which the DNS server must obtain a fresh copy of the resource record. A TTL value of 0 indicates that the resource record should be used just once and not cached.

Queries and Resolvers

Clients query DNS servers by means of *resolvers*. A resolver is typically a piece of code running on a DNS client that carries out the DNS queries. The resolver sends queries (on behalf of the client) to the server and caches replies. Each query is sent using a User Datagram Protocol (UDP) datagram, described in RFC 768. Clients can issue two types of queries: *recursive* and *iterative*. A recursive query from a client causes a DNS server to contact another DNS server when the first server is unable to satisfy a client request. This recursion can be cascaded so that the second server can contact a third server and so on until the request is satisfied. Clients most typically issue an iterative query, wherein a server that does not have the required information returns pointers to other servers that might be able to provide the information. Iterative queries are less stressful for servers. A resolver typically caches the values returned by a DNS server in an effort to improve performance and lower the load on the DNS server. Recall that the resource record returned by a DNS server contains a TTL value that denotes how long a cached entry is considered valid.

A resolver needs to process "soft" errors—errors due to network problems—with care. An aggressive retry mechanism would only increase network packets when the network is already facing problems. On the other hand, the resolver could end up reporting an error when the entry might have successfully reached the server, had the resolver retried.

A DNS query contains three fields:

- The DNS domain name for which information needs to be retrieved.
- The type of resource record desired. This is either one of the defined types; a superset, such as an asterisk (*) to indicate that resource records of any type should be returned; or MAILB to indicate that resource records related to a mailbox should be returned.
- The class of resource records desired. This can be one of the defined class types or a superset, such as an asterisk to indicate any class.

The query response usually takes one of three forms:

- An error indicating that the name specified in the query does not exist
- A "soft" error indicating that the information is temporarily unavailable but might later be available
- A set of one or more resource records that meets the criteria specified in the query

DNS Zones

For convenience, the DNS name space is divided into *zones*. A zone is created by logically cutting the link between a node and its parent. The resulting isolated subtree is the zone. A server has full authority over its zone. When a server in a zone is presented with a query, the server either returns the requested information or returns a referral to a server that has authority over the subdomain that the query refers to. Figure 6-4 shows a hypothetical DNS name space divided into zones.

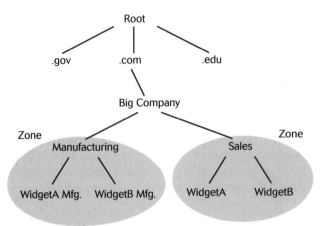

Figure 6-4   *A hypothetical DNS name space divided into zones.*

DNS Replication

Each DNS zone has a name server. For reliability, the server is replicated at least twice. One server is designated the master and the others are designated slaves. All updates are made only on the master, and the slave servers periodically poll the master to acquire the updates. These updates are called *zone transfers*. The master/slave relationship is limited to zone transfers; as far as queries (from resolvers) are concerned, all name servers within a zone are considered equal.

DNS Transport Protocols

DNS implementations must support queries over UDP and should support queries over Transmission Control Protocol (TCP). It is unacceptable to drop UDP support when a server also offers TCP support. TCP offers a more reliable way of accomplishing a query, and TCP is also able to handle cases in which the result of a query returns a vast amount of data. On the other hand, UDP offers the advantage of a lower overhead. Both the UDP and TCP queries use port 53. In practice, zone transfers are performed using TCP, whereas resolvers use UDP. Some clients attempt to locate a server using IP broadcast or multicast packets. DNS servers might support such queries, but they are not required to do so.

Dynamic Domain Naming System

Dynamic DNS is an amalgamation of technologies that dynamically assign IP addresses, for example Dynamic Host Control Protocol (DHCP) and DNS technologies. DHCP (described in Chapter 3, "More About Transports") provides the means to manage IP addresses in a dynamic manner. IP addresses are leased to DHCP clients. DNS, on the other hand, provides a fairly static database of IP addresses and domain names. The entries in the DNS database are updated in a master database through human intervention and propagated by means of software to other DNS servers. Dynamic DNS combines these two technologies. The DHCP server notifies the "local," or secondary, DNS servers whenever it leases an IP address or terminates the lease on an IP address. The secondary DNS server propagates the change to a primary DNS server if appropriate. The dynamic DNS update messages may be sent using UDP or TCP as a transport mechanism.

Another difference between Dynamic DNS and DNS is the flow of information. With DNS, information flows from a primary DNS server to a secondary DNS server. With Dynamic DNS, the flow of information is reversed, moving from a secondary server to a primary one. Dynamic DNS is described in RFC 2136.

The X.500 Specifications

Open Systems Interconnection (OSI) defined X.500 in 1988 with a series of specifications. These specifications were extended in 1993. OSI's objective was nothing less than to define a global directory service. The marketplace reality has been a little harsh in that X.500 has not captured the widespread acceptance that was expected. Among the reasons for this relative lack of acceptance are the complexity of the protocols, the amount of resources required to implement and run the protocols, the lack of a business case for implementation, and security concerns about making previously guarded data publicly available.

The X.500 specifications define an information model that determines how information is stored in a directory. X.500 stores directory entries in a directory service database, called a *Directory Information Base* (DIB). Each entry is defined by a number of attributes. An attribute has a type and a value. The type of an attribute determines its syntax—that is, the kind of information possible for the value. An attribute might have multiple values. An entry has a variable number of attributes, some mandatory and some optional. Each entry has a named attribute objectClass, whose value determines which of the other attributes are mandatory and which are optional. Examples of the values an objectClass attribute can take are Person, State, Country, and so on. Examples of other attributes are surname, common name, organizational unit value, and so on.

The entries are arranged hierarchically in the directory service database. This structure is referred to as the *Directory Information Tree* (DIT). The DIT might be distributed in a geographic hierarchy or an organization hierarchy across multiple directory servers. Each entry is uniquely identified by a *distinguished name* (DN), which is a collection of attribute-value pairs that identify a country, organization, organizational unit, and common name. When some information is omitted from a distinguished name (and a default value is provided), the resulting entity is called a *relative distinguished name* (RDN).

An example of a distinguished name, as depicted in Figure 6-5, is /c=USA, /o=Aumsoft, /ou=Documentation, /cn=Dilip

X.500 requires that a client establish a session with the directory server before the client is able to perform any operation. This is done by means of the bind operation that lets a client provide credentials to the server. The security provided can range from a simple clear-text password to a public key–based cryptography algorithm. A client closes the session via an unbind operation.

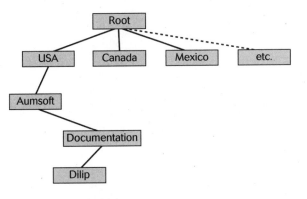

Directory Information Tree

Figure 6-5 *An example of a distinguished name, /c=USA, /o=Aumsoft, /ou=Documentation, /cn=Dilip.*

Once the client has established a session, it can perform search, read, modify, add, delete, or abandon operations. The search operation retrieves entries with attributes that meet some specified criteria, or *search filter*. The result of a search operation might be an entry, a series of entries, or a subtree. The read operation simply fetches the attributes for a specified entry. The modify operation is used to change existing entries. X.500 defines a modifyRDN operation to modify the name of an entry. X.500 also defines add and delete operations for adding and deleting entries. X.500 defines an abandon operation that is used to cancel an operation that has not yet completed.

Each operation and its result can be signed using the client's or server's public key.

Applications access the information in the directory service database in a way similar to a resolver, by means of a client-side interface. This client-side interface is referred to as the *Directory User Agent* (DUA). The DUA accesses information stored on the directory server by means of a protocol called *Directory Access Protocol* (DAP). DAP is an application-level protocol that specifies the use of an OSI transport stack. Implementing an OSI transport stack requires a nontrivial effort not just in terms of development costs but also in terms of hardware required to run the protocol stack. Information can be exchanged among various directory servers by means of the *Directory System Protocol* (DSP), which is discussed later in this section. The X.500 1993 specification describes the *Directory Information Shadowing Protocol* (DISP), which defines replication among X.500 directory servers. Figure 6-6 shows the various X.500 components and protocols.

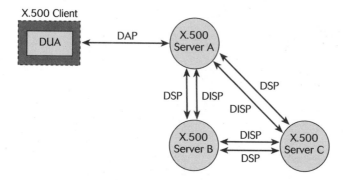

Figure 6-6 *The X.500 components and protocols.*

Replication is used to distribute the load between various servers, to provide a degree of redundancy, and also for efficiency. Replication is also used to move the information to a server that is more readily accessible. X.500 specifies that no matter which server a client accesses, the client is presented with the same view of the data. A server that might not have the requested piece of information satisfies this specification by *chaining*, which means that it contacts another server, or by *referral*—asking the client to contact another server. The chaining is accomplished using the DSP. DSP is used exclusively for communication between X.500 servers, but this interaction between servers happens as a result of action taken by the DUA. Figure 6-7 illustrates the concept of chaining.

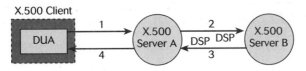

Figure 6-7 *X.500 chaining.*

In the figure (and the two following), the numbers on the arrows designate the order in which the various exchanges occur. First the X.500 client sends an X.500 query to Directory Server A. Server A does not have the required information and decides to contact Server B. Server B replies to Server A, at which point Server A replies to the client.

Figure 6-8 illustrates the concept of referrals.

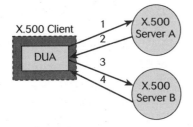

Figure 6-8 *X.500 referrals.*

In this figure, the X.500 client sends a query to Directory Server A. Again, Server A does not have the required information. Server A sends a reply to the client. The reply consists of information that essentially says, "I (Server A) do not have the required information. Try Server B." The client contacts Server B, and then Server B replies to the client.

Figure 6-9 shows the concept of X.500 *multicasting,* which is similar to chaining. However, with multicasting, the request for information is simultaneously passed to more than one server. Each server returns an answer or returns an error if it cannot process the request. The client receives a single response.

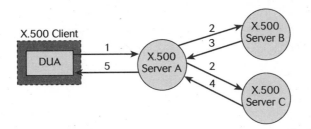

Figure 6-9 *Multicasting.*

Lightweight Directory Access Protocol

Lightweight Directory Access Protocol (LDAP) is now an open standard Internet protocol for accessing directory services. LDAP has its roots in the X.500 DAP. LDAP was first defined in RFC 1487. LDAP version 2 is the current standard and is defined in RFC 1777, which supersedes RFC 1487. LDAP was established to provide a simpler implementation of some limited aspects of X.500. The University of Michigan has the most famous implementation of LDAP. Recently, a host of companies including Netscape and Microsoft have declared their intention to "adopt" LDAP in their commercial offerings, causing some people to believe that LDAP is now the standard Internet directory service.

The main differences between LDAP version 2 and X.500 are as follows:

- LDAP runs over TCP/IP, whereas the X.500 DAP requires an OSI stack.

- LDAP provides a simplified version of a bind command. LDAP clients can bind anonymously (that is, without providing a password) or they can provide a clear plain-text password. X.500 provides for cryptographically stronger mechanisms.

- LDAP does not provide a read or list command. A client can achieve the equivalent functionality by means of an appropriate search command.

- An LDAP client connects to only a single server at a time. The LDAP server cannot return a referral to the client in response to a query from the client.

- LDAP uses much simpler encoding for data compared with X.500.

The University of Michigan has implemented a C library with which an LDAP client can link. This is described in RFC 1823, an informational RFC. The library allows a C client to use simple function calls that use only text strings. Using this library, one can write a C program that can send LDAP queries such as search and read. Refer to the commands described in the section "The X.500 Specifications" for details.

System Administrators often raise questions concerning LDAP security issues. LDAP allows access limitations to be specified for every defined distinguished name—a system administrator can define the rights a user is allowed on a per-DN and per-path basis. These rights can be:

- None—the user is prevented from accessing any information
- Compare—the user can compare DN values
- Search—the user can search for a DN and be informed of its existence
- Read—the user can read the DN attribute values
- Write—the user can modify the DN attribute values
- Delete—the user can delete the DN

LDAP version 3 is, strictly speaking, still a work in progress. The Internet Engineering Task Force (IETF) has not yet officially frozen the LDAP version 3 specification. The expected offerings in LDAP version 3 include the following:

- LDAP version 3 provides a model wherein the LDAP server need not be an X.500 server. The older LDAP model (version 2) provided for a client to send queries as specified in the LDAP protocol. In the older model, a front-end processor at the server converted the LDAP query to a DAP query and presented that to the server. The new model (version 3) no longer requires the conversion between LDAP and DAP. The LADP models are illustrated in Figure 6-10.

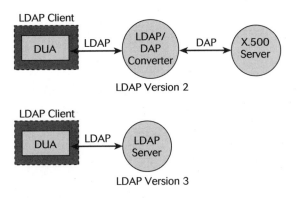

Figure 6-10   *The LDAP Models.*

- An LDAP server can now return a referral in response to a client query.
- LDAP version 2 specified the object classes and attributes as part of the protocol. Thus, the directory was not extensible. With LDAP version 3, clients can interrogate a server to discover the range of object classes and attributes. This implies that new attributes can be defined when required, and that LDAP clients will be able to discover the presence of these new attributes.
- LDAP version 3 permits the use of Unicode for character representation, thus allowing for more flexibility and internationalization.
- LDAP version 3 allows for increased security by permitting X.509 certificates to be used. X.509 is the specification that describes the format of the certificate. Version 3 also specifies a mechanism for the client to use the Secure Sockets Layer (SSL).
- LDAP version 3 defines *Connectionless LDAP* (CLDAP), which is a form of LDAP that is particularly suited for applications that need to make simple queries and get a fast response. CLDAP uses UDP as a transport mechanism to carry the queries and responses.

References

DNS

RFC 2136, "Dynamic Updates in the Domain Name System"

RFC 1591, "Domain Name System and Delegation"

RFC 1480, "The U.S. Domain"

RFC 1183, "New DNS Resource Record Definitions"

RFC 1101, "DNS Encoding of Network Names and Other Types"

RFC 1035, "Domain Names—Implementations and Specification"

RFC 1034, "Domain Names—Concepts and Facilities"

RFC 1032, "Domain Administrator's Guide"

RFC 974, "Mail Routing and the Domain System"

RFC 920, "Domain Requirements"

X.500

RFC 1309, "Technical Overview of Directory Services Using the X.500 Protocol"

RFC 1308, "Executive Introduction to Directory Services Using the X.500 Protocol"

RFC 1279, "X.500 and Domains"

LDAP

RFC 2256, "A Summary of the X.500(96) User Schema for Use with LDAPv3"

RFC 2255, "The LDAP URL Format"

RFC 2254, "The String Representation of LDAP Search Filters"

RFC 2253, "Lightweight Directory Access Protocol (v3): UTF-8 String Representation of Distinguished Names"

RFC 2252, "Lightweight Directory Access Protocol (v3): Attribute Syntax Definitions"

RFC 2251, "Lightweight Directory Access Protocol (v3)"

RFC 1960, "A String Representation of LDAP Search Filters"

RFC 1959, "An LDAP URL Format"

RFC 1823, "The LDAP Application Program Interface"

RFC 1798, "Connectionless Lightweight X.500 Directory Access Protocol"

RFC 1777, "Lightweight Directory Access Protocol"

RFC 1487, "X.500 Lightweight Directory Access Protocol"

7

Discovery and Management

THIS CHAPTER DESCRIBES SOME POPULAR TOOLS used to tune and manage networks. I've included only those tools that have a status similar to a protocol. For example, tools for dumping routing tables are an essential part of network management, but they are not discussed here because no protocol is associated with them. (Routing protocols are discussed in Chapter 2, "Basic Transports and Plumbing.") RFC 1470, "FYI on a Network Management Tool Catalog: Tools for Monitoring and Debugging TCP/IP Internets and Interconnected Devices," provides a more comprehensive list of tools. RFC 1574, "Essential Tools for the OSI Internet," is another excellent reference.

Echo

The echo protocol is used to test for packet loss on network hardware and servers. A variety of network resources (hosts, routers, servers, and so on) support the echo protocol for diagnostic reasons. An echo operation consists of sending a request from the local system and returning a response from the remote system. The echo-request (ERQ, type code 30) packet is used to troubleshoot a remote system. When the remote system is working, it responds with an echo response (ERP, type code 31), which includes the entire echo-request packet for later study. Details about the echo protocol are available in RFC 862 and RFC 1575.

Ping

Ping is a method for detecting the availability and the bandwidth and performance of a remote network resource. The ping command is one of the basic tools used to troubleshoot network problems. Ping is sometimes considered an acronym for Packet Internet Groper.

One method of implementing ping is by using the Internet Control Message Protocol (ICMP) echo message. Another method of implementing ping is by using the echo protocol (discussed above) over either Transmission Control Protocol (TCP) or User Datagram Protocol (UDP). If the echo-request and echo-response packets work, a ping operation is considered successful.

A ping utility usually sends multiple packets to the server. The utility notes each round-trip time in addition to the percentage of success and failure rates of all the packets it sends. Another useful feature of ping utilities is that they can display the route buffer of returned packets, which helps determine problems with related network resources. Ping utilities normally also have options to control the size of the packet, the number of packets to send, and the amount of time to wait before sending the next packet.

Ping is discussed in RFC 1574.

Traceroute

Traceroute is another network debugging tool. It is similar to ping, showing detailed information about the network routes that packets take.

Network packets travel through a variety of routers and backbones before they reach the destination server. The response packet often travels a different route home. The traceroute utility shows each hop a packet makes in its travels from local source to target system. Traceroute is useful to determine how your Internet connection is managed from your local Internet Service Provider (ISP) up to the backbone and down through the ISP of the target system.

One method of implementing traceroute is by a sequence of packets with increasing time-to-live (TTL) values. A TTL value is set to produce an immediate timeout, which causes the hop to return the packet. TTL values are increased for subsequent hops until the destination address is reached. While simple and widely supported, this method generates a large number of packets and does not trace the return path of a packet. Another way in which traceroute can be implemented is to use a new Internet Protocol (IP) traceroute option, which can be used in conjunction with an ICMP echo packet. This method generates fewer packets and traces the return path of a packet.

Traceroute utilities normally have options that you can use to control the time to wait for a response, the number of packets to send, and the number of network hops to stop after.

When using traceroute, keep in mind that different protocols have different bandwidth needs. While protocols such as Network News Transfer Protocol (NNTP) can tolerate some delays, protocols such as multicast backbone (MBone) do not, and too many hops or too many delays at a particular hop can cause network latency problems that prevent such protocols from working.

Identification Protocol

The Identification Protocol (also known as the Ident protocol or ident), described in RFC 1413, provides basic user identification about TCP-based protocols. The Identification Protocol used to be called the Authentication Server Protocol, but it has been renamed to indicate its strength in identifying a user.

Ident is often used by servers for better log files or basic identification verification. Given another TCP protocol, such as Telnet, Simple Mail Transfer Protocol (SMTP), File Transfer Protocol (FTP), Internet Relay Chat (IRC), NNTP, or Hypertext Transfer Protocol (HTTP), a server can use ident to help identify a user. Doing so helps prevent some of the problems associated with the faking of user accounts with these protocols.

Ident is a connection-based protocol that uses TCP port 113. The ident server—often called identd on UNIX systems—reads a string that identifies the user of that client process. This information can be used to augment log files of user activity or used to terminate connections that fail to meet identification needs (for example, fake e-mail). The availability of ident information should not preclude the use of strong authentication in a protocol because ident can be faked by knowledgeable users.

The two common errors in ident protocol queries involve invalid TCP port values and unrecognized users (processes that don't have a recognizable user, or users that have hidden their identification).

Whois and Whois++

Whois is a protocol for finding information about networks, domains, and organizations. The whois service runs on a series of servers located on the Internet. Whois clients send requests to the servers. Whois servers return information such as the server name, information about the organization, administrators and their contact information, as well as an IP address. Whois is similar to the finger protocol, the difference being that almost all servers run the finger protocol, but only certain servers run the whois protocol. Whois is meant to be used only for lightweight queries, not for extensive querying.

In mid-1992, the whois protocol was extended and renamed whois++. Whois++ is not compatible with whois. The main differences between whois++ and whois are that whois++ imposes a structure on the information returned from the server and also allows for server-to-server communication.

The data stored in whois++ servers is stored as a series of database records. Each record consists of various fields that are stored as an attribute-value pair. An example of an attribute-value pair is Email:hacker@atlarge.com. Special keywords, #FULL and #END, indicate the beginning and end of each record. The #FULL keyword is usually followed by a keyword indicating the template type of the record. For example, the keyword USER indicates that the record provides information about a user.

Whois++ servers communicate with each other in a manner that resembles database replication. The knowledge that servers exchange with one another is known as *forward knowledge*. The advantage to forward knowledge is that when a client interrogates some particular server, the server can return a referral (or pointer) to a server that has the required information. Server-to-server communication is performed according to the Common Indexing Protocol (CIP). CIP is a protocol defined by the Find working group of the Internet Engineering Task Force (IETF). (For more information, see http://www.ietf.cnri.reston.va.us/html.charters/find-charter.html.) Two other IETF working groups that study this area are Access, Searching, and Indexing of Directories (ASID; http://www.ietf.cnri.reston.va.us/html.charters/asid-charter.html); and Integrated Directory Service (IDS; http://www.ietf.cnri.reston.va.us/html.charters/ids-charter.html).

CIP enables servers to exchange a condensed form of information called centroids. Centroids provide a superset of the information the server has but lose some distinctions as to which record contains a certain piece of information. The result is that a query might return a false positive—in other words, a server might return a referral, but when you follow the referral, no data is available. A server will never return an indication that no data is available when some data is actually available (a false negative).

References

RFC 1914, "How to Interact with a Whois++ Mesh"

RFC 1913, "Architecture of the Whois++ Index Service"

RFC 1835, "Architecture of the Whois++ service"

RFC 1834, "Whois and Network Information Lookup Service; Whois++"

RFC 1575, "Echo Function for CLNP"

RFC 1574, "Essential Tools for the OSI Internet"

RFC 1470, "FYI on a Network Management Tool Catalog: Tools for Monitoring and Debugging TCP/IP Internets and Interconnected Devices"

RFC 1413, "Identification Protocol"

RFC 1393, "Traceroute Using an IP Option"

RFC 954, "NICNAME/WHOIS"

RFC 862, "Echo Protocol"

8

Searching

ONE OF THE BIGGEST PROBLEMS OF THE INFORMATION AGE is sorting through all the available information to find what you need. The advent of the World Wide Web (WWW) has made online information easier to access, but at the same time the amount of online information has increased dramatically. Navigating through all this information is still a difficult task.

Early on, you could traverse the Web only via *link pages*—links to other pages. Next came *index sites,* such as Yahoo!, which create a large number of links to a variety of topics. Index sites are sometimes also available as printed Internet directories. However, these services do not cover all information—only the information that has been discovered by the index editors.

Now we have *search engines,* which are generally servers that hold a large amount of data (often full-text data) about a large collection of content. They let users do keyword searches to find specific information within this collection.

Early File Location and Transfer Methods

Before the Web protocols came to predominate on the Internet, a variety of other methods were used to locate and transfer documents. In this section, we'll discuss these other methods.

Archie

Before the Web, files were made available on the Internet primarily via File Transfer Protocol (FTP) servers. Users had to know the names of the various FTP servers (there are many) and the kind of information (types of files) available on each server. It was difficult for most users to deal with so many servers.

Archie is an information system designed to enhance data stored on FTP servers. First an Archie server creates a list of information about the files and resources it knows about—for example, storing the related meta-information about a file (filename, subfolder, size, date, and so forth). The information about files on multiple FTP servers can be combined into a single Archie database. This data is normally updated at regular intervals to accommodate new and updated files on the FTP servers.

Once this Archie information database is available, it is offered to the user. This happens by means of batch mode interactions to Archie servers via e-mail daemons or through interactive clients via Telnet, Web, and other protocols. Using the Archie system, a user doesn't have to memorize all the FTP servers in the world and can retrieve a file based on a partial filename or a subfolder name.

Gopher

Named after the mammal, Gopher is a protocol for burrowing through the Internet. It is a distributed document delivery system that uses a client/server model. The Gopher client presents a hierarchy of resources (servers, subfolders, and documents) to the user, which can be traversed until the resulting documents are located and retrieved. Users can select an item from this list (often using numbers in nongraphical systems or a mouse in graphical systems) or enter search text to narrow the document search. This is similar to browsing a catalog in a library.

Most Gopher users start at the top of a Gopher server and look through the hierarchical list of folders or through the results of a query to the Gopher search server to obtain a list of filenames to retrieve.

The Gopher client/server protocol is a simple, stateless protocol that communicates over Transmission Control Protocol (TCP) port 70. The client sends a line of text to the server, and the server responds with a body of text; both use simple characters as field delimiters. The list of server results includes actual resource names as well as descriptive names. In addition to being Hypertext Transfer Protocol (HTTP) clients, most Web browsers are also Gopher clients.

With the advent of the Web, the popularity of the Gopher protocol has waned because Web protocols (along with Web-based search engines) provide similar functionality. Gopher is described in RFC 1436.

Veronica

Veronica is a resource-discovery system for most of the public Gopher servers. Veronica is to Gopher as FTP is to Archie. The Archie protocol enhances the FTP protocol by allowing a single search to find multiple documents in multiple folders on multiple FTP servers. Similarly, the Veronica protocol enhances the Gopher protocol by allowing a single keyword search to find multiple documents in multiple folders on multiple Gopher servers ("Gopher space").

Veronica has new server-side software to gather the information from the various Gopher servers. Once Veronica obtains the data, it stores that data on a Gopher server that is accessible by a Gopher client via the Gopher protocol. The term *Veronica* is an acronym for "very easy rodent-oriented netwide index to computerized archives."

Jughead

Similar in concept to Veronica, Jughead is also related to Gopher. Jughead provides keyword searches of Gopher servers.

Z39.50

Z39.50 is the Information Retrieval Service Definition and Protocol Specification for Library Applications. It was created to solve problems common to searching multiple databases, which normally requires system-specific and database-specific knowledge.

Z39.50 defines rules and procedures for the behavior of two diverse systems that communicate to perform database searching and information retrieval. The Z39.50 protocol can be *stateful*—that is, the server can obtain additional information from the client in multiple steps. A query can also be made in a single step.

The Z39.50 standard is controlled by the National Information Standards Organization (NISO), which is also known as Committee Z39 of the American National Standards Institute (ANSI). NISO maintains information retrieval standards for information-related industries, including libraries and publishing. NISO's latest version of Z39.50, approved in 1995, is slated to replace the 1991 Search and Retrieve (SR) standard approved by the International Organization for Standardization (ISO) in 1991.

Z39.50 has two URL schemes, a Z39.50 Session URL (Z39.50s prefix, multistate interactive mode) and a Z39.50 Retrieval URL (Z39.50r prefix, single-state mode, for well-known data); both are defined in RFC 2056. For more details about Z39.50, see RFCs 2056, 1729, and 1625.

Wide Area Information Server

The Wide Area Information Server (WAIS) project is another full-text information retrieval system. It provides client software, server software, and a network protocol to allow users to locate information across a variety of databases using English-like queries. The WAIS protocol uses a derivation of the Z39.50 protocol.

As with Gopher, the popularity of the WAIS protocol has waned because Web protocols (along with Web-based search engines) provide similar functionality.

Harvest

The Harvest Information Discovery and Access System is a distributed indexing system that gathers, extracts, organizes, searches, caches, and replicates information. A Harvest server consists of multiple components, including gatherers, brokers, object caches, and replication managers. These components can be configured to search a variety of data formats and provide output in a variety of formats. The components store data in Harvest's Summary Object Interchange Format (SOIF), a structured indexing format that enables sophisticated queries.

There is no explicit Harvest client or Harvest client/server protocol. Users access Harvest through a Web browser, which talks to the Harvest server indirectly through the HTTP server.

As powerful as Harvest is, with the advent of the Web, its popularity has waned as the popularity of vendor-specific search engines that provide data to users via Web protocols has increased. However, some Web-based search engines use Harvest to create their content.

Web Catalogs and Web Search Engines

With the explosive growth of the Web, it became imperative to develop tools with which clients could locate documents of interest on the Web. These tools present the client with a Hypertext Markup Language (HTML) form. The client fills out the form, including key words or subjects of interest for which documents need to be located, and sends it to the server using HTTP. At the server, the form is processed using Common Gateway Interface (CGI) script and the Internet Server Application Programming Interface (ISAPI). (See Chapter 12, "World Wide Web Basics," and Chapter 13, "Advanced Web," for details on HTML, HTTP, CGI and ISAPI). This processing involves use of a database or index residing at the server.

This database can be generated (and subsequently accessed in an Internet search) by using either a subject catalog or a search engine. Each of these has some advantages and disadvantages. A subject catalog is likely to return fewer and older—but more relevant—documents than a search engine. However, this is true only for nonexotic subjects. Search engines are more likely to return a lot of information, including more recent data and documents, but some of it may not be relevant. Given the size of the Web, no single search engine or subject catalog database is likely to contain information about all the documents on the Web. One part of the Web might be covered by one database but not by another.

Subject Catalogs or Directories

As explained previously, one of the early methods of searching the Web was based on creating a catalog of subjects that included the URLs of documents relevant to the subject. The subject catalog was conceived as similar to a library subject catalog. When compiling the subject catalog, software can be used to locate the URLs for the subject, but some human interaction is required to decide which URLs should be presented when documents for a particular subject are requested. Yahoo! (http://www.yahoo.com) is a well known example of such a subject catalog.

Web-Based Search Engines

All Web search engines consist of two main components: one to retrieve information from a database and another to build a database of the information relevant to the subject of the search. The database of relevant information is built by means of software programs that are often referred to as *robots, crawlers, spiders,* or *worms.* Lycos, AltaVista, Infoseek, Inktomi, and Excite are examples of Web-based search engines.

The various search engines differ from one another. Some of these differences include:

- The extent of the Web covered by the search engine robot
- The frequency with which the search engine robot visits a Web site
- The logic a search engine uses in deciding whether a particular document should be returned in response to a search
- The extent to which a search can be defined and refined
- The kinds of documents (HTML, non-HTML, multimedia, and so forth) about which the robot collects information

Each of the search engines cover a varying amount of data and have features that might be common or unique. Some examples follow, but these should not be considered a comprehensive list. AltaVista and Lycos claim to index URLs in the tens of millions. The AltaVista robot follows the robots.txt protocol (described in the following section) and can efficiently process large amounts of data quickly. The Lycos robot also honors the robots.txt protocol. The Lycos robot searches more popular Web pages before other pages. The Lycos robot also analyzes Web pages to build inferences about multimedia contents of a page. The HotBot robot also follows the robots.txt protocol. The HotBot robot attempts to search the Web without putting an undue load on a Web site. It indexes a certain portion of a Web site and then returns to that site later.

Search engines can be general purpose or special purpose; for example, a search engine can retrieve from a database documents pertinent only to a particular field, such as medical information or the articles of one publication.

There is also a category of search engines called *meta-search*. Meta-search engines do not build a database of their own. Instead, they submit the search simultaneously to multiple search engines and then refine and amalgamate the results.

Web Robots

The Web consists primarily of Web servers that store data and the users that request this data. However, users with Web browsers are not the only clients. Some clients belong to the variety of software known as Web robots, crawlers, or spiders (among other names).

Web robot software, which is often automated, traverses a Web site and retrieves all available documents. This is one of the main reasons to build a database of information for a Web search engine. Behind the scenes of any good Web search engine is a busy Web robot. Web robots also have a variety of other uses, including validating HTML documents, validating hypertext links in HTML documents, and copying HTML documents.

Robot Exclusion Protocol

Web robots are primarily HTTP clients. They crawl through HTML documents and they can crawl through other data via other protocols, such as Network News Transfer Protocol (NNTP), FTP, and e-mail. Wherever a large amount of data is stored, there is usually some software posing as a user, sorting through the data for some other purpose.

For various reasons, sometimes Web administrators do not want robots to visit their sites or certain sections of their sites. If this is the case, the Robot Exclusion Protocol can be used. This protocol is a voluntary method for instructing robots how to traverse a Web site. It is primarily used by HTTP server administrators, but it can also be used by HTML authors.

The main method of controlling robot behavior is via a file named robots.txt, which is located in the root folder of an HTTP server. When a robot first accesses a site, it checks for this file before progressing further. If the file does not exist, it means the Web administrator does not have any specific instructions for the robot. This robots.txt file is a plain ASCII text file. It consists of User-Agent lines describing the HTTP_USER-_AGENT string of an agent and Allow and Disallow lines describing what files and folders are off limits. For each specified User-Agent, one or more Allow or Disallow lines are listed, telling where that robot can or cannot visit. For example, a robots.txt file might consist of three directives:

```
# robots.txt for http://www.example.org/, webmaster@example.org
# don't let BadRobot go anywhere, except the bad robot file
User-agent: BadRobot
Disallow: /
Allow: /bad-robots-read-this.html

# let GoodRobot go anywhere
User-agent: GoodRobot
```

```
Disallow:
# don't let any robots in the mirrors and archives subfolders
User-agent: *
Disallow: /mirrors
Disallow: /archives
```

Robot META Tag

In addition to creating a robots.txt file in the root folder of a Web site, an HTML author can also include robot directives in an individual HTML document, which some robots look for. This is useful for HTML authors who are part of a large site and don't have administrative control of the root folder of the site. (The robots.txt file is only valid in the root folder.) For example, this method might be useful for a personal home page on a public-access Internet Service Provicer (ISP) site.

The HTML META tag is used to embed these HTTP headers in the document. The syntax for this tag is:

```
<META NAME="ROBOTS" CONTENT="NOINDEX, NOFOLLOW">
```

The valid directives for the Robots META tag include:

INDEX—index the document

NOINDEX—do not index the document

FOLLOW—follow the links in the document

NOFOLLOW—do not follow the links in the document

The directives can be placed in a single META tag value, delimited by commas.

Future Standards and Protocols

This section describes protocols that are in their infancy but that could well end up influencing search protocols on the Internet.

The Robot Guidance Project

The Robot Guidance Project is a new effort that intends to go beyond the Robot Exclusion Protocol. The current standard is concerned primarily with the exclusion of robots and does not provide much positive guidance for them. This new standard is expected to address topics such as including a finer granularity of input for content creators, working with protocols and document types beyond HTTP and HTML, and including multiple new ways to offer positive guidance for the robot instead of only negative exclusion rules.

Common Indexing Protocol

The Common Indexing Protocol (CIP) is a new effort of the Internet Engineering Task Force (IETF) Find working group. CIP is a common protocol for exchanging indexing information and is based on concepts from previous protocols, including Whois++, X.500 (LDAP), and CCSSO. It also uses a version of Harvest's Summary Object Interchange Format structured indexing file format. This standard is in its infancy but will be worth following.

References

ftp://boombox.micro.umn.edu/pub/gopher

gopher://veronica.scs.unr.edu:70/11/veronica

http://lcweb.loc.gov/z3950/agency

http://www.wais.com

http://harvest.transarc.com

http://info.webcrawler.com/mak/projects/robots/robots.html

http://www.botspot.com/robotguidance

http://www.ietf.org/html.charters/find-charter.html

RFC 2056, "Uniform Resource Locators for Z39.50"

RFC 1729, "Using the Z39.50 Information Retrieval Protocol"

RFC 1625, "WAIS Over Z39.50"

RFC 1436, "The Internet Gopher Protocol (a Distributed Document Search and Retrieval Protocol)"

Information
Retrieval

P
A
R
T

III

9

Electronic Mail Messaging

ELECTRONIC MAIL (E-MAIL) IS ONE OF THE MOST popular messaging applications for the Internet. This chapter offers details about the major e-mail protocols used on the Internet.

Electronic mail has its roots in proprietary e-mail systems. Commercial e-mail systems were initially developed mostly on mainframes and minicomputers. Mail users worked from terminals connected to the mainframe or minicomputer. IBM's Professional Office System (PROFS) is an example of such an e-mail system.

The next commercial wave of e-mail implementations was featured on local area networks (LANs). These implementations were notable for their lack of support of protocol standards. A file server (also called a message store) acted as the e-mail server. Personal computers on the LAN exchanged e-mail by writing to files stored on the file server. The file server provided file sharing over network operating systems such as Microsoft LAN Manager or Novell NetWare. E-mail could be routed from one store to another via proprietary protocols or implementations that did not strictly adhere to standards. The two message stores could be on the same LAN or they could be connected over a wide area network (WAN) using dial-up facilities. Examples of a LAN–based e-mail system are Microsoft Mail and Lotus cc:Mail. LAN–based e-mail works very well at the departmental level. Unfortunately, however, it does not scale to a higher level and the administrative problems created in connecting a number of e-mail servers (probably one or more per department) can be significant. Figure 9-1 on the following page illustrates this situation.

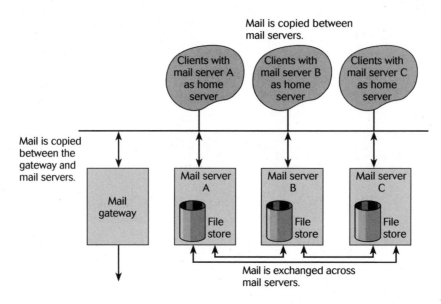

Mail is copied between
mail servers.

Mail is copied
between the
gateway and
mail servers.

Mail is exchanged across
mail servers.

Figure 9-1   *The architecture of an e-mail system that works well at the departmental level.*

The next generation of LAN–based e-mail systems used remote procedure calls (RPCs) to let clients converse with the message store. This generation of message store runs a number of processes that constitute the e-mail server; it is no longer just a file server. The advantages to this kind of e-mail system are that it is a more secure system and provides server-based processing capability. Facilities like security and server-based processing allow the building of applications, such as a workflow application, on top of e-mail. An extremely simplistic explanation of a workflow application is one that allows server processing of highly structured e-mail based on the contents of the e-mail fields. This would be useful in an insurance company, for example. A telephone operator could enter a claim, and the server would route the claim to different people for processing. The e-mail might wend its way from a claims processor to an adjuster and then to the accounts payable department, with each recipient updating the e-mail field contents.

Notwithstanding the type of e-mail system that is used, a few basic terms defined here can be generally applicable. E-mail can be generated by a human or by a computer program. The human does so by means of a user interface running on a personal computer, a mainframe, or a minicomputer. This user interface software typically interacts with another piece of software—a dynamic-link library (DLL) or other library—that provides the functionality needed to interact with the e-mail server. The library, or the combination of the library with the user interface, is referred to as the *user agent*. The user agent connects to an e-mail server, typically over a LAN or a dial-up connection. The e-mail server the user connects to is known as the home server for that user, and it is to this server that the user sends e-mail, expecting the server to direct the e-mail appropriately. The home server is also the location at which e-mail addressed to the user arrives when sent by other users. The e-mail server forwards e-mail to other servers using a piece of software called a *mail transfer agent* (MTA). A message might traverse a number of MTAs before it arrives at the home server for the e-mail addressee. Figure 9-2 illustrates this situation and depicts the various flavors of e-mail protocols that are applicable at each stage.

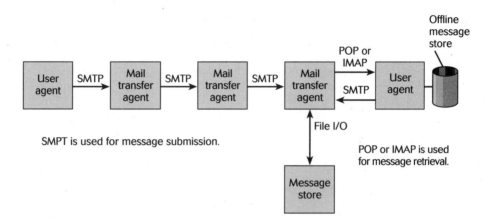

Figure 9-2 *E-mail travels via MTAs until it arrives at a specified home server; different protocols apply at each stage.*

Another paradigm for describing modern-day client/server e-mail is expressed in terms of the *offline*, *online*, and *disconnected* models.

- Offline model: The client connects to the server from time to time and downloads all e-mail. After the messages are downloaded, they are deleted from the server. All further processing of the messages happens on the client and the server has no further knowledge of any of these messages. This is the model used by Post Office Protocol, described later in this chapter. Internet Message Access Protocol (IMAP, also described later in this chapter) can support this model as well, but IMAP is at its best when used in the online and disconnected models.

- Online model: The client establishes a session with the server and all e-mail processing occurs during the session. All e-mail processing occurs on the server with the client driving the processing. Examples of implementations that use this model are IMAP, Network File System (NFS), and Common Internet File System (CIFS).

- Disconnected model: This is a mix of the offline and online models. The client connects, downloads some selected messages, and processes them offline. At some later stage, the client reconnects and uploads the changes back to the server. (The changes could be edits within a message or an address book, message deletes, message replies, and so on.) The server is the main repository for the messages, with the client acting as a temporary storage facility. IMAP can operate using this paradigm.

The following sections describe the e-mail protocols depicted in Figure 9-2, as well as some other e-mail protocols.

The RFC 822 Message Format

RFC 822 defines the format for e-mail messages; that is, RFC 822 defines what Post Office Protocol 3 (described in the next section), Simple Mail Transfer Protocol (SMTP), and other e-mail transport protocols carry or transport. RFC 822 defines a message as consisting of two major components: an envelope and message contents.

The envelope contains information pertinent to transporting and delivering the message. The envelope also contains information required to reply to the message. This information is usually conveyed by means of a line of text that begins with a keyword, is followed by a value, and ends with a carriage return and/or linefeed character. Examples of keywords are: "From," "Reply To," and so on. Thus the envelope contains an e-mail address for the sender and one for the receiver at the least.

The message contents are further subdivided into two parts: the header and the body. The header contains information that is generated automatically by the user agent at the sending node and updated by every MTA that handles the message. The header contains a message ID as well as date and time stamps that identify when each MTA handled the message. The user agent at the receiving node might compress, reformat, or even hide the message header. Nevertheless, the header is very much present. The body contains the actual message, or text, that the sender generated. The sender can be a human or a computer program. The message body is set off from the header by means of a null line, which is a line that contains only a carriage return (CR) character and a linefeed (LF) character.

Many of the RFC 822 implementations on the Internet assume that no line within a message is longer than 1000 bytes and that no message is larger than 64 KB. Since a sender is generally unaware of a message's path and whether it will pass through intermediate nodes that have this implementation, the message has to be encoded before it is sent and then decoded at the receiving user agent.

Post Office Protocol

Post Office Protocol (POP) is an e-mail protocol that's applicable to the offline model of client/server e-mail. POP has been revised a number of times: POP3 is version 3 of the protocol. POP3 is described in RFC 1939.

With POP, all pending messages destined for an e-mail client are downloaded to that client when it connects and queries for new e-mail. A POP client cannot selectively download messages from the e-mail server: it's an "all or nothing" situation. After the messages are downloaded, the e-mail client can delete or modify any message without interacting further with the e-mail server.

A POP3 client sends commands to a POP3 server and awaits the responses. A POP3 command is line based, represented in ASCII, and the command starts with one of a limited set of keywords. A POP3 response consists of either a single line or multiple lines. The first line of a response indicates success or failure status by means of the ASCII text *+OK* or *-ERR,* respectively. A multiple-line response is terminated by a line that consists of a single period (dot) followed by a carriage return and linefeed. To prevent confusion, a process called *dot stuffing* is provided whereby any line that begins with a dot but is not the terminating line is "stuffed" with an extra dot by the server and then stripped off by the client.

POP3 is described in terms of a *state machine.* A state machine is a hypothetical machine that can only be in a number of predetermined states. The machine reacts to input by switching from one state to another when certain criteria are met. There are three possible states within the POP3 protocol: the authorization state, the transaction state, and the update state. When a client establishes contact with the e-mail server, that server is in the authorization state. Once the client establishes its identity and successfully provides credentials, the transaction state is entered. When the client sends a QUIT command, the update state is entered. After processing is accomplished in the update state, the state machine reverts to the authorization state. Certain commands can be used only in certain states. Table 9-1 on the next page summarizes the POP3 commands and their parameters, appropriate state, and description. Parameters in square brackets are optional.

POP3 provides for a client to send credentials (username and password) so that access to the e-mail can be regulated. If the client uses the USER command, the password will flow as plain ASCII text. An extension of POP3 defines a way for the password to be encrypted before transmission by means of a command called APOP. Using the APOP command, the POP3 server sends an ASCII greeting to the client when the client first connects. The greeting consists of a string that is unique for every client connection.

The client appends its plain-text password to the string received from the server and then computes the MD5 digest of the resulting string. The client sends the username and the MD5 digest as parameters within the APOP command.

Table 9-1   Summary of POP3 Commands

Command	Parameters	State	Description
USER	UserName	Authorization	Identifies the mailbox on which the client wishes to operate.
PASS	Password	Authorization	Provides the server with a plain text password for the mailbox identified by the USER command. This command, on success, causes a state transition.
APOP	Name, Digest	Authorization	Provides a means of sending the password in a secure manner. The Name parameter identifies the mailbox, and the Digest parameter is an MD5 digest string; see RFC 1321 for information regarding MD5. This command causes a state transition.
STAT	None	Transaction	The server is requested to send back statistics about the mailbox, such as the number of messages and the total size in bytes.
UIDL	[Msg#]	Transaction	If a parameter is specified, the server returns the unique identifier for that message. If no parameter is specified, the server returns a unique identifier for all messages. Each identifier is unique across POP sessions.
LIST	[Msg#]	Transaction	If a parameter is specified, the server returns that parameter's message number and size. If no parameter is specified, the server returns the message number and size of each message.
RETR	Msg#	Transaction	The server sends the full text of the message identified by the parameter.
DELE	Msg#	Transaction	The server marks for deletion the message identified by the parameter. The deletion occurs when the client sends the QUIT command.
RSET	None	Transaction	The server resets all messages marked for deletion. This is an "undo" for all DELE commands issued so far.
TOP	Msg#, n	Transaction	The server returns the first n lines of the message identified by the Msg# parameter. The parameter n must be a non-negative integer.
NOOP	None	Transaction	The server returns a positive response.

▶ Table 9-1   Summary of POP3 Commands

Command	Parameters	State	Description
QUIT	None	Transaction and Authorization	The client wishes to close the session. If the server is in the Transaction state, it enters the Update state to delete any messages marked for deletion and sends a positive response. This command causes a state transition from Transaction to Update and then to Authorization. If the server is in the Authorization state when this command is issued, the session is terminated, without the server entering the Update state.

Another extension of POP3 defines a command called XTND XMIT. This extension can be used instead of SMTP (described in the next section) to transfer mail from the client to the server. However, this extension has not been widely implemented.

On the other hand, POP3 has been very widely implemented. As of this writing, almost all the ISPs provide e-mail access to the end user using POP3 clients. POP3 servers listen on TCP port 110. POP3 is described in RFCs 1957, 1939, and 1725.

Simple Mail Transfer Protocol

As the name implies, Simple Mail Transfer Protocol (SMTP) is a simple protocol used to transfer e-mail. SMTP is typically used to transfer e-mail from a client to a server as well as from a server to another server.

SMTP is a request-response protocol. The commands and responses are ASCII text–based and terminated by CR and LF characters. Responses also contain a three-digit numeric code that indicates the return status. This numeric code can be used to drive a protocol state machine.

SMTP is layered over the Transmission Control Protocol (TCP). Typically, after a TCP connection is established, the sending SMTP sends a HELO command that allows the sender to identify itself. Next the sending SMTP sends a MAIL command. The other SMTP server hopefully responds with an OK, indicating that it is ready to receive e-mail. The sending SMTP then sends an RCPT command that identifies the intended recipient of the e-mail. The receiving SMTP indicates whether it is willing to accept mail for that recipient. If a mail message is intended for multiple recipients, each recipient's receipt of mail is negotiated in this manner. After this negotiation is accomplished, the message is sent. The e-mail message is indicated by an SMTP DATA command. SMTP provides a VRFY command that can be used to verify the existence of a given user mailbox and to receive detailed information about that user. SMTP provides an EXPN command that is used to expand mailing lists. SMTP also defines a TURN command that is used to turn the connection around—that is, the direction of e-mail flow is reversed so that the sending SMTP server now offers to become the recipient. Some administrators prefer to disable the VRFY and TURN commands because of security considerations.

When an SMTP server receives e-mail for a recipient, it might indicate an advisory error using a response code value of 251. This value is followed by a string that indicates the correct address for the intended recipient. The receiving SMTP server owns responsibility for further routing of the message. A receiving SMTP server can also respond with a different response—number 551, that is also followed by a string and the e-mail address. In this case, the receiving SMTP server is declining to accept the e-mail so the sending SMTP still owns responsibility for the e-mail message.

SMTP is designed to efficiently transfer multiple messages to a single recipient or to multiple recipients within a single client/server session. RFC 821 describes the SMTP transport protocol. RFC 822 describes the message structure used by SMTP— in other words, RFC 822 describes the syntax and semantics of e-mail messages that are transported via the protocol described in RFC 821. Later RFCs extended the message structure.

SMTP servers route e-mail based on the Domain Name Service (DNS) domain name of the intended recipients. (See the section on DNS in Chapter 8, "Searching.") SMTP servers route e-mail messages based on the *MX records* in the DNS. An MX record registers a domain name and associates an SMTP relay host to which e-mail for that domain should be sent.

Table 9-2 presents a summary of the SMTP commands. The command names are case insensitive, but the parameters can be case sensitive (for example, a mailbox name).

Table 9-2   SMTP Commands

Command	Description
HELO	Identifies the client to the server
MAIL	Initiates a mail transfer
RCPT	Identifies a single message recipient; typically follows a MAIL command
DATA	Follows a RCPT command; indicates all message recipients have been identified, and initiates data transfer
SEND	Substitute for MAIL command; rarely used now
SOML	Substitute for MAIL command; rarely used now (SOML stands for SEND OR MAIL)
SAML	Substitute for MAIL command; rarely used now (SAML stands for SEND AND MAIL)

Table 9-2 SMTP Commands

Command	Description
VRFY	Used by a client to verify that a given user/mailbox exists; some servers can fail this command for security reasons
EXPN	Used by a client to verify the existence of a given mailing list and to expand that mailing list
HELP	Asks what commands the server supports
NOOP	No operation; server is expected to respond OK
QUIT	Client sends this command to close the session
RSET	Reset the session; current transfer (if any) is canceled
TURN	The client offers to exchange roles with the server to deliver mail in the reverse direction; rarely used

SMTP servers listen on TCP port 25. SMTP is described in RFC 821.

SMTP Extensions

A number of SMTP extensions have been defined, and these are registered with the Internet Assigned Numbers Authority (IANA), a unit of the Internet Architecture Board (IAB). (For more information, see http://www.iana.org.) The SMTP extensions are defined in such a manner that they are backward compatible. This means that an extension is not used if either one of a pair of SMTP servers does not implement the extension. SMTP servers that don't require these extensions don't need to implement them. SMTP extensions that have been defined include the following:

- RFC 2197 defines extensions for batching of SMTP commands. This means that multiple SMTP commands can be sent through a single TCP send operation. On the Internet, some SMTP sessions occur over high-latency networks (that is, the time between the transmission and receipt of an SMTP request may be very great). Batching multiple SMTP commands over such a network leads to efficiencies in mail transmission. RFC 2197 defines a way for servers to indicate that they fully support this batch facility.

- RFC 1830 defines extensions that facilitate transmission of large amounts of data. The need to terminate each line with a CR and LF character is eliminated by RFC 1830. Also, large binary attachments can be transmitted "as is" without encoding them using Base64 or quoted printable encoding.

- RFC 1845 defines an extension that allows for an SMTP transfer to be tagged as a transaction. If the TCP session (and thereby the SMTP session as well) is broken, a new session can be established that continues the (old) transaction. This facilitates efficient transfer of large amounts of data.

- RFC 1869 defines a protocol by which an SMTP server can indicate to an SMTP client which SMTP service extensions it supports. This protocol is defined so that existing SMTP implementations don't need to be changed unless the features of the service extensions are to be requested or provided.

- RFC 1870 defines an SMTP extension that allows an SMTP client to indicate the size of the message it is transferring. The server can respond as to whether it is willing to accept the message. This facility is required because with Multipurpose Internet Mail Extensions (MIME), the size of SMTP messages can be larger and the receiving SMTP server might not have enough resources (memory, disk space, and so on) for handling the message.

- RFC 1891 defines an SMTP extension that allows an SMTP client to specify the nature of message delivery status notifications (DSNs) and whether they should be generated. The client can specify that the DSN should include the contents of a message and any other information that allows the sender to identify the message recipients and the transaction in which the original message was sent.

- RFC 1985 defines an SMTP extension that allows two SMTP machines to transfer e-mail in one direction and then to transfer e-mail queued up for transmission in the opposite direction in a secure manner. This is accomplished by defining a new SMTP command, named ETRN.

- RFC 2034 defines an SMTP extension whereby an SMTP server can indicate to an SMTP client that it is returning enhanced status codes. These enhanced status codes were not part of the original SMTP specification and may not be understood by all SMTP implementations.

UNIX-to-UNIX Copy Protocol

Strictly speaking, UNIX-to-UNIX Copy Protocol (UUCP) is a file-transfer protocol. The protocol is also used to transfer e-mail by wrapping the e-mail with a thin address envelope and then invoking UUCP. Typically, UUCP is used as an alternative to SMTP when e-mail is being transferred over a dial-up connection. See RFC 976 for details.

Internet Message Access Protocol Version 4

Internet Message Access Protocol (IMAP) is more suitable when the e-mail client software is running on a laptop computer. With IMAP, a user can selectively download messages or even just parts of messages. This feature is highly useful when accessing e-mail over a slow telephone line from a laptop computer. RFC 2060 describes

IMAP in terms of a state machine. For each state, the client can issue a limited number of IMAP commands to the e-mail server. Some of these commands can cause a transition into another state, wherein a different set of commands would be applicable. Figure 9-3 shows the IMAP state machine as described in the IMAP RFC.

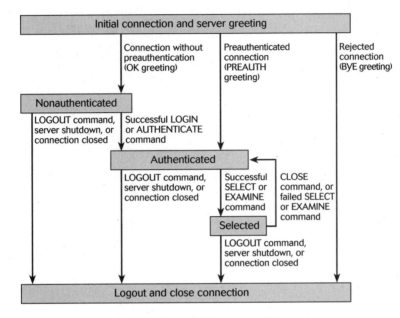

Figure 9-3   *The IMAP state machine as described in RFC 2060.*

With IMAP, the client can download selected messages from a mail server and then disconnect. In the disconnected state, the client can modify any or all of the messages. In order to allow synchronization, IMAP assigns each message a unique identifier that is valid across any IMAP sessions that the client might establish.

IMAP commands consist of an identifier and a command name, followed by parameters, if any exist. The server returns a tag in its response. The tag allows the client to associate the response with a command. This is necessary because IMAP allows the client to issue multiple commands without waiting for a response. Obviously, the client needs to ensure that each tag is either unique or, if the client uses a pool of tags, that the pool is large enough so that a particular tag is not reused before the server response containing that tag is received. The server can generate responses that are not associated with any particular outstanding command. These are called *untagged responses,* and they use the special asterisk (*) tag.

IMAP results include the following:

- OK indicates successful completion of a previously sent command. OK can also indicate that additional information has been included when sent as an untagged response.
- NO indicates unsuccessful completion of a previous command when tagged; it is used to convey warnings when untagged.
- BAD indicates a bad command or argument when tagged; it indicates a serious protocol problem when untagged.
- PREAUTH is always untagged; it indicates that there is no need for a LOGIN command.
- BYE is always untagged; it indicates that the server is ending the session.

IMAP commands are summarized in the following table. Parameters in square brackets are optional.

Table 9-3   Summary of IMAP Commands

Command	State	Parameters	Description	Result
NOOP	All	None	Used as a "keep alive" to reset timers on server	OK, BAD
CAPABILITY	All	None	Server responds with an untagged response indicating its capabilities; the only capability defined for now is IMAP 4	OK, BAD
LOGOUT	All	None	Client indicates end of session; server responds with an untagged BYE response	OK, BAD
AUTHENTICATE	Nonauthenticated	Authentication mechanism name	Client indicates authentication mechanism; defined authentication mechanisms are Kerberos V4, S/KEY, and GSSAPI (described in Chapter 6)	OK, NO, BAD
LOGIN	Nonauthenticated	User ID, password	Provides clear text user ID and password; not as secure as the AUTHENTICATE command	OK, NO, BAD
CREATE	Authenticated	Mailbox name	Creates a mailbox	OK, NO, BAD
DELETE	Authenticated	Mailbox name	Deletes a mailbox	OK, NO, BAD

Table 9-3   Summary of IMAP Commands

Command	State	Parameters	Description	Result
SELECT	Authenticated	Mailbox name	Selects a mailbox for which the client will issue further commands; server responds with untagged responses detailing information about the mailbox as well as the response to the SELECT command	OK, NO, BAD
EXAMINE	Authenticated	Mailbox name	Same as the SELECT command except that the mailbox box is opened in read-only mode	OK, NO, BAD
RENAME	Authenticated	Old mailbox name, new mailbox name	Renames a designated mailbox	OK, NO BAD
SUBSCRIBE	Authenticated	Mailbox name	Adds the given mailbox to the list of subscribed mailboxes	OK, NO, BAD
UNSUBSCRIBE	Authenticated	Mailbox name	"Undoes" the SUBSCRIBE command; removes a given mailbox from the subscribed list	OK, NO, BAD
APPEND	Authenticated	Mailbox [flags] [date-time] message	Appends a designated message to the specified mailbox; other parameters (if present) are appended to the message	OK, NO, BAD
LIST	Authenticated	Context, mailbox	Allows the user to list a subset of available names; the context argument provides the server with additional context	OK, NO, BAD
LSUB	Authenticated	Context, mailbox	Same as LIST command except that the server limits its response to mailboxes that subscribed via the SUBSCRIBE command	OK, NO, BAD
STATUS	Authenticated	Mailbox	Requests the status of the named mailbox	OK, NO, BAD
FETCH	Selected	Message set, message item name	Retrieves data pertinent to a message; data could be parts of a message or the whole message	OK, NO, BAD

▶ **Table 9-3   Summary of IMAP Commands**

Command	State	Parameters	Description	Result
STORE	Selected	Message set, message item name, message item data	Changes data associated with specified message; by default the changed value is returned in an untagged response	OK, NO, BAD
CHECK	Selected	None	Requests implementation-dependent checkpointing of the currently selected mailbox; the resulting mailbox state is stored to disk	OK, BAD
EXPUNGE	Selected	None	Deletes all messages marked for deletion	OK, NO, BAD
SEARCH	Selected	[character set], [search criteria]	Searches mailbox for messages that match given criteria	OK, NO, BAD
COPY	Selected	Message set, mailbox name	Copies specified messages into specified mailbox	OK, NO, BAD
UID	Selected	Command name, command arguments	Indicates specified command (COPY, FETCH, STORE, or SEARCH) that should be executed with unique identifiers, rather than message sequence numbers, as input	OK, NO, BAD
X	Selected	Implementation defined	Experimental implementation-dependent command	OK, NO, BAD
CLOSE	Selected	None	Deletes messages marked for deletion; causes a transition to authenticated state	OK, NO, BAD

IMAP is more complex than POP3 and is harder to implement. IMAP also puts more demands on storage resources at the e-mail server, since old messages might accumulate on the server. On the other hand, it is more likely that a decent backup strategy is in place at the e-mail server, thus protecting data integrity. Also, IMAP allows the possibility of implementing groupware applications, since server-side mail processing as well as shared mailboxes are supported features. (A shared mailbox is a mailbox that can be accessed by multiple recipients.) IMAP also allows for searches to be implemented on e-mail still residing on the server, without downloading the mail to the client.

When TCP is used, the IMAP server listens on port 143.

At this writing, both Microsoft and Netscape have committed to shipping IMAP e-mail client and server software. SunSoft, ICL, and NetManage also have IMAP e-mail software implementations.

IMAP is described in RFCs 2060, 1731, and 1730.

Multipurpose Internet Mail Extensions

RFC 822 describes the structure of the message transported by SMTP. Because of shortcomings with the message structure, RFCs 2049, 2048, 2047, 2046, and 2045 define Multipurpose Internet Mail Extensions (MIME) as an alternative description of the message structure that SMTP can transport.

Prior to MIME, the Internet was limited by its ability to transport only ASCII data—that is, data was transported as bytes, but the highest bit of each byte had to be 0. MIME addresses this deficiency by allowing the transport of binary data—that is, data with any combination of values for the 8 bits in a byte. Note that MIME enhances the capabilities of e-mail messages as defined in RFC 822; MIME is not a replacement for RFC 822. Further, this enhancement is done in a manner that is backward-compatible.

MIME Body Types

RFC 822 defines a message as simply text with no structure. MIME defines a number of content types for text and binary data. Each basic type can have further subtypes. The message size is limited to 64 KB, and messages larger than this need to be broken into smaller messages and then reassembled at the destination. MIME permits recursion—in other words, a MIME message can contain a body part that is itself a MIME message, and so on. The six MIME body types are described in the following sections.

Text

The Text type is used to carry the body of the message. A subtype value of Plain is the default and corresponds to the RFC 822 content. Other possible subtypes include values to indicate Rich Text Format (RTF). RTF supports special character formatting such as italic or boldface. The Text type permits the character set to be US-ASCII, or ISO-8859-1 through ISO-8859-10.

Image

The Image type is used to indicate that the specified data carries images. The defined subtypes are GIF (Graphic Image Format) and MPEG (Motion Picture Experts Group).

Audio

The Audio type indicates sound data, such as voice or music.

Application

The Application type allows data to be carried that is specific to an application, such as a Microsoft Excel spreadsheet or a Microsoft Word document. The possible subtypes include:

- *Octet-Stream*, which indicates data that has no associated application
- *Office Document Architecture* (ODA), which indicates the data associated with a Microsoft Office application
- *PostScript* (from Adobe), which indicates high-quality print data

Structured

The Structured type is sometimes referred to as a multipart type. The Structured type does not carry data per se, but it carries a combination of the types already enumerated above. There are four subtypes defined for the Structured type:

- *Alternative,* which indicates that the same data is presented in different formats, such as plain ASCII, RTF, or Word (.doc) format. The receiving e-mail application is free to pick any one of the data types, depending on its capabilities.
- *Digest,* which indicates that the content is a message digest. Each of the body parts is a message in its own right. Gateways need to pay particular attention to this subtype, since they need to process such digest messages appropriately.
- *Parallel,* which indicates that the different parts should be rendered simultaneously—for example, audio and video data.
- *Mixed,* which indicates that the message consists of a mix of different parts, such as text, audio, or video.

Message

The Message type indicates that the body part contains messages. The subtypes are:

- *RFC 822,* which indicates an e-mail message.
- *Partial,* which indicates that the message is a partial message. This is used to send the message in parts when the message exceeds 64 KB in size.
- *External Body,* which is used to indicate a reference to a file that is external to the e-mail message. This is typically used to indicate a reference to a large file that can then be downloaded using File Transfer Protocol (FTP).

MIME Encoding Techniques

MIME encoding techniques are used to transform data from a form in which all 8 bits are in use into a form in which the data is represented using 7-bit ASCII. This ensures that the data can be successfully transferred through the Internet, where a lot of the e-mail transport can handle only ASCII data. Prior to MIME, this transfer was accomplished using UUENCODE to encode the data and UUDECODE to decode the data. (See Chapter 4, "Encoding Standards," for more about UUENCODE and UUDE-CODE.) In the MIME header, a field called *Content Transfer Encoding* is defined with one of six possible values. These values are described in the following sections.

Quoted-Printable

Quoted-Printable encoding is used for data in which the majority of the characters are already 7-bit ASCII (for example, a message in the Scandinavian language). The intent of this encoding technique is to leave the ASCII characters alone and encode only those characters that have their high bits (of an 8-bit byte) turned on. The result is that most of the message is readable, even without being decoded.

Base64

The *Base64* encoding technique renders the data unreadable without being decoded and results in the message being expanded by a factor of one third. The encoding algorithm converts a group of three 8-bit characters (24 bits) into four 6-bit ASCII characters (24 bits). Bits from an original character are distributed among multiple characters that are output by the encoding technique. All characters are transformed into the 65 characters that are common among US-ASCII, EBCDIC, and ISO 646. These characters are known as the *Base64 alphabet* and are shown in Table 9-4 on the following page.

Characters in the encoded stream that are not part of the Base64 alphabet are ignored when the message is decoded. This permits insertion of extra CR and LF characters into the data stream to ensure that the message can pass through intermediate e-mail gateways.

Binary

The *Binary* value indicates that there is no encoding, that non-ASCII characters might be present, and that the lines might be too long for SMTP to be able to successfully transport the message.

Table 9-4 Base64 Alphabet

Value	Encoding	Value	Encoding	Value	Encoding	Value	Encoding
0	A	17	R	34	i	51	z
1	B	18	S	35	j	52	0
2	C	19	T	36	k	53	1
3	D	20	U	37	l	54	2
4	E	21	V	38	m	55	3
5	F	22	W	39	n	56	4
6	G	23	X	40	o	57	5
7	H	24	Y	41	p	58	6
8	I	25	Z	42	q	59	7
9	J	26	a	43	r	60	8
10	K	27	b	44	s	61	9
11	L	28	c	45	t	62	+
12	M	29	d	46	u	63	/
13	N	30	e	47	v		
14	O	31	f	48	w	(pad)	=
15	P	32	g	49	x		
16	Q	33	h	50	y		

Seven-Bit

The value *Seven-Bit* indicates that there is no encoding, that the characters are all ASCII, and that the lines are short enough for SMTP to be able to successfully transport the message.

Eight-Bit

The value *Eight-Bit* indicates that there is no encoding, that non-ASCII characters might be present, and that the lines are short.

X-Token

The value *X-Token* indicates that the encoding technique is privately negotiated between the sending and the receiving SMTP servers.

The intent behind explicitly defining the Binary, Seven-Bit, and Eight-Bit formats is that even though they currently have no encoding mechanisms defined, future implementations might be able to recognize the different natures of their underlying data and deal with them appropriately.

Secure/Multipurpose Internet Mail Extensions

Secure/Multipurpose Internet Mail Extensions (S/MIME) defines a protocol for adding security to electronic messaging. S/MIME provides privacy by encrypting a message, and authentication by allowing the inclusion of digital signatures. S/MIME is currently being developed under the auspices of an IETF working group. Details of the IETF working group can be found at http://www.ietf.org/html.charters/smime-charter.html. This working group has put out for comments a number of RFC drafts, which can be found at this Web site. Details of S/MIME can also be found at http://rsa.com/smime.

The S/MIME standard calls for encrypting the message contents using a symmetric cipher and then encrypting the key using a public-key algorithm. Because of U.S. government regulations, S/MIME recommends using the RC2 algorithm in cipher block chaining (CBC) mode, using a 40-bit key while sending messages. (RC2 is discussed in Chapter 5, "Cryptography and Security Basics.") If a separate version of an application is implemented that is limited to the United States, the S/MIME standard recommends implementing Data Encryption Standard (DES) or Triple DES for content encryption.

S/MIME requires support for MD2 and MD5 as the digest algorithms for messages that are being received. MD2 and MD5 are also described in Chapter 5. For messages being sent, MD5 is the recommended digest algorithm.

S/MIME requires support for X.509 version 1 certificates for message receipt. The S/MIME standard recommends support for X.509 version 2 and version 3 certificates for message receipt. Support for X.509 version 1 certificates is recommended for messages being sent.

For outgoing messages, support for RSA key sizes ranging from 512 bits to 1024 bits is required, subject to clarifications from the U.S. government. The S/MIME standard recommends support for key sizes up to 2048 bits.

S/MIME uses X.509 certificates. VeriSign has set up the required infrastructure to issue and support X.509 certificates. RSA Data Security sells a toolkit called TIPEM that includes C object code for digital signatures, digital certificates, and message formatting. A number of companies, including Microsoft, Lotus, VeriSign, Netscape, and Novell, have announced support for S/MIME.

MIME Object Security Services, or PEM-MIME

MIME Object Security Services (MOSS) is a draft proposal (RFC 1848) that could very well replace Privacy Enhanced Mail (PEM). (See the next section for a description of PEM.) Remember that MIME defines an e-mail message as consisting of a number of different parts. S/MIME applies a single security standard to the whole message—

that is, to all the parts within the MIME message. MOSS provides a mechanism to encrypt different parts of the message using different algorithms or different keys for the same algorithm. MOSS is sometimes referred to as PEM-MIME. One criticism often applied to MOSS is that the standard is not rigorous enough. MOSS is so loose in its definition that it does not preclude the possibility of a MOSS-compliant e-mail agent generating a message that is unreadable by a different e-mail agent that is also MOSS-compliant.

Privacy Enhanced Mail

The roots of Privacy Enhanced Mail (PEM) can be traced back to the workings of the Privacy and Security Research Group that was mandated by the Internet Architecture Board (IAB) in the mid-1980s. PEM is documented in RFC 1421.

PEM provides a number of features:

- Confidentiality, in that a message is intelligible only to its intended recipients. This confidentiality applies not only when the message is in transit (as in traveling over a LAN) but also while the message is stored in a recipient's mailbox.

- An authentication service, which ensures that a message purporting to be from a certain sender is indeed from that sender.

- An integrity service, which ensures that the message received is exactly what was sent—that is, the message has not been modified.

- Nonrepudiation, which means that the sender of the message cannot later claim to have never sent the message. In other words, it can be proved that the message received by the recipient could only have come from the sender.

Note that PEM messages are designed to use SMTP as a transport mechanism, and PEM assumes that the message is in RFC 822 format. All of the information specific to PEM is encapsulated within two strings "-----*BEGIN PRIVACY-ENHANCED MESSAGE-----*" and "-----*END PRIVACY-ENHANCED MESSAGE-----*". To ensure proper delivery of the message, PEM user agents use the canonical form for the PEM message content—that is, the message is converted to an ASCII form, and CR and LF are inserted at the end of each line. After the message has been put in canonical form, it is encrypted and signed, and then it is encoded into ASCII using the Base64 encoding technique. (See the section on MIME earlier in this chapter.)

PEM uses DES in CBC mode to encrypt the message. The symmetric-cipher key used by DES is sent to each recipient in an encrypted form, using a public key signature algorithm. PEM uses X.509 certificates to validate the public keys of the intended recipients.

A free noncommercial implementation of PEM called RIPEM is available from RSA Data Security. See the text file at ftp://ripen.rsa for more information.

Pretty Good Privacy

Pretty Good Privacy (PGP) leverages private key cryptography, public key cryptography, and message digests (all described in Chapter 5, "Cryptography and Security Basics"). PGP ensures message confidentiality (only the intended recipient can decrypt and read the message) and message authentication (the recipient can be sure of the identity of the sender). But keep in mind that, strictly speaking, PGP is used to ensure privacy of files, not just privacy of e-mail.

To ensure confidentiality, PGP encrypts a message with a randomly generated 128-bit key using the International Data Encryption Algorithm (IDEA) symmetric block cipher. This key is then placed in a message header, which is encrypted using the RSA public key cipher. The e-mail recipient's public key is used as the key for the RSA cipher. The recipient decrypts the header using the recipient's private key to recover the randomly generated key that's embedded in the message.

To ensure authentication, a technique called digital signatures (see Chapter 5) is used. The message is processed using MD5, which produces a 128-bit hash. The hash is then encrypted using RSA, with the sender's private key being the input key for RSA. This encrypted hash is prefixed to the message. The recipient extracts this encrypted hash and decrypts it using the sender's public key. The recipient also decrypts the message and independently computes the MD5 hash of the message. The computed MD5 hash should be identical to the decrypted hash.

PGP provides for three different key lengths:

- A "casual" option that has 384-bit keys
- A "commercial" option that has 512-bit keys
- A "military" option that has 1024-bit keys

PGP stores a user's public and private key in files called *keyrings* on a computer disk. These keys are stored in an encrypted form. Each user has to provide a password to access the keys. The MD5 message digest algorithm is used to produce a digest of the password phrase. This message digest is used as the key to encrypt the keys with the IDEA cipher. PGP has a crucial weakness that is common to public key cryptography systems: how to ensure that a public key is correct and belongs to a particular user.

The digital signature produced by PGP and the encrypted message can have the most significant bit of a byte set. These messages may or may not be successfully transmitted through e-mail servers because some servers assume that the most significant bit is always reset. PGP provides a scheme of mapping every three characters into four characters, with the most significant bit clear.

PGP is available on a wide variety of platforms, including Microsoft Windows, DOS, UNIX, Macintosh, and VMS. Both freeware and commercial versions of PGP are available. Some versions do not meet U.S. export requirements. An international version of PGP, called PGP5I, was created by printing PGP5 code in a book and then exporting the book (but not the code). The code was then scanned into a computer. This export version meets U.S. government requirements.

PGP is described in RFCs 2015 and 1991. See http://www.pgp.com for more details.

Mailing Lists and List Servers

The sections above describe different protocols for transporting e-mail. Mailing lists and list servers are examples of the application of these protocols.

List servers provide a convenient way for a user to obtain information and participate in discussions. The only knowledge required by the user is how to send and receive e-mail. List servers are simply e-mail distribution servers. A number of different lists can be created on a server. E-mail sent to a list server is distributed to all members of the list. Implementations of the list server system exist for various operating systems, including flavors of UNIX and Microsoft Windows NT. Each entry in a list server list can be up to eight characters in length. (For interoperability, this length is eight characters irrespective of the underlying operating system.)

People can join and leave list servers by sending e-mail to a special mailbox on the list server. Often, this e-mail is "read" by software that automatically processes requests and draws only misformed messages to the attention of the human administrator. There is no convenient way for a human to ask an e-mail client or any list server system, "What are the lists of which I am a member?" The human user is expected to keep track of this information by maintaining a diary or some such mechanism. Commands exist that allow a user to ask to be removed from all list servers. Periodically, the list server sends "probe" messages to the list, which generate e-mail nondelivery receipts for every client whose e-mail address is no longer valid. Those who receive such messages can simply ignore them. The list server uses the nondelivery messages to prune the list of subscribers for various reasons. If a user is going on vacation, for example, the list server might be instructed by the user to retain the user's subscription but not send any e-mail during the vacation time. All interaction with the list server, including setting and resetting options, is accomplished by means of e-mail.

One disadvantage of the list server mechanism is that a user's mailbox can get flooded with e-mail messages sent to the entire list. To work around this problem, the subscriber might elect to receive only digests of all the messages sent to the list (all within a single message) rather than each individual message. The advantages of using list server lists, however, is that the process is simple and users can collect a lot of interesting or useful information if the participation in the list is of a high quality. All this occurs simply by means of e-mail, without users having to learn a new system and its associated commands.

The existence of various list server lists might be detected by means of Web search engines. Information collection and retrieval protocols, such as Gopher and Veronica, can also help. A user can also subscribe to a "list of lists," in which an announcement is made (via an e-mail message) every time a new list is added. List server lists exist for various topics, including programming specialties, social causes, and hobbies.

News and Usenet

Usenet allows users to have discussions in public forums called *newsgroups*. A message that's sent to the newsgroup is forwarded to every user who subscribes to the newsgroup. Usenet is the name given to a loosely coupled network of computers that exchange e-mail messages. The messages are tagged with particular subjects or headers. These headers identify the newsgroup to which the message belongs. The message is called an *article*. This exchange of articles among servers as well as between clients and servers is accomplished using the Network News Transfer Protocol (NNTP), described in the next section.

The major difference between Usenet and a list server is in the way a user accesses and receives information. With Usenet, the user has to fire up a news reader and download messages. The subscriber can look at article headers and then retrieve the full text for only selected articles. With a list server, however, the subscriber receives e-mail directly in his or her mailbox.

Newsgroups are not centrally administered. They are essentially self-policing mechanisms. Newsgroups are named according to a particular convention: names consist of multiple components, each separated by a dot. The first component indicates the category of the newsgroup (for example, *soc*, as used in soc.culture.india). The major newsgroup categories (identified by the leading component) are shown in Table 9-5.

Table 9-5 Major Newsgroup Categories

Group Name	Description
biz	Dedicated to business-related issues
comp	Related to computers, computer software, networking, and other computer-related issues
sci	Dedicated to science-related subjects
soc	Dedicated to social and cultural issues
talk	Provided for lengthy discussions and debates

Table 9-5 Major Newsgroup Categories

Group Name	Description
news	Dedicated to discussion of news and information
rec	Dedicated to recreational activities such as the arts, hobbies, and so on
misc	Associated with miscellaneous issues that do not fit any of the other major categories
alt	Limited distribution category whose content has a wider latitude than other groups

For more details, see RFC 1036.

Network News Transfer Protocol

Network News Transfer Protocol (NNTP) defines a standard for

- Clients to post news articles to servers
- Clients to retrieve and read news articles from servers
- Articles to be exchanged between news servers

NNTP is similar to SMTP. For example, NNTP messages must use the ASCII character set, and NNTP commands are in the form of simple ASCII text. Commands are ASCII lines with the command name followed by optional parameters that are specific to the command involved. Each command is terminated by ASCII CR and LF characters. Like SMTP, the NNTP responses consist of a three-digit code followed by ASCII text. The three-digit code can be used to drive a protocol state machine, whereas the text can be displayed for human consumption. Responses are terminated by the same CR/LF sequence. When a command results in the server sending back more data, such as an article body, each line is terminated by the CR/LF sequence. The end of the response is indicated by a line with a single dot (.) followed by a CR/LF. Just as in SMTP, dot stuffing is employed; any line that begins with a dot will have the dot doubled, then a CR/LF appended at the end for sending, and the extra dot stripped by the receiving server.

NNTP responses consist of three digits. The first digit conveys information about the success or failure of the message. Table 9-6 describes the semantics of the first digit of the NNTP response code.

Table 9-6   First-Digit NNTP Response Code Semantics

1xx	Informative message
2xx	Command OK
3xx	Command OK so far; send the rest
4xx	Command was correct but could not be performed
5xx	Command incorrect or unimplemented; serious error

The second digit in the response code indicates the function response category. Table 9-7 summarizes the semantics for the second digit of the NNTP response code.

Table 9-7   Second-Digit NNTP Response Code Semantics

x0x	Connection, setup, and miscellaneous messages
x1x	Newsgroup selection
x2x	Article selection
x3x	Distribution functions
x4x	Posting
x8x	Nonstandard implementation–specific extensions
x9x	Debugging output

NNTP provides 15 commands that a client can issue to the server. Note that an NNTP server might occasionally act as a client when NNTP messages are being relayed. Table 9-8 summarizes the NNTP commands. Square brackets identify optional parameters. Angle brackets, where shown, are syntactically required.

Table 9-8   Summary of NNTP Commands

Command	Arguments	Description
ARTICLE	<msg-id>	Retrieves the text of the message specified by *msg-id*
ARTICLE	[*nnnn*]	Retrieves the text of the message specified as article index number *nnnn*
BODY	<msg-id>	Retrieves the body associated with the message specified by *msg-id*
BODY	[*nnnn*]	Retrieves the body associated with the message specified as article index number *nnnn*

Table 9-8 Summary of NNTP Commands

Command	Arguments	Description
GROUP	GroupName	Selects *GroupName* as the current group and returns the numbers of the first and last articles, as well as an estimate of the number of articles in the group
HEAD	<msg-id>	Retrieves the header associated with the message specified by *msg-id*
HEAD	[*nnnn*]	Retrieves the header associated with the message specified as article index number *nnnn*
HELP	none	Provides an ASCII text response detailing commands implemented by the server
IHAVE	<msg-id>	Client informs the server that it has the message specified by *msg-id*; if the server sends a positive response, the client transfers the entire message; if the server sends a negative response, the client must not send the message
LAST	none	Moves the current article pointer back to the previous article within the same newsgroup
LIST	none	Returns a list of group names; for each group the *msg-id* of the first and last messages is returned, with an indication of whether posting to that group is permitted
NEWSGROUPS	date, time, [GMT], [<dist>]	Returns a list of newsgroups created since specified date and time; time is in server's time zone but can be optionally specified as GMT; *dist* is optional and used to restrict the list of newsgroups returned
NEWNEWS	newsgroups, date, time	Returns message IDs of new messages in specified group since specified date and time
NEXT	none	Moves current article pointer to next article in current newsgroup
POST	none	Used to post new messages to server; server can respond positively or negatively

Table 9-8   Summary of NNTP Commands

Command	Arguments	Description
QUIT	none	Terminates the session
SLAVE	none	Informs the server that the client is another slave server
STAT	msg-id	Similar to ARTICLE except that no text is returned; typically used to position current article pointer
XOVER	none	Not described in RFC 977; de facto standard command that retrieves header information for a group of articles using a single command

NNTP is documented in RFC 977.

Future Applications

E-mail has become an extremely important application, a development made possible by the widespread adoption of standards. Future applications are expected to include a standard method of storing and exchanging e-mail address book information. Another example of applications that are still needed are those designed to exchange schedule and calendar information over the Internet. The Application Configuration Access Protocol (ACAP), described in RFC 2244, may be one step toward these applications. This is a protocol that might be worth watching.

References

Post Office Protocol

RFC 2195, "IMAP/POP AUTHorize Extension for Simple Challenge/Response"

RFC 1957, "Some Observations on Implementations of the Post Office Protocol (POP3)"

RFC 1939, "Post Office Protocol Version 3"

RFC 1734, "POP3 AUTHentication Command"

IMAP

RFC 2195, "IMAP/POP AUTHorize Extension for Simple Challenge/Response"

RFC 2193, "IMAP4 Mailbox Referrals"

RFC 2180, "IMAP4 Multi-Accessed Mailbox Practice"

RFC 2060, "Internet Message Access Protocol—Version 4"

RFC 1733, "Distributed Electronic Mail Models in IMAP4"

RFC 1732, "IMAP4 Compatibility with IMAP2 and IMAP2BIS"

RFC 1731, "IMAP4 Authentication Mechanisms"

SMTP

RFC 2197, "SMTP Service Extension"

RFC 2034, "SMTP Enhanced Error Codes"

RFC 1985, "SMTP Service Extension—ETRN"

RFC 1891, "SMTP Delivery Status Notifications"

RFC 1870, "SMTP Size Declaration"

RFC 1869, "SMTP Service Extensions"

RFC 1845, "SMTP Checkpoint/Restart"

RFC 1830, "Binary and Large Message Transport"

RFC 0822, "Standard for the Format of ARPA Internet Text Messages"

RFC 0821, "Simple Mail Transfer Protocol"

MIME

RFC 2231, "MIME Parameter Value and Encoded Word Extensions: Character Sets, Languages, and Continuations"

RFC 2184, "MIME Parameter Value and Encoded Word Extensions: Character Sets, Languages, and Continuations"

RFC 2112, "The MIME Multipart/Related Content-Type"

RFC 2049, "Multipurpose Internet Mail Extensions (MIME) Part Five: Conformance Criteria and Examples"

RFC 2048, "Multipurpose Internet Mail Extensions (MIME) Part Four: Registration Procedures"

RFC 2047, "MIME (Multipurpose Internet Mail Extensions) Part Three: Message Header Extensions for Non-ASCII Text"

RFC 2046, "Multipurpose Internet Mail Extensions (MIME) Part Two: Media Types"

RFC 2045, "Multipurpose Internet Mail Extensions (MIME) Part One: Format of Internet Message Bodies"

RFC 1927, "Suggested Additional MIME Types for Associating Documents"

RFC 1896, "The Text/Enriched MIME Content-Type"

RFC 1741, "MIME Content Type for BinHex Encoded Files"

RFC 1740, "MIME Encapsulation of Macintosh Files—MacMIME"

RFC 1641, "Using Unicode with MIME"

RFC 1556, "Handling of Bi-Directional Texts in MIME"

RFC 1437, "The Extension of MIME Content-Types to a New Medium"

RFC 1428, "Transition of Internet Mail from Just-Send-8 to 8-bit-SMTP/MIME"

RFC 1344, "Implications of MIME for Internet Mail Gateways"

Secure E-Mail

RFC 2312, "S/MIME Version 2 Certificate Handling"

RFC 2311, "S/MIME Version 2 Message Specification"

RFC 2015, "MIME Security with Pretty Good Privacy (PGP)"

RFC 1991, "PGP Message Exchange Formats"

RFC 1848, "MIME Object Security Services"

RFC 1847, "Security Multiparts for MIME: Multipart/Signed and Multipart/Encrypted"

RFC 1424, "Privacy Enhancement for Internet Electronic Mail: Part IV: Key Certification and Related Services"

RFC 1423, "Privacy Enhancement for Internet Electronic Mail: Part III: Algorithms, Modes, and Identifiers"

RFC 1422, "Privacy Enhancement for Internet Electronic Mail: Part II: Certificate-Based Key Management"

RFC 1421, "Privacy Enhancement for Internet Electronic Mail: Part I: Message Encryption and Authentication Procedures"

Other References

RFC 2244, "ACAP—Application Configuration Access Protocol"

RFC 1211, "Problems with the Maintenance of Large Mailing Lists"

RFC 1036, "Standard for Interchange of USENET Messages"

RFC 977, "Network News Transfer Protocol"

RFC 976, "UUCP Mail Interchange Format Standard"

RFC 0402, "ARPA Network Mailing Lists"

10

File Transfer and File Systems

THIS CHAPTER BEGINS WITH A DISCUSSION of the protocols used to transfer files between two computer systems. Before the advent of the World Wide Web, File Transfer Protocol (FTP) and Trivial File Transfer Protocol (TFTP) were probably the most popular ways to transfer files over the Internet. Of course, one can now use a Web browser to retrieve a file and save it locally.

The latter part of this chapter discusses file systems, including Common Internet File Systems (CIFS) and WebNFS. (*NFS* stands for Network File System.) Both of these file systems were originally created for file sharing over a local area network (LAN) and were later repositioned (with suitable changes) for the Internet.

File Transfer Protocol

FTP is a popular and somewhat secure way to move files across a wide variety of computers. FTP uses Transmission Control Protocol (TCP) as a transport mechanism to move data. It permits a user to provide credentials to a server and then list folders and transfer files in either direction. FTP allows a client to initiate file transfer between the client and the FTP server, as well as between two other remote machines.

FTP Model

RFC 959 defines the FTP model in terms of a user/server model, as illustrated in Figure 10-1 on the following page.

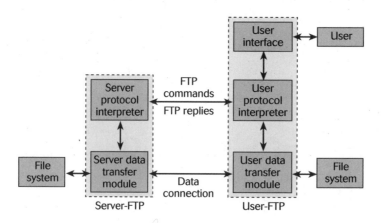

Figure 10-1 *The FTP user/server model.*

FTP is a fairly complex protocol that establishes two TCP connections, one for transferring data and one for transferring commands. Each FTP host has a Protocol Interpreter (PI) module that is responsible for interpreting and acting on FTP commands and responses. Each FTP host also has an FTP Data Transfer (DT) module that is responsible for handling data. The PI and DT modules on each host are connected by some means, the definition of which is beyond the scope of the RFC 959 specification. FTP uses Telnet as the PI by executing the Telnet module or by completely reimplementing the Telnet protocol. FTP commands are sent as plain text. FTP responses are plain text as well and consist of a three-digit number followed by some text. The number is intended to be used by software to determine the step to be taken next. The text is to be read by the user. Each command generates one or more responses.

Data Types

FTP transfers files by converting data from the data type stored on the source to a neutral data format (on the wire). The neutral data format is then converted to the type that is native to the target computer. If the total number of computers that FTP supports is n, a direct brute force conversion matrix would require $n \times n$ conversion implementations. Using a neutral format breaks this down to $2 \times n$ conversion implementations. The neutral data format is Network Virtual Terminal ASCII (NVT-ASCII).

The data types defined by FTP are as follows:

- NVT-ASCII
- EBCDIC, which is used mostly on mainframe computers

- IMAGE, which describes binary executable files that are to be treated as a series of 8-bit bytes or octets
- LOCAL, which describes binary executable files with a specified byte size

The client identifies the data type for the benefit of the server by using an FTP command called the TYPE command.

File Structure

FTP defines a number of file structures in order to accommodate a wide variety of computers. These are as follows:

- *File*, in which the file being transferred is simply a stream of bytes.
- *Record*, in which the file being transferred is a series of records.
- *Page*, in which the file being transferred is a series of data blocks. This mode is used for random access files (files that have some data and a lot of "holes" between the data).

Transmission Modes

FTP specifies three possible modes for data transmission:

- *Stream mode,* which treats the file as a sequence of bytes. This mode can be used with any data type. When the file structure is of type Record, special two-byte control characters are used to indicate the end of a record (EOR) and the end of a file (EOF). If the file structure is of type File, the EOF is indicated by the sending computer closing the data connection.
- *Block mode,* in which the file is transmitted as a number of blocks. Each block is preceded by a header, which contains the size of the block and a descriptor. The descriptor specifies whether the block is the last block in the file or the last block in a record. The descriptor also has a bit that indicates whether the data is reliable. This bit is used when voluminous data, such as geologic or atmospheric data being read off a medium, results in a media error. The descriptor can also specify whether a block is a Restart Marker. Restart Markers allow the receiver to specify the last received Restart Marker and request that the file transfer be reinitiated from that point.
- *Compressed mode,* which is used to transfer files efficiently and utilize network bandwidth optimally. The compression is fairly simple, where a string of x replications of a data byte are compressed into 2 bytes.

Error Recovery

FTP relies on TCP to present the data in order, without any loss and without any data being repeated. FTP provides for restarting the file transfer if the transfer mode used was block or compressed.

FTP Commands and Responses

FTP commands are ASCII strings that are accompanied by optional parameters. FTP defines commands to provide user credentials, navigate folders, store and retrieve files, specify data types, specify the transmission mode, obtain server status, and so forth. Refer to RFC 959 for complete details. RFC 959 specifies that an FTP implementation must contain certain commands but can optionally implement the other commands.

All FTP commands require the server to provide a response. Some commands elicit multiple responses from the server. Each response consists of a three-digit numeric code followed by a text string. The text string can be displayed for the benefit of human users, while the numeric code is typically used to drive a state machine.

RFC 2228 describes optional FTP commands that the FTP client and server may implement. When both the client and server implement these commands, the commands provide for authentication (the server can indeed be sure the client is who it claims to be), data integrity, and confidentiality on both the data and command channels (the two TCP connections that FTP uses for transferring data and commands). This means that the server and client can determine whether a third party has corrupted the data or command. The data and command are also encrypted so that a third party that gains access to the TCP packets can't make any sense of them. The encryption key (see Chapter 5, "Cryptography and Security Basics," for information about encryption) is distributed using a channel external to FTP, such as a courier, a predetermined key, or e-mail.

FTP servers listen on TCP port 21. FTP is described in RFC 959.

Anonymous FTP

Some sites act as repositories of information that is intended for widespread dispersion and is meant to be freely available. Anonymous FTP provides free access to this information. To access this information, a user typically needs to know just the archival site name and a starting filename or directory path. The archival site creates a special account with the username "anonymous." This account is only allowed to login, navigate a limited number of directories, and retrieve (but not write or deposit) a limited number of files. The archival site might accept any string including "guest" as the password, but might also request the user to provide its e-mail address as the password. Anonymous FTP is described in RFC 1635.

FTP and Firewalls

As described above, the FTP protocol uses two TCP connections, one for transferring data and another for transferring commands. The client sends a command to the FTP server that is listening on port 20. Using its port 21, the server initiates a TCP connection for transferring data to the same port the client used for sending its request. Since different clients usually do not use the same port for sending requests, the FTP server will be initiating a TCP session to a port that cannot be determined in advance. This presents a problem since firewalls typically block incoming sessions to unknown ports. RFC 1579 suggests modifications in both FTP clients and servers that work around this problem.

Trivial File Transfer Protocol

TFTP, as the name indicates, is a simple way of transferring files between two computers. TFTP uses User Datagram Protocol (UDP) to manage the movement of data. It does not define a mechanism for a user to provide credentials such as user name and password; hence, TFTP can be used only to transfer files to and from areas that are accessible to any user. TFTP is only capable of moving files and does not provide the functionality of navigating, listing folders, and so forth.

TFTP transfers data in fixed-size blocks of 512 bytes. It uses a fixed-size window of one data block—each data block must be acknowledged before the next one can be sent. Note that both the computers involved send and receive packets. One sends data blocks and receives acknowledgment that the data blocks were successfully received. The other receives data blocks and sends acknowledgment packets. Each computer must time out and retransmit if the expected acknowledgment or data block is not received. Almost all errors cause the file transfer to be terminated. Once a file transfer has been terminated, there is no provision to restart the transfer and copy the rest of the file. RFC 1783 extends the TFTP protocol by describing a mechanism to negotiate the block size for file transfer. With this option, the block size can be set to a value from 8 through 65464. RFC 1784 introduces an option to negotiate time-out values, with possible values from 1 through 255. RFC 1784 also describes an option to specify the size of the transferred file.

TFTP server implementations usually provide some means of configuring the paths to which access is permitted by TFTP. This is reasonable given the insecure nature of TFTP. TFTP implementations are simple and small enough to be provided in programmable read-only memory (PROM) for diskless workstations.

The TFTP server listens on UDP port 69. TFTP is described in RFC 1350, and TFTP extensions are described in RFC 1785, 1784, 1783, and 1782. The extensions attempt to add many options to TFTP.

Common Internet File System

CIFS is a protocol that defines a standard for remote file access over the Internet and intranets. It defines ways for a client to request file services from a server. An extension of CIFS called Common Internet File Systems/Enterprise defines ways for clients to discover CIFS servers and protocols for clients to request other services such as print services. CIFS is based on the Server Message Block (SMB) protocol and is readily available on a number of platforms, including Microsoft Windows 95, Microsoft Windows NT, and many flavors of UNIX.

A potentially confusing aspect of CIFS is that there are a number of dialects of the SMB technology. A dialect is negotiated between the client and server when a session is established. All these dialects are considered CIFS, just as WebNFS includes Sun Microsystems' Network File System (NFS), versions 1, 2, and 3. Another point worth mentioning is that each dialect contains optional extra capabilities. Simply enumerating a negotiated dialect does not necessarily define the feature set completely. Some SMB dialects have been adopted as standards by the Open Group (formerly X/OPEN). Microsoft is trying to get CIFS adopted as an informational RFC by IETF. CIFS complements HTTP and FTP and should not be considered a replacement for either.

CIFS provides a number of benefits. Here are a few:

- It provides file sharing and locking semantics, allowing multiple clients to access and update the same resources. The same mechanisms also allow clients to do aggressive read-ahead/write-behind caching because a comprehensive cache coherency strategy is provided.
- It attempts to cache files on the clients and has an elegant cache coherency mechanism named *opportunistic locking* (oplock, for short). When a client opens a file, CIFS opens the file and attempts to have the server grant an oplock. If the oplock is granted, the client can cache write data (at the client) and also do predictive read-ahead. When another client asks the server to open the same file, the server sends an oplock break SMB to the first client.

The first client can then flush its data, get a byte range lock on portions of the file, and so forth. At that point, the client stops caching the file, and the server can grant a second client appropriate access to the file.

- It can run efficiently over slow dial-up lines.
- It allows for file and folder names in any character set, not only English.
- It can operate over connection-oriented and connectionless protocols (such as TCP and UDP).
- It allows for batching of requests. That is, a number of requests can be collected at the client and then sent to the server all at once. The goal is to minimize the number of round-trips over the wire.

To access a file on a server, the client must be able to parse a Uniform Resource Locator (URL) and extract the server name. CIFS defines two ways for the client to resolve a server name to an address: One method is to use NetBios name resolution; the second and preferred way is to use Domain Name System (DNS) name resolution. (DNS is discussed in Chapter 3, "More About Transports.") DNS is the preferred method because it provides greater interoperability.

CIFS offers the ability to read and write selected portions of a file. A file transfer using CIFS can easily be restarted from the last known checkpoint. FTP would require that everything be copied again. The fact that the Internet is not a reliable medium (connections are often interrupted) adds weight to the argument for CIFS.

Figure 10-2 on the following page illustrates some of the SMBs exchanged in a rather simplistic scenario and explains some of the prominent fields sent or returned in SMB commands or responses. The intent of the figure is to acquaint the reader with SMB technology. A lot of the details about each SMB have been omitted from the figure; for more information, see the latest CIFS specification.

CIFS implementations exist in every computer running Microsoft Windows (including Windows 3.1, Windows 95, and Windows NT). A number of other vendors, including Intergraph, Data General, Intel, and Network Appliance, have announced support for CIFS. Other vendors have been shipping CIFS-compliant software for years, including IBM (IBM LAN Server), Novell, Banyan, Digital Equipment (PATHWORKS), AT&T (Advanced Server for UNIX), smba (NetNames), Santa Cruz Operation (LAN Manager), and Hewlett-Packard (Advanced Server 9000).

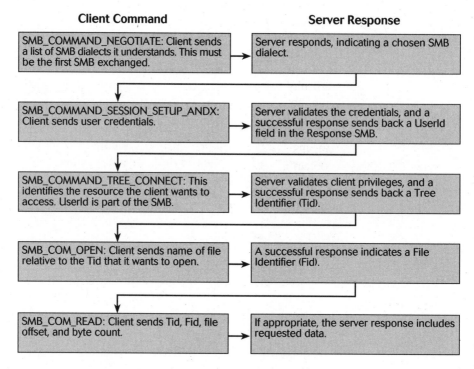

Client Command   **Server Response**

SMB_COMMAND_NEGOTIATE: Client sends
a list of SMB dialects it understands. This must
be the first SMB exchanged.

Server responds, indicating a chosen SMB
dialect.

SMB_COMMAND_SESSION_SETUP_ANDX:
Client sends user credentials.

Server validates the credentials, and a
successful response sends back a UserId
field in the Response SMB.

SMB_COMMAND_TREE_CONNECT: This
identifies the resource the client wants to
access. UserId is part of the SMB.

Server validates client privileges, and a
successful response sends back a Tree
Identifier (Tid).

SMB_COM_OPEN: Client sends name of file
relative to the Tid that it wants to open.

A successful response indicates a File
Identifier (Fid).

SMB_COM_READ: Client sends Tid, Fid, file
offset, and byte count.

If appropriate, the server response includes
requested data.

Figure 10-2   *Some SMB commands and responses in a simple CIFS scenario.*

WebNFS

WebNFS is based on NFS, a technology from Sun Microsystems. NFS provides a file
system that maps remote disks or shares to a local driver. NFS version 2 became a
standard with the publication of RFC 1094. RFC 1813 describes NFS version 3. NFS
is based on remote procedure call (RPC) and is often described as a stateless protocol. A stateless protocol is a request-response protocol; once the response has been
sent or received, no further information pertaining to the other end of the connection needs to be retained.

The definition of WebNFS covers the use of any version of NFS (1, 2, or 3) as applied
to the Web. Prior to version 3, NFS relied on UDP as the defined transport mechanism. NFS version 3 introduced TCP as the transport mechanism. NFS in its native
form works poorly on high-latency, low-bandwidth networks such as dial-up connections to the Internet. One problem is that NFS requires an RPC call to the port
mapper service in order to obtain a port number on the NFS server to which the client

can send its request. WebNFS differs from NFS in that a WebNFS client can always assume that the WebNFS server is listening on port 2049. Another disadvantage of NFS is the overhead involved in an RPC call to mount the file system and obtain a handle. WebNFS solves this by providing a predefined handle signified by a length of 0. A third difficulty is that NFS requires a client to evaluate the pathname one component at a time, obtaining a handle to each component. For example, consider the case in which a client tries to print a file named /folder1/folder2/myfile.txt. NFS first obtains a handle to folder1, then a handle to folder2, and finally a handle to myfile.txt. In contrast, WebNFS permits a client to evaluate full paths all at once. In this example, WebNFS can obtain a handle to myfile.txt in one fell swoop.

WebNFS also offers some advantages over FTP and HTTP. It can reopen and start copying files from the last known position when a connection is re-established after being lost. WebNFS servers scale better, serving more clients faster than can FTP and HTTP servers. Until HTTP byte-range read features become more widely implemented, WebNFS will have an edge because its clients can read selected portions of a file rather than only the whole file. Sun contends that WebNFS scales much better than HTTP, and it claims a performance factor of 3:1 in favor of WebNFS. However, when all is said and done, WebNFS should be considered a complement to HTTP and FTP rather than a replacement. Sun has announced plans for a Java-based implementation of WebNFS.

References

http://www.cifs.com

ftp://ietf.org/internet-drafts/draft-leach-cifs-v1-spec-01.txt

RFC 2228, "FTP Security Extensions"

RFC 1813, "NFS version 3 Protocol Specification"

RFC 1785, "TFTP Option Negotiation Analysis"

RFC 1784, "TFTP Timeout Interval and Transfer Size Options"

RFC 1783, "TFTP Blocksize Option"

RFC 1782, "TFTP Option Extension"

RFC 1635 "How to Use Anonymous FTP"

RFC 1579, "Firewall Friendly FTP"

RFC 1350, "The TFTP Protocol"

RFC 1094, "NFS: Network File System Protocol Specification"

RFC 959, "File Transfer Protocol"

Text Conferencing

ONE OF THE PRIMARY FEATURES OF THE INTERNET is that it allows users to interact with each other. Many of these interactions do not occur in real time but use messages sent via e-mail or news protocols instead. This chapter covers two additional methods for text-based interactive communications—Internet Relay Chat and multi-user dungeons.

Internet Relay Chat

Internet Relay Chat (IRC) provides a basic, text-based method that allows multiple users to communicate interactively. IRC has its roots in interactive messaging in the bulletin board system (BBS) community.

Each IRC server hosts multiple channels of conversations, with multiple clients participating on each channel. The channels cover a variety of topics, such as investing, technical subjects, games, sports, regional issues, and language-specific subjects. In fact, you can probably find an IRC channel for just about any subject.

Channels are dynamic in nature, much more so than mailing lists or newsgroups. Given their timeliness, some virtual events are scheduled for a particular date and time so that a user can join the channel when others are connected.

In the simplest case, multiple IRC clients talk to a single IRC server. Typically, multiple IRC servers (connected via an undirected acyclic graph) form an IRC network. An IRC client connects to a single IRC server on the IRC network but can access the channels and users on the other IRC servers. Additionally, there are multiple IRC networks, such as Eris-Free Net (EFnet) and Undernet. Although it is uncommon, it is possible in some cases to connect these separate IRC networks by means of a gateway.

Most people use IRC client software instead of a Telnet client to handle conversations and to help with metacommands and macros. An IRC bot, or robot, is a special kind of IRC client software that is computer generated rather than human operated.

IRC Protocol

The IRC protocol is described in RFC 1459. This client/server protocol uses Transport Control Protocol/Internet Protocol (TCP/IP) over ports 6660-6669. It is an 8-bit protocol, with most commands using the US-ASCII text character set.

Three different communication methods are used with the IRC protocol: client to client, one to many (one to a list, to a channel, or to a host/server mask), or broadcast (to all IRC servers on that network).

The IRC protocol uses more than one dialect. For example, Undernet uses the same client/server protocol but a different server/server protocol.

Normally, text messages are sent via the IRC protocol. Sometimes, however, a dialect is used to transfer binary files from one client to another. The Direct Client to Client (DCC) dialect is one example of a dialect that is used this way.

IRC Commands

The IRC protocol contains a variety of commands that cover a variety of categories—mainly connecting a server with another server or with a client, obtaining information about a user or a server, manipulating channels, or sending messages from a client. A few of the commands are optional and are not necessarily supported by all IRC servers and clients. Table 11-1 lists all the IRC commands

Table 11-1   IRC Commands

Command Name	Syntax
Admin	ADMIN [<Server>]
Away (optional)	AWAY [<Message>]
ChannelMode	MODE <Channel> {[+|−]|o|p|s|i|t|n|b|v} [<Limit>] [<User>] [<BanMask>]
Connect	CONNECT <TargetServer> [<Port> [<RemoteServer>]]
Error	ERROR <Message>
Info	INFO [<Server>]
Invite	INVITE <Name> <Channel>
Ison (optional)	ISON <Name>{ <Name>}
Join	JOIN <Channel>{,<Channel>} [<Key>{,<Key>}]

Table 11-1 IRC Commands

Command Name	Syntax
Kick	KICK <Channel>{,<Channel>} <User>{,<User>} [<Comment>]
Kill	KILL <Name> <Comment>
Links	LINKS [[<Server>] <Mask>]
List	LIST [<Channel>{,<Channel>} [<Server>]]
Names	NAMES [<Channel>{,<Channel>}]
NickName	NICK <Name> [<HopCount>]
Notice	NOTICE <Name> <Text>
Operator	OPER <User> <Password>
OperWall (optional)	WALLOPS <Message>
Part	PART <Channel>{,<Channel>}
Password	PASS <Password>
Ping	PING <Server1> [<Server2>]
Pong	PONG <Server> [<Server2>]
PrivateMessage	PRIVMSG <Receiver>{,<Receiver>} <Message>
Quit	QUIT [<Message>]
Rehash (optional)	REHASH
Restart (optional)	RESTART
ServerQuit	SQUIT <Server> <Comment>
Server	SERVER <Server> <HopCount> <Information>
Stats	STATS [<Query> [<Server>]]
Summon (optional)	SUMMON <User> [<Server>]
Time	TIME [<Server>]
Topic	TOPIC <Channel> [<Topic>]
Trace	TRACE [<Server>]
UserMode	MODE <Name> {[+|−]|i|w|s|o}
User	USER <User> <Host> <Server> <RealName>
UserHost (optional)	USERHOST <Name>{ <Name>}
Users (optional)	USERS [<Server>]
Version	VERSION [<Server>]
Who	WHO [<Name> [<o>]]
WhoIs	WHOIS [<Server>] <NameMask>[,<NameMask>[,...]]
WhoWas	WHOWAS <Name> [<Count> [<Server>]]

Multiuser Dungeons

A multiuser dungeon (MUD) is a virtual environment in which users interact with each other and with computer-created characters and scenery. A MUD might also be called a multiuser dimension or a multiuser dialog, depending on whom you talk to and the intended purpose of that particular MUD.

A MUD allows each user to assume a character in a virtual environment and to explore that environment. A MUD also allows a user to interact with other human-controlled and computer-controlled characters. MUDs have a variety of purposes; a popular one is to allow users to participate in adventurous combat simulations.

A MUD environment is mostly text based. Users enter text to "talk" with other users, the MUD uses text to describe scenes to users, and a MUD client usually enters short keyboard commands to control interactions with the MUD server.

There is a name for every MUD that exists in the world. First, many MUD codebases have been developed since the earliest MUD was created about 1980. These include MUD, LPMUD, DikuMUD, TinyMUD, TinyMUCK, TinyMUSH, MOO, and many others. Many codebases are dialects of earlier ones, although a few new ones exist. (MUD users and developers are often quite zealous about their dialects.) Second, each MUD world normally has a unique name, often with the suffix "MUD" ("FooMUD," for example). New MUD users might be overwhelmed with the number of different MUD names.

A MUD is implemented by using a MUD server, which stores the MUD world and coordinates the interactions among multiple users. Each user connects to the MUD server by using either a Telnet client (with a purely text-based user interface) or a MUD client (often with a friendlier user interface). MUD clients and servers often work over port 4201 and normally use the TCP/IP protocol, but the protocol sometimes varies based on the MUD codebase.

In addition to assuming a virtual character in a MUD world, some users become wizard characters, which have administrative abilities for that MUD world. Some users augment their characters, turning them into cyborgs by means of MUD client software. There are also bots, which are purely computer-created characters.

Some MUD servers provide a related service via the Remote WHO (RWHO) server. A client can talk to this server via Telnet over port 6889 to obtain a list in WHO format of users on that MUD server.

Web-Based Chats

Other types of text conversations have been created on the Internet in addition to those that are based on IRC or MUDs. With the popularity of World Wide Web protocols, some people have added chat functionality to their Web pages. Often these pages use existing IRC-like technologies connected through the HTTP server by means of a gateway. Other times, they use new technologies. Implementations vary widely, some being basic scripts that take input from users and append them to a chat session file, often viewable in an HTML editor.

References

<news:alt.irc>

<news:rec.games.mud.announce>

RFC 1459, "Internet Relay Chat Protocol"

The Web

P
A
R
T

IV

12

World Wide Web Basics

THE WORLD WIDE WEB (WWW), A SET OF INTERNET protocols and software that present information in a hypertext format, became very popular in the mid-1990s. The famous Mosaic browser, developed at the National Center for Supercomputing Applications (NCSA), was the first graphical Web browser and helped to popularize the Web. The Web was developed in 1989 by Timothy Berners-Lee at the European Laboratory for Particle Physics (CERN). Today the World Wide Web Consortium (W3C) oversees standards related to the Web.

Hypertext is used to construct documents that reference other documents with links, which are easily selectable by novice users. The Web was one of the first Internet protocols to use hypertext to make navigating through large amounts of nonsequential information on the Internet easy and efficient. Instead of having to know an arcane File Transfer Protocol (FTP) command line, a user could click a link on a page to view a file. Computer science degrees were no longer required to obtain information on the Internet.

The Web made use of the existing protocols Multipurpose Internet Mail Extensions (MIME) and Transmission Control Protocol/Internet Protocol (TCP/IP) to help package and transfer data. It integrated the use of other existing protocols (such as FTP and Telnet) as well. Protocols developed for the Web include Uniform Resource Locators, Hypertext Transfer Protocol (HTTP), Hypertext Markup Language (HTML), and Common Gateway Interface (CGI), which I'll describe in this chapter.

NOTE

This chapter assumes knowledge of TCP/IP and MIME.

Uniform Resource Locators

A Uniform Resource Locator (URL) is an address for a network resource. A URL is similar to a filename but also includes a server name and information about the kind of network protocol the resource uses. A URL also sometimes includes user name information and protocol-specific arguments and options.

Web pages use URLs to link to other pages. URLs include many other popular network commands, pointers to FTP-based files, Usenet (a worldwide network of UNIX systems used as bulletin boards by special-interest discussion groups) news messages, Finger and Gopher queries, and so forth.

All this information existed before URLs, but URLs make it much easier to embed this information in such a way that programs can use it, providing the crucial data in a hyperlinked environment. Indeed, before URLs, it was a fairly clumsy process to provide all the server, file, protocol, user, and argument information, especially for users that were new to the Internet. URLs set the stage for easier-to-use hypertext-based commands.

A URL can be broken down into the following parts:

> <scheme>:<scheme-specific name>

where the <scheme> is the protocol or scheme being used ("http," "ftp," and so on), and the <scheme-specific name> varies in format based on the scheme.

Many URL schemes use the following format:

> <protocol>://<user>:<password>@<host>:<port>/<path>

where <user> is the username, if necessary (for example, with FTP using nonanonymous login); <password> is the password for the username; <host> is the domain name of the network host, such as "fictionalcorp.com," or its Internet Protocol (IP) address in x.x.x.x numeric notation; <port> is the IP port number to connect to (if not specified, the protocol's default value is assumed); and <path> is the data associated with the URL, often subdirectory/filename information.

A URL for a Web page might read something like http://www.fictionalcorp.com/corpinfo/sales.html

The "http" part indicates that the URL is using the HTTP protocol. The "www.fictionalcorp.com" part of the URL names the server to which the user wants to connect. The "/corpinfo/sales.html" part is the subdirectory and filename of the HTML document for the Web page.

Table 12-1 describes some popular URL schemes.

Table 12-1   Popular URL Schemes

Scheme	Description
http	Hypertext Transfer Protocol
https	Hypertext Transfer Protocol encrypted over Secure Sockets Layer (SSL)
mailto	E-mail address
ftp	File Transfer Protocol
finger	Finger protocol
gopher	Gopher protocol
wais	Wide Area Information Server
news	Usenet news
nntp	Usenet news via Network News Transfer Protocol (NNTP)
snews	Usenet news via SSL-encrypted NNTP
file	Host-specific filenames
jdbc	Java Database Connector database object
irc	Internet Relay Chat session
telnet	Telnet interactive session
tn3270	IBM 3270 terminal interactive session
afs	Andrew File System global filenames
nfs	Network File System filenames
cid	Content identifier (Content-ID–based messages)
mid	Message identifier (Message-ID–based messages)
z39.50r	Z39.50 query retrieval
z39.50s	Z39.50 query session

However, a shorter URL—http://www.fictionalcorp.com—points to the "home page" of that server, and HTTP servers have a default filename (often "default.html" or "index.html") for subdirectories in which no file is named. This URL could probably be more explicitly mapped to the following URL: "http://www.fictionalcorp.com/default.html."

For FTP, the syntax is similar. The file bar.txt in the subdirectory /foo on the FTP server ftp.fictionalcorp.com would be packaged into a URL as ftp://ftp.fictionalcorp.com/foo/bar.txt.

Because the World Wide Web currently enjoys great popularity on the Internet, many popular browsers assume the "http://" prefix for URLs that don't explicitly have one.

Traditionally, domain names often explicitly included protocol information. For example, a company's FTP server might have been named ftp.fictionalcorp.com, while its HTTP server would have been named www.fictionalcorp.com. With the advent of URLs, however, a company could use the name fictionalcorp.com for both servers. They would then include the relevant protocol information for resources used on that server by specifying, for example, ftp://fictionalcorp.com/public/foo.txt or http://fictionalcorp.com/.

A partial or relative URL is one that does not include a protocol, host, port, or path but rather includes only the relative resource name. For example, Bletch.html, when referenced by the Web page http://www.fictionalcorp.com/foo/bar.html, is a relative form of http://www.fictionalcorp.com/foo/bletch.html.

As stated earlier, URL syntax varies according to the URL scheme. For example, HTTP uses "#" after the HTML filename to indicate an anchor. The URL http://fictionalcorp.com/foo.html#disclaimer refers to the "disclaimer" section of the document foo.html.

Instead of a subdirectory and filename, a URL can include other resource information. An NNTP URL uses the form:

nntp://<host>:<port>/<newsgroup>/<article>

where <newsgroup> is the name of the newsgroup and <article> is the article number.

In general, only alphanumeric characters should be used in a URL, because most special characters are reserved or unsafe to use directly. Reserved characters include ";", "/", "?", ":", "@", "=", "&". Unsafe characters include "<", ">", """, "#", "%", "{", "}", "|", "\", "^", "~", "[", "]", "`".

If a resource name contains a character that is reserved or not in the US-ASCII character set, the name should be URL-encoded. You perform URL encoding by replacing the character with three new characters: the percent symbol (%) followed by the two hexadecimal digits that represent the value of the character.

Hypertext Transfer Protocol

HTTP is the main method that Web protocols use to transfer data between a server and a client. It is a simple method. Prior to the Web and HTTP, FTP was the primary input/output (I/O) protocol method used to transfer files on the Internet.

HTTP is a small, fast I/O protocol that understands URLs and is intended for hypertext/hypermedia environments. It is stateless, unlike FTP, and has only a few commands, or methods. HTTP uses MIME, making it extensible for multiple media formats and different I/O purposes.

HTTP is a client/server protocol that uses a request/response model. An HTTP client, or user agent (often a Web browser), connects to an HTTP server by using a URL and requests a resource, such as an HTML document.

This request/response model uses MIME to encapsulate the requested data. The data traffic between HTTP client and server resembles e-mail conceptually. It consists of data (the message body) and metadata (the message headers). HTTP transfers data in MIME format, and the metadata includes the information necessary to transfer the data between the HTTP server and client. However, HTTP assumes binary connections, which traditional MIME (with its 7-bit e-mail gateway limitations) cannot.

Usually, there are HTTP clients (Web browsers) and HTTP servers (Web servers). There can also be proxy/gateway servers, which act as servers to a client and then act as a client to another server to resolve the original client's request through a gateway (for example, the firewall between a company's intranet and the Internet).

Traditionally, HTTP clients/servers talk over TCP/IP using port 80, the default TCP port assigned to HTTP. However, other ports can be used if specified in the URL. Additionally, HTTP does not assume TCP/IP and can be used with other reliable protocols.

A Web browser often views a Web page that consists of multiple objects, such as the HTML document itself and multiple images (GIF, JPEG, PNG, and other files). Most HTTP clients will have one thread (with one connection to the server) to read the initial HTML document and then start multiple threads (each with its own connection to the server) to read the other necessary files. The connection is established by the client for the request and ended by the server for the response.

Messages

HTTP messages are normally requested from the HTTP client and responded to by the HTTP server. Request messages have a Request-Line that shows the request, and Response messages have a Status-Line that shows the answer and the message body (or entity) that shows the actual data.

Commands

Compared to other I/O protocols, HTTP has only a few commands, which are also known as methods. Only three—GET, HEAD, and POST—are required to be implemented. Four other methods—PUT, DELETE, LINK, and UNLINK—are also defined but these are not as widely implemented.

GET

The GET command retrieves a resource from a server and sends it to a client. The syntax of this command is as follows:

GET <URL> HTTP/1.0

For example, an HTTP client would request the file foo.html from the server www.fictionalcorp.com with a GET command of:

GET www.fictionalcorp.com/foo.html HTTP/1.0

By using the If-Modified-Since header field, a "conditional GET" command can be implemented, retrieving a resource only if it has been modified after a given date.

HEAD

The HEAD command is very much like the GET command, but it returns only meta-information about the URL and does not return the file itself: there is no entity-body in the response. Clients should use the HEAD command instead of the GET command when they are interested only in testing URLs for availability or changes.

POST

While the GET and HEAD commands get information from the server, the POST command is used to send data from a client to a server. Most Web documents are read-only, and users with Web browsers generally do not send new files to their server. However, users often fill out HTML forms (for example, requesting a printed catalog be mailed to them); the HTML form information is sent from the HTTP client to the HTTP server via the POST command.

PUT

The PUT command is less common than the POST command (and not as widely supported). It sends data from the HTTP client to the HTTP server.

DELETE

The DELETE command is used by an HTTP client to tell the HTTP server to delete a specific URL on the server. It is not widely supported because of the anonymity of HTTP clients and the read-only nature of the Web.

LINK

The LINK command is used to link a specific URL with other resources. It is not widely supported.

UNLINK

The UNLINK command is used to unlink a specific URL from other resources. It is not widely supported.

Status Codes

HTTP defines a set of status codes that clients and servers need to understand in order to transfer messages. These codes fall into the categories listed in Table 12-2.

Table 12-2   HTTP Status Code Categories

Status Code Category	Status Code Numbers	Description
Informational	100–199	Application-specific messages.
Successful	200–299	The request was successfully processed.
Redirection	300–399	The client needs to initiate further action in order to process the request. This is often done by the client without the user's knowledge.
Client Error	400–499	Client-side problems.
Server Error	500–599	Server-side problems.

Each HTTP status code consists of a numeric value followed by a text string, which may include additional meta-information. Table 12-3 lists the status code and its description. In addition to the status codes defined in the HTTP specification, status codes may be defined by applications.

Table 12-3   HTTP Status Code Descriptions

Status Code	Description
200 OK	No error, the request succeeded.
201 Created	The POST request has been fulfilled.
202 Accepted	The asynchronous request was received. The request has been accepted but not necessarily acted upon.
204 No Content	The request succeeded, but there is nothing for the client to display; this is useful meta-information for responses that do not need to be displayed to the user.

Table 12-3   HTTP Status Code Descriptions

Status Code	Description
300 Multiple Choices	The requested resource is available from multiple locations. The list of choices is returned in the response. The server's preferred choice is included in the Location field in the response.
301 Moved Permanently	The requested URL has permanently moved to a new URL (specified in the Location field in the response); all subsequent references to this resource should use the new URL.
302 Moved Temporarily	The requested URL has temporarily moved to a new URL (specified in the Location field in the response); subsequent references to this resource should continue to use the original URL.
304 Not Modified	The conditional GET request worked; however, the document has not been modified since the date in the If-Modified-Since field.
400 Bad Request	The request was not understood; the client should send an updated request.
401 Unauthorized	If this was an anonymous request, it must be authenticated; if it was an authenticated request, it was denied.
403 Forbidden	The server is unwilling to grant the request, often due to invalid authorization.
404 Not Found	The server did not find a specific URL.
500 Internal Server Error	An unexpected server error has occurred.
501 Not Implemented	The server does not support this request.
502 Bad Gateway	The proxy/gateway server has received an invalid response from the server it contacted.
503 Service Unavailable	The server is temporarily unable or unwilling to handle the request; this is normally due to server overload or maintenance.

Header Fields

HTTP messages have a variety of header fields that can be used in requests and responses. Some are specifically used for client requests, some for server responses. Some are not supported by some clients or servers. The fields are described in the following sections.

Accept

The Accept field lists the media types that can be used to respond to this request. Most clients indicate that all media types are acceptable by using an asterisk (*) in this field, and pass unrecognized media types to the user, asking the user to associate the relevant MIME type.

Accept-Charset

This field lists the character sets—besides the US-ASCII and ISO-8859-1 defaults—that the client can support.

Accept-Encoding

This field is similar to the Accept field but restricts the acceptable Content-Coding response values.

Accept-Language

The Accept-Language field is similar to the Accept field but limits the number of acceptable natural languages used in the response.

Allow

The Allow field lists the commands (GET, HEAD, and so forth) that are supported by the server (and thus allowed by the client).

Authorization

This field is needed for HTTP servers that don't allow anonymous access to some resources. It sends user's credentials with the request.

HTTP provides a simple challenge-response authentication mechanism to use when anonymous access is not appropriate. It also allows for multiple authentication mechanisms. In the HTTP basic authentication mechanism, the username and password are encrypted using unsecure MIME base64 encoding. Other HTTP clients and servers support other more secure methods, such as the Microsoft Windows NTLM method.

In conjunction with a "401 Unauthorized" response, the server includes a WWW-Authenticate header field describing the authentication methods it supports. The client then resubmits the request, including an additional authorization header field with user credentials for that authentication mechanism. If the server does not accept these credentials, it responds with status "403 Forbidden."

Content-Encoding

This field describes the encoding mechanism (zip, compress, and so on) of the media to be used for decoding the data.

Content-Language

The Content-Language field describes the natural language of the intended audience.

Content-Length

This field describes the size of the message body sent. For the HEAD command, it indicates how large the data would have been if the GET command had been used.

Content-Type

This field describes the media type of the message body. The Content-Type field is normally "text/html" for HTML documents. For the HEAD command, this field indicates the media type the data would have been if the GET command had been used.

Date

This field indicates the date and time at which the message originated.

Expires

The Expires field gives the date and time after which data should be considered invalid. While the field will not force a refresh of the data, HTTP clients should not cache data in their history after this expiration date. A date format (albeit an invalid format) of 0 indicates that the data expires immediately.

From

This field gives the e-mail address of the requesting user. It is used for log-in purposes, not for user authentication. Automated HTTP clients such as robots should include the e-mail address of a person responsible for starting the robot, in case there are errors.

If-Modified-Since

This date/time field is used as a modifier with the GET command only to obtain the resource if it has changed; it is good for caching clients. If nothing has changed, the "304 Not Modified" status code will be returned.

Last-Modified

This field notes when the data was last modified.

Link

The Link field provides relationships such as links between the data and some other resource, hierarchical structure, and navigation paths.

Location

This field defines the exact URL at which the resource was located in cases of automatic redirection (status codes 300–399).

MIME-Version

This field indicates the version of the MIME protocol being used.

Pragma

The Pragma field is a general-purpose field for implementation-specific directives. One common pragma is "no-cache," which indicates that the data should not be cached.

Referer

This field allows the client to specify the URL from which the requesting URL was obtained. This helps determine "back-links," which are used to track bad links and advertising revenue. This back-link may be private information, and so HTTP clients should enable a user interface to disable the use of this field; unfortunately, most popular browsers today do not do this.

Retry-After

This field specifies a measure of time in which services will be unavailable. It is used in conjunction with the status code "503 Service Unavailable."

Server

This field defines the name and version of the HTTP server.

Title

This field indicates the descriptive title of the entity.

URI

This field lists some or all of the Uniform Resource Identifiers (URIs) that this resource can make available.

User-Agent

This field defines the name and version of the HTTP client.

WWW-Authenticate

This field is used for nonanonymous access, using a simple challenge/response authentication scheme. The credential information is not encrypted. See the subsection describing the Authorization field earlier in this section for more information.

HTTP 1.1

The current version of HTTP is version 1.1. This version is supported by all major clients (browsers) and Web servers. HTTP 1.1 is described in RFC 2068. The notable changes in HTTP 1.1 (compared to HTTP 1.0) relate to improved performance. (See http://www.w3.org/Protocols/HTTP/Performance for complete details on the performance improvement and case studies.) These changes include the following:

- Persistent Connections. HTTP 1.1 sets up fewer TCP connections than HTTP 1.0. HTTP 1.0 sets up and tears down a TCP connection for each HTML application request. HTTP 1.1 creates a TCP connection that persists across multiple requests. Doing so also allows a single TCP segment to carry multiple requests. Persistent connections provide better performance than the Netscape extension referred to as HTTP "Keep Alive" because they operate more efficiently in situations involving proxy servers.

- HTTP 1.1 supports compression/decompression, which means files can be transferred between a client and a server in a compressed state, reducing network load.

- Virtual hosting. HTTP 1.1 supports a single Web server (with a single IP address) having multiple domain names. This situation occurs frequently now, when a commercial Internet service provider (ISP) hosts multiple domains.

- HTTP 1.1 supports multiple languages.

- HTTP allows byte range transfers, meaning that only selected ranges of a file or document need to be transferred. This is especially useful when a TCP connection is dropped, because the whole document need not be transferred again. Transfer can begin at the last known checkpoint.

Hypertext Markup Language

HTML is a simple data format providing a simple markup language used for Web hypertext. HTML can be used to represent a variety of hypertext documents. Often HTML files are static documents; via gateways (see the section "Common Gateway Interface" later in this chapter), HTML can be used to represent dynamic data, such as information from databases. For information on Dynamic HTML (DHMTL), and using languages such as Microsoft Visual Basic, Scripting Edition (VBScript) that don't require CGI, see Chapter 13, "Advanced Web."

HTML is a simplified version of Standard Generalized Markup Language (SGML), a formal defining document system. The HTML markup is simple, yet powerful enough to represent most common documentation. HTML is the "text/html" Internet Media Type and MIME Content Type.

HTML-based documents, using hyperlinks (represented as URLs) and sent via HTTP, represent the fundamental nature of the Web.

Early versions of HTML were informally defined. The markup language was first formally defined and widely supported as HTML version 2.0. HTML version 3.2 was the next major version and was also widely supported. HTML version 4.0 has just been released. Some of the features of HTML 4.0 are explained in more detail in Chapter 13, "Advanced Web." The notable differences between HTML versions 3.0 and 4.0 include the following:

- Standardized style sheets
- Support for bidirectional languages

- Frame improvements
- Table improvements
- Support for mathematical characters
- Support for braille and speech

The W3C has also made available an HTML validation service. This service can be used to validate that HTML content meets HTML 4.0 standards. Details can be obtained from http://validator.w3.org.

Special Characters

HTML has some reserved characters. To specify one of these characters in text or in a URL, use the name string or number string indicated in the following table.

Table 12-4   Special Characters in HTML Text

Character	Name String	Number String	Description
HT	N/A			Tab

LF	N/A	
	Linefeed

CR	N/A		Carriage return
SP	N/A	 	Space
NBSP			Non-breaking space
"	"	"	Quotation mark
&	&	&	Ampersand
<	<	<	Less than symbol
>	>	>	Greater than symbol
®	®	®	Registered trademark symbol
©	©	©	Copyright symbol
<any>		&#<number>;	Any ISO 8859-1 numeric value

Tags

HTML uses tags to describe and delimit a document. Tags are used to create headings, paragraphs, lists, formatting, and hyperlinks. Tags are case insensitive.

Most HTML tags come in pairs, with each pair consisting of a starting tag and an ending tag. A starting tag is delimited with "<" and ">". An ending tag is delimited with "</" and ">". For example, to display the text "Foo" in boldface font, the HTML pair of <B></B> tags would be used:

    <B>Foo</B>

Some tags have only a starting tag and do not have an ending tag. For example, to add an explicit line break after the text "Bar", the <BR> tag would be used:

Bar

Some tags cannot be nested.

Comments can be used in HTML documents. Comments begin with "<!--" and end with "-->".

Document Layout

HTML documents have a formal layout, as shown in the following example:

```
<!DOCTYPE HTML PUBLIC "-//W3C//DTD HTML 3.2 Final//EN">
<HTML>
<HEAD>
<TITLE>
<!-- document title -->
</TITLE>
<!-- other headers -->
</HEAD>
<BODY>
<!-- document body -->
</BODY>
</HTML>
```

HTML version 3.2–compliant pages use the <!DOCTYPE> header. The pair of <HTML></HTML> tags surround the entire document. The pair of <HEAD></HEAD> tags surround the metadata of the document, including the pair of <TITLE></TITLE> tags. The pair of <BODY></BODY> tags surround the data of the document.

Headers

Within the <HEAD> section are various metadata tags, including the pair of <TITLE></TITLE> tags, that describe the document.

BASE

This tag is a full URL, used to provide a base address for resolving relative URLs.

ISINDEX

This tag represents a set of hyperlinks from which the user can choose by providing keywords for the HTML browser to search.

LINK

This tag links the page to a related resource. This link may be a style sheet or index page, copyright information page, other version of the document, and so forth.

META

This tag provides an extensible way of specifying metadata, often via an HTTP header, to be used by HTTP clients and servers. Each <META> tag contains a name/value pair.

<META HTTP-EQUIV="<name>" CONTENT="<value>">

<META NAME="<name>" CONTENT="<value>">

In the <META> tag, <name> is the name of the header and <value> is the value of the header. If "HTTP-EQUIV" is specified instead of "NAME," the <META> tag is intended to be used as an HTTP header.

SCRIPT

This tag is used to include a script, written in a script language such as VBScript or JavaScript, in a document. See Chapter 13, "Advanced Web," for more information on scripting.

STYLE

This tag is used to add a style sheet to a document. See Chapter 13 for more information about style sheets.

TITLE

This tag is a description of the document, often displayed by the Web browser in the title bar of its window.

Links

The pair of <A></A> tags define a hyperlink "anchor." An anchor normally specifies a link to another document, using an absolute or relative URL; for example:

<A HREF="http://www.fictionalcorp.com/default.html"></A>

Sometimes a link is given to a fragment of another document, using a URL followed with a "#<fragmentname>" suffix:

<A HREF="http://www.fictionalcorp.com/default.html#copyright"></A>

Within a page, a fragment name can be defined as follows:

<A NAME="foo"></A>

Once defined, a link to a fragment within the same document can also be specified:

<A HREF="#foo"></A>

Outside the document, the link can be specified as in this example:

<A HREF="http://www.fictionalcorp.com/default.html#foo"></A>

Images

The <IMG> tag is used to display an image in the document. The image can be in a format such as Graphics Interchange Format (GIF), Joint Photographic Experts Group (JPEG) File Interchange, Portable Network Graphics (PNG), and so on. The <IMG> tag format is as follows:

```
<IMG SRC="<url>" ALT="<name>:">
```

where <url> is the URL to the image file, and <name> is the text description of the image. The ALT attribute should be specified for HTML user agents that cannot display the image, such as text-mode browsers.

Image Maps

An obvious feature of a graphical hypertext environment is the capability it provides to click on an image. Instead of having a list of all of the countries of the world, it may be more intuitive to display a graphical map of the world and let users click on the regions that interest them.

To accomplish this in HTML requires the ability to use an image as hypertext and to calculate the pixel coordinates of the image where the user selected it to determine what hypertext link to use.

HTML uses image maps to achieve this functionality. A few things are required to do this. First an image is needed. Then it's necessary to break down the image into regions for different selections. For example, a map of the world can be broken down by defining polygons for the various country borders.

A few shapes, using different coordinate systems, can form a map. A rectangle includes the left-x/top-y, right-x/bottom-y values. A circle includes the center-x/center-y and radius values. A polygon includes the x1/y1, x2/y2, …, xN/yN value pairs.

This coordinate data is then used with the HTML <MAP> element to associate it with the relevant hypertext link. For example, the polygon that represents India would be associated with a URL for India.

There are two kinds of image maps, client-side and server-side. For a server-side image map, the first kind to be used, the browser relies on the server to do the calculations and jump to the appropriate hyperlink. In a client-side image map, which was developed later as an extension to HTML (and is not part of the main specification), all functionality is performed on the client-side—no server is required. To handle offline clients viewing local file content (where a server is not present) and to conserve network traffic, client-side image maps are a reasonable method to use in modern browsers.

General Formatting

HTML defines six heading levels. The <H1> tag denotes the largest level, while the <H6> tag denotes the smallest. To insert a paragraph separator, use the <P> tag. To insert a line break, use the <BR> tag. To divide a section of text using a horizontal rule, use the <HR> tag.

Italic text is represented by the <I> tag. Emphasized text (normally rendered in italic) is represented by the <EM> tag. Bold text is represented by the <B> tag. Strong emphasis (normally rendered in bold) is represented by the <STRONG> tag.

Text to be displayed in a larger font is represented by the <BIG> tag. Text to be displayed in a smaller font is represented by the <SMALL> tag. To indicate subscript text, use the <SUB> tag. To indicate superscript text, use the <SUP> tag.

When citing the title of a book or other citation, use the <CITE> tag. When citing a block of source code, normally best displayed in a monospaced font, use the <CODE> tag. When citing text typed by the user, use the <KBD> element. When citing a sequence of sample literal characters, use the <SAMP> element. When citing preformatted text, useful for fixed-font text that has existing line breaks, use the <PRE> element.

When indicating an example element, which assumes that 132 characters fit on a line, use the <XMP> element. When indicating a listing, which assumes that 80 characters fit on a line, use the <LISTING> element.

When citing address related information (author name, contact information, signature, and so on), use the <ADDRESS> element. When indicating a text quote from another source, use the <BLOCKQUOTE> element.

BODY

After the <HEAD> of a document, but before the content of a document, the HTML <BODY> element is used to initialize various characteristics of the document. It defines the document's style, including background image; font type, size, and color; and document margin. Today with the advent of cascading style sheets, many of the <BODY> features aren't used as often.

Lists

Various kinds of lists can be made in HTML. Unordered lists use the <UL> tag. Ordered lists use the <OL> tag. Definition lists use the <DL> tag. Directory lists use the <DIR> tag. Menu lists use the <MENU> tag. Within each list, each item is surrounded by a pair of <LI></LI> tags.

Tables

A table of data displayed in rows and columns is created with the <TABLE> tag. The table header row is created with the <TH> tag. Each row is created with the <TR> tag. Each cell is created with the <TD> tag.

Forms

HTML forms allow user input into the HTML user agent and are normally sent off to a server for processing via the HTTP POST command. An HTML form is a template of data. Most forms require that a CGI application reside on the HTTP server in order to operate. (See the section "Common Gateway Interface" later in this chapter for more information.)

A form has the following definition:

```
<FORM ACTION="<url>" METHOD=GET|POST>
<!-- form data -->
</FORM>
```

where ACTION specifies the URL to be run when the form is executed, and METHOD is the HTTP method (either GET or POST).

HTML forms support a variety of input fields. For normal text, there is the Text field. For passwords and other text that will not be visible, there is the Password field. These fields can have a default value as well as a maximum input length. There are also checkboxes and radio boxes; these can be set up to be checked or unchecked by default. For lists, there is the Select field; in a list of items, a default value can be selected, and a flag can be set to let the user choose a single entry or multiple entries. For information that the server requires but the user does not need to see, there is the Hidden field. And to make a form work, there are the Submit and Reset fields, which cause the form to take action.

Frames

Originally HTML was displayed as a single page rendered in a single display area. HTML frames provide a method to display multiple HTML windows, either sub-windows of the main window or separate windows.

A common use of frames is to split a Web page. Often, one row or column is separate from the rest of the page and can be scrolled. Site-specific navigational links are often stored in a small frame, and the main frame is used to display the intended content.

Frames are described to the browser by defining the frame's layout. This special HTML document uses a <FRAMESET> element instead of a <BODY> tag. The <FRAMESET> element defines the various frames of the layout; for each frame, the URL is specified as well as a variety of row, column, and border layout information. Optionally this frameset document can also define a layout for browsers that don't implement (or that allow users to opt not to use) frames, using the <NOFRAME> element.

The <FRAME> element is used to define an individual window in a frameset. The <FRAME> element specifies the name of the window and capabilities such as scrolling, resizing, or drawing a border around the window.

Given the limited, linear nature of Back and Next buttons, the navigational model of a Web browser is not well suited for use with multiwindowed frames. A poorly designed Web site that uses frames can confuse more than help a user. While frames are a powerful addition to HTML, they are not universally liked.

NOTE

For information about the <EMBED>, <APPLET>, <APP>, and <OBJECT> tags; Java applets; Plug-Ins; ActiveX controls; and other code, see Chapter 13, "Advanced Web."

Common Gateway Interface

The Common Gateway Interface (CGI) is a platform-independent interface used to run software in conjunction with an HTTP server. It allows for "gateway" connectivity between non-HTTP servers and other forms of data. One of the most popular forms is a database gateway, which is used for Web representations of data stored in a database.

The HTTP server executes the CGI process, which is often a stand-alone application. A CGI application is initiated by an HTTP client, specifying a URL that points to the CGI application. The HTTP server executes this CGI application and returns the output to the HTTP client.

CGI defines the interface between HTTP servers and CGI applications, including command line, parameters (environment variables), input, and output.

Script-based software is frequently used, often in the Perl language, so that CGI applications are commonly referred to as *CGI scripts*.

Arguments

A sample URL for a CGI application without parameters is as follows:

http://www.samplecorp.com/cgi-bin/foo.cgi

A URL passes parameters to the CGI application by appending a question mark (?) and the subsequent arguments to the URL, for example:

http://www.samplecorp.com/cgi-bin/foo.cgi?a=1

The command line is accessed via the argc/argv arguments to main().

Environment Variables

Data is passed from the HTTP server to the CGI application using environment variables. For C language bindings, these environment variables are accessed by means of the C runtime function getenv(). Table 12-5 describes the CGI environment variables.

Table 12-5   CGI Environment Variables

Variable	Description
AUTH_TYPE	Describes the HTTP authentication mechanism.
CONTENT_LENGTH	The same as the HTTP Content-Length header.
CONTENT_TYPE	The same as the HTTP Content-Type header.
GATEWAY_INTERFACE	The CGI specification version to which the server conforms, normally CGI/1.1.
HTTP_*	A method to retrieve HTTP headers by prefixing the HTTP header with "HTTP_".
PATH_INFO	The path to the CGI application from the URL.
PATH_TRANSLATED	The path to the CGI application in the server operating system–specific file naming conventions.
QUERY_STRING	The URL-encoded search string; the query part of the URL.
REMOTE_ADDR	The IP address of the requesting agent, normally the HTTP client.
REMOTE_HOST	The fully qualified domain name (if available) of the requesting agent, normally the HTTP client.
REMOTE_IDENT	The name (if available) of the requesting agent.
REMOTE_USER	The user name of the requesting agent (if an authentication method is used).
REQUEST_METHOD	The HTTP command (method) requested.
SCRIPT_NAME	The name of the CGI application.
SERVER_NAME	The name of the server, either a fully qualified domain name or an IP address.
SERVER_PORT	The port on which the request was received.
SERVER_PROTOCOL	The name and version of the protocol (normally HTTP/x.x) that accesses a request.
SERVER_SOFTWARE	The name and version of the server software.

Input and Output

Input from the client (of the size defined by CONTENT_LENGTH) is read from stdin. Output to the client is sent by writing to stdout. Sometimes the output is enclosed in the MIME message body. At other times, if the REQUEST_METHOD was GET or HEAD, the output is available as a separate file, pointed to by the Location header. CGI uses the HTTP status codes.

Security

Since CGI allows clients to execute software on servers, security precautions for writing and hosting CGI applications should be taken. Server administrators need to ensure that dangerous software is not accessible to HTTP clients, and CGI software should be carefully reviewed to check for security holes.

Future Protocols

The W3C is working on a protocol that will succeed HTTP, dubbed HTTP-NG (for Next Generation). The main design goals for HTTP-NG are as follows:

- Simple: HTTP-NG must be simple so that it can be easily implemented and maintained.
- Extensible: HTTP-NG must be easily extensible to provide for needs that are not perceived during design.
- Scalable: HTTP-NG must scale effectively whether used in a small local intranet or with the Internet.
- Efficient: HTTP-NG must be more efficient than HTTP. As it stands now, HTTP does not lend itself well to high-latency networks because it is a single request/response protocol. HTTP is also fairly verbose in nature, with each request and response having a high overhead. HTTP-NG will address these and other deficiencies.

Details of HTTP-NG can be obtained from the W3C Web site at http://w3.org/Protocols/HTTP-NG/Activity.html

References

http://www.w3.org

http://www.w3.org/MarkUp

http://www.w3.org/Protocols

http://hoohoo.ncsa.uiuc.edu/cgi/overview.html

RFC 2070, "Internationalization of the Hypertext Markup Language"

RFC 2068, "Hypertext Transfer Protocol—HTTP 1.1"

RFC 1945, "Hypertext Transfer Protocol—HTTP 1.0"

RFC 1942, "HTML Tables"

RFC 1867, "Form Based File Upload in HTML"

13

Advanced Web

CHAPTER 12, "WORLD WIDE WEB BASICS," defined a basic Web architecture, using Uniform Resource Locators (URLs) to name resources, Multipurpose Internet Mail Extensions (MIME) to bundle resources, Hypertext Transfer Protocol (HTTP) to transfer resources, Hypertext Markup Language (HTML) to display resources, and the Common Gateway Interface (CGI) to provide basic HTTP server extensibility. These technologies remain the core of the Web, but new protocols have evolved quickly and from many sources. This chapter describes many innovations on the basic architecture, including extending the Web client and server, scripting, and Java applications.

Extending the Web Client

Originally, a Web browser was simply a tool that displayed text and that could follow hyperlinks to retrieve that text. Various innovations have extended the capabilities of Web browsers. Today, a Web browser is often viewed as a universal client because it performs the functions that were previously handled by several dedicated clients.

MIME Helper Applications

Web browsers have grown in their ability to read information attached to an HTML document. A Web browser uses the HTTP Accept header to tell the Web server what types of information it understands. At the very least, most browsers understand HTML documents and a few image file formats. Even though they are not designed to be responsible for understanding other types of content, such as sound files, movie files, and a variety of application specific files (such as Microsoft Word documents, Microsoft Excel spreadsheets, and computer-aided design [CAD] data files), most browsers accept all forms of media from the Web server—whether or not they are comprehensible. This allows the Web to be used for uncommon and as-yet-undefined media formats beyond the usual HTML and image file formats.

When encountering formats that it does not understand, the browser looks in a simple MIME database (created and maintained by the browser and/or client operating system) to find a "MIME helper application" that is listed on the client as being responsible for that media type. For example, on a Microsoft Windows system, the Media Player might be responsible for Moving Pictures Experts Group (MPEG) movies, and Word might be responsible for Word documents. For media types that have no helper application listed, Web browsers normally ask the user what to do with the media type. The user needs to associate the data with a specific application, or tell the browser to cancel the data transfer.

HTTP Cookies

Because HTTP was designed to provide a stateless transaction, Web browsers originally treated content as read-only. But before long, owners of Web sites wanted a way for the server to save session information on the Web client, to be retrieved later. For example, Web shopping site producers wanted to give client customers a transaction ID, to help associate the various HTTP transactions with a single customer. Advertisers on Web sites sought to track information about the places on a site visited by the users, to help build demographic databases and personalize sites with dynamic content.

To meet these goals, Netscape proposed and implemented *HTTP Cookies*, small amounts of data that the Web server saves and can later retrieve from the client system. Cookies quickly gained popularity. Eventually, the early specification was replaced with RFC 2109 and addressed privacy concerns related to the collection of personal information.

Cookies are normally used by CGI and related server-side code. They are managed by Web browsers, called *HTTP User Agents*. Browsers normally store the data in a database or in one or more files; more sophisticated browsers allow the user to reject cookies from servers, and to delete previously saved cookies.

Cookies are implemented via two new HTTP headers, Cookie and Set-Cookie. A cookie transaction is initiated by the server asking the client to save a cookie. The server sends the data via the Set-Cookie header. If the client is able and willing to do so, it saves the data. Later, if the user revisits the site or any URL associated with the cookie, the browser returns the data via the Cookie header.

These headers include multiple properties, which are defined in attribute-value pairs. The properties of a cookie include:

- <name>=<value>: <name> is the name of the cookie, and <value> is the value of the data of the cookie.

- domain=<domain>: the name of the server with which to associate the cookie.

- path=<path>: the relative path on the server with which to associate the cookie.

- secure: if this property is present, the cookie is to be used over a secure connection only; today this normally means an HTTPS transaction—HTTP plus Secure Sockets Layer (SSL).

- comment=<comment>: a description of the use of the cookie.

- Max-Age=<seconds>: the lifetime of the cookie.

- version=<version>: the version of the Cookie specification. For RFC 2109, the value is 1. The original specification did not use this property.

Client Pull and Server Push

Client pull and *server push* are two related capabilities that make HTML documents more dynamic. Both methods require additional MIME capability on the Web client, and they are designed to be used by server-side applications that also understand this new MIME format.

Normally, a Web client obtains data from a Web server in a single HTTP transaction. Client pull and server push can make a logical transaction last longer by sending data several times, with each new set of data replacing the previous set.

Using client pull, the server sends data and control information to the client. The control information normally provides a way to update the data or a new URL for the client to go to. A new HTTP response header (containing the Refresh=<seconds> property) controls the timing of the update.

With server push, the client maintains an open connection to the server. When the server sends data to the client, the client displays the data and waits for the server to send subsequent data, which the client uses to refresh the original data. This continues until the server decides to close the connection. The MIME type of "multipart/mixed" is used to implement this.

These two capabilities are not in wide use today. Other client-side and server-side technologies are used more widely, and not all Web browsers support client-pull and server-push methods.

A number of new products have sprung up that claim to be push products. Given the nature of the Web, which is primarily a pull medium (in other words, a client searches for information and retrieves it, thus pulling the information), it is hard to see where the push comes from. In reality, so called push technologies can also be characterized as pull technologies with some fancy enhancements. The enhancements might consist of filtering performed at the client or at the Web server. The client might contact a Web server that it believes has content of interest, or the client might contact some intermediary, or broker, and explain via preferences or some other mechanism what the client is interested in. The broker could then alert the client when an interesting event (as defined by the client preferences) took place. In order of increasing complexity, the various products can be classified into three categories:

- Notification
- Scheduled Pull
- Channels

These categories are described in the following sections. A single product could very well be classified under more than one of these categories—they are not mutually exclusive.

Notification

In a notification scenario, the client registers with a Web server and awaits a notification that something of interest has happened. The event could be one that is almost always likely to happen, for example the *Wall Street Journal* updating its main page, or the event could be something such as an airline ticket price meeting certain criteria or a stock reaching a certain price. The notification can be by means of an e-mail message that contains the information from the Web page of interest. The notification might also simply be an e-mail message or some other event such as a numeric pager call that indicates that the client should poll the Web server and pull down the page.

Scheduled Pull

A scheduled pull includes an array of technologies that can be categorized as *dumb pull* or *smart pull*.

With a dumb pull, the client visits Web sites of interest periodically and pulls down Web pages for viewing off line. Products that perform a dumb pull differ in how deeply they will search a Web site, whether they can search Web sites that require authentication (such as a user ID and password), and whether they share the cache with the browser or not.

With a smart pull, the client pulls down only those Web pages that have changed or starts searching a Web page only when a notification is received.

Channels

With channels, a large amount of data is being pushed. If HTTP is used as the transport mechanism, the client periodically polls for updates or items of interest. Information is grouped by items of interest into "streams," and the stream, or channel, has a proprietary format, depending on the vendor. The situation is similar to using a TV satellite dish for pay TV, where different companies require using a different satellite dish.

Microsoft uses Channel Definition Format (CDF; described later in this chapter). Netscape has a channel product it calls Netcaster. A number of companies have come up with interesting channels. McAfee has SecureCast, which carries information related to viruses. CyberMedia has a product named Oil Change that carries information about software updates.

One problem with existing push technologies is that they do not scale effectively. When a large number of clients are polling for updates, the Web server and the infrastructure is inundated with requests and responses. Stopgap solutions to help alleviate the load on the network exist in the form of products that let clients poll a broker or a local server. The idea behind a broker is that information of interest to a lot of clients is mirrored to another server that is closer to the client. The network load is moved off part of the network because the mirroring pushes the data only once over that part of the network. Previously, the data had been pushed to multiple clients independently of each other. In the future, the push products are expected to use IP multicasting to enhance scaling and, at the same time, move closer to a real push solution.

Netscape Plug-Ins

Web browsers were originally extensible only via MIME helper applications, which were separate processes with separate windows. Netscape *plug-ins* are designed to extend the browser in an integrated manner. A plug-in is a separate module that appears to be integrated with the browser.

The plug-in interface was designed to integrate applications seamlessly into the browser, to support data types not supported intrinsically by the browser, and to leverage operating system–specific code and thus support the migration of existing applications that take advantage of the Web.

When the browser finds a MIME type that it does not understand, it looks to see whether a plug-in has registered to support it. If so, the browser loads the plug-in or creates a new instance of a previously loaded plug-in. The browser calls the plug-in's NPP_Initialize function when the plug-in is first loaded, and it calls NPP_New when a new instance is created. When the window containing the plug-in is closed, the browser calls the plug-in's NPP_Destroy function to delete the instance, and later it calls NPP_Shutdown when the last instance is unloaded.

The plug-in API provides interfaces that work with the browser to exchange information and share system resources. The categories of interfaces provided include event handling, window management, memory management, data stream buffer management, and printing.

Macromedia Shockwave

Shockwave was developed by Macromedia in an effort to bring multimedia to the Internet in general and to HTML pages in particular. Shockwave is a technology that consists of a number of products. A Shockwave object is created using one of several authoring tools from Macromedia, such as the well-known product called Director. The Shockwave object is then referred to on a Web page. A Web browser client that attempts to view a Web page referring to a Shockwave object must have a Shockwave viewer, which is available from Macromedia and its partners at no cost. For Microsoft Internet Explorer, the Shockwave viewer is an ActiveX object. For Netscape Navigator, the Shockwave viewer is a plug-in. Shockwave technology supports audio, video, animation, and the processing of user input such as mouse clicks. Shockwave also includes a scripting language and a technology to compress and decompress Shockwave objects.

Macromedia sells the technology to create Shockwave objects and gives away the technology to view Shockwave objects. Director and Authorware, also from Macromedia, are two commercial products that can be used to create Shockwave objects. Shockwave viewers are available for a number of platforms, including all versions of Windows and the Macintosh. The viewers are also bundled with Web browsers and computers.

Macromedia positions its products for usage on the Internet and intranets and also for the development of multimedia training and education software. More information may be obtained from the Macromedia Web site at www.macromedia.com.

Java Applets

Java applets are small, platform-independent programs that run within the context of a browser's HTML document. These programs add dynamic information to the static document—audio, video, access to spreadsheet or database data, and so forth. As with HTML documents, Java applets are stored on Web servers, and are downloaded by the Web client to the local system using HTTP.

The Java programming language is a portable object-oriented language, loosely based on C++. Instead of compiling to native code, Java source code (using a .java source file) is "compiled" into byte codes (using a .class byte code file), and run by the Java Virtual Machine (VM).

The Java language has a set of APIs that are portable to a variety of operating systems and platforms. These APIs provide basic functionality (window management, memory management, user input, and so on) and are grouped into packages.

Java applets are a special form of Java applications. They are not meant to be run as stand-alone programs; an applet needs to be embedded in another application. Normally, it is embedded in an HTML document and run by a Java-enabled Web browser. An applet has a restricted security context, cannot access the client's system, and can talk only with the server that hosted it. Java applets have a special package, called java.applet, that provides interfaces between an applet and its environment (the browser and the HTML documents).

Java applets are inserted into an HTML document via an APPLET tag. This tag indicates the initial window size for the applet, parameters for the applet, and the location from which the browser can download the .class file, among other things.

GIF Animations

Given the various technologies created to make a Web client more intelligent, it is ironic that more of these solutions have not been used as widely as the simple GIF image. The GIF file format was originally used by Web browsers to display a single image. However, a lesser-used version of the GIF specification enables multiple images to be stored in a single file, with rudimentary timing information about how to cycle through the images—similar to common movie file formats, but without sound.

When popular Web browsers started supporting GIF animation, this low-technology solution became widely used. For example, the popular Java applet sample "Tumbling Duke" had multiple GIF files and a Java applet to load the files and hand-animate them. However, this client-side functionality can easily be replaced by a single, simple GIF animation. Web site artists use GIF animations in many creative ways to make a static

Web site more dynamic. Advertisers use GIF animations to pass on extra information to the user, and some Web sites use animations to include multiple advertisements in a single ad panel.

Platform for Internet Content Selection

The Platform for Internet Content Selection (PICS) is a method for labeling content. It's primarily used to rate content so that software can help control access by children to questionable content; the PICS method can also be used for other content filtering and content identification uses.

A rating service provides content labels in a variety of ways. For HTML documents on the Web, the label is associated with the content by use of the META tag to create an HTTP PICS-Label header. A rating service uses a rating system, or scale of values for labeling. Movies in the United States are rated using a scale starting with G, PG, PG-13, and so on. Television has a similar rating system.

When content is associated with a rating service and a particular rating system, filtering software can be used to control access to content that meets specific criteria. There is a variety of products for parents to help control access to questionable content by children. Many modern Web browsers have built-in PICS awareness.

Platform for Privacy Preferences Project

Platform for Privacy Preferences Project (P3P) is an initiative started by the World Wide Web Consortium to define a standard way for a Web site to display its privacy practice and for a user to exercise preferences over that practice. For example, a site might indicate that it will provide information if the user provides certain information in exchange. The user might be willing to give only certain information, and might want to provide certain information only after confirmation. P3P does not define a new technology but uses existing technology to achieve its objectives. In particular, P3P depends on Extensible Markup Language (XML), cookies, and digital signatures. For more details, please refer to http://www.w3.org/p3p/overview.html.

Cascading Style Sheets

The Cascading Style Sheet (CSS) mechanism is an HTML language specification used to associate styles (fonts, colors, spacing, margins, positioning, and so on) with the elements of an HTML document.

A *style sheet* is a collection of formatting rules that can be applied to multiple documents. As a result, it acts as a template does in a desktop publishing application. A style sheet, like a template, allows the same "look" to be applied automatically to each occurrence of a particular element in every document to which the style sheet is attached. For example, all top-level headings might be set to use the Arial font at 20 points in boldface type. The "cascading" aspect in CSS is the allowance of multiple style sheets, with rules of precedence for a single document.

A style sheet can be associated with an HTML document in a variety of ways. The style sheet can be contained in a separate file, which can be referenced by multiple documents that each use a LINK tag in the head section of the HTML document:

```
<LINK REL="stylesheet" TYPE="text/css" HREF="foo.css">
```

Style sheet information can be embedded within an HTML document by using a STYLE tag in the head section of the document; this style information then applies to the entire document. Style sheet information can also be placed within a specific element of an HTML document by using the STYLE attribute of that element.

CSS provides much more control over HTML, increasing HTML's viability in Web publishing.

Extensible Markup Language

Extensible Markup Language is a technology that is now being developed under the auspices of the World Wide Web Consortium (W3C). XML complements HTML and is based on Standard Generalized Markup Language (SGML). Whereas HTML describes a set of commands that define how data is laid out on a page, XML allows the data on an HTML page to be described by the type of information it represents. One direct consequence of this distinction is that search engines can return more meaningful hits. For example, using XML, a search engine might be able to distinguish whether the word "cookie" in an HTML page applies to the Internet or to a tasty dessert.

XML allows browser clients to download an HTML page just once and then manipulate the page off line, without referring to the server. The client can view the data in any meaningful way desired and can manipulate the data; for example, XML would, ideally, allow a client to perform actions such as extracting a hotel's name and address from the result of a search and then feeding the data into a mapping program that would print out driving directions.

XML Syntax Details

XML uses the Unicode character set for encoding. This means that XML can be used with a wide variety of international languages. Unicode has associated encodings for purposes of transmission. XML uses Universal Transformation Format-8 (UTF-8) by default. (For information about Unicode and UTF-8, see Chapter 4, "Encoding Standards.")

Unlike HTML, XML is case sensitive and white space is relevant.

XML has some reserved characters that have special meaning. For example, the characters "<" and ">" need to be encoded as "&lt" and "&gt" respectively. The sentence "25 > 24 and 25 < 26" would thus be encoded as "25 &gt 24 and 25 &lt 26" in XML.

XML syntax is very similar to that of HTML and consists of a series of tags and annotated text. The major difference is that the XML tags indicate what the data represents, rather than how the data should be represented. Another difference is that the tags are limited in HTML, whereas XML has unlimited potential because users can define their own sets of tags.

XML syntax consists of a series of elements. Each element consists of a beginning tag, contents, and an ending tag, as in this example:

<PERSON>

<LASTNAME>Gates</LASTNAME>

<FIRSTNAME>Bill</FIRSTNAME>

</PERSON>

In this example, the element PERSON begins on the first line and ends on the last line of the example. As shown, elements can contain other elements. Simple XML documents can be self-contained and self-describing. Complex XML documents are described using an external file called a *Document Type Definition file*.

Document Type Definition File

A Document Type Definition (DTD) file specifies the valid syntax for an XML document. In particular, a DTD file enumerates the elements that can appear in a particular XML document and the relationships among different elements. An XML document may or may not have a DTD associated with it.

XML and SGML

As previously stated, XML is based on Standard Generalized Markup Language (SGML). XML is a simplified form of SGML that lends itself readily to transmission across networks by reducing complexity while promoting ease of use and interoperability across platforms and applications. A form of XML document called "well-formed" does not need an associated DTD file and can thus be transmitted over networks more easily. SGML has no equivalent to a well-formed XML document. A different form of XML document called "valid" does require an associated DTD file and does have an SGML-equivalent concept.

XML Vocabularies

Simply put, an XML DTD file constitutes a *vocabulary*. A vocabulary is the collection of elements defined by a DTD file and the rules for constructing valid instances of those elements. The following sections describe some XML vocabularies. More are expected to be defined in the future.

Channel Definition Format

Channel Definition Format (CDF) is a vocabulary defining the structured view of data available for push delivery on Web sites. This includes descriptions of the various channels, a schedule for when the data is to be pushed, and so forth. CDF first shipped with Microsoft Internet Explorer version 4.

Open Software Description

Open Software Description (OSD) is a standard vocabulary jointly developed by Microsoft and Marimba to facilitate advertising, downloading, and installation of software across the Internet. The OSD specification was submitted to W3C in the latter part of 1997.

Resource Description Framework

Resource Description Framework (RDF) is being developed under the auspices of W3C to create a means of describing metadata (data about data) that can facilitate searching for resources or information on the Web. RDF is based on Apple's Meta Content Format, a technology later acquired by Netscape.

Open Financial Exchange Format

Open Financial Exchange (OFX) is a standard vocabulary for representing data exchange between a financial application (such as Intuit Quicken or Microsoft Money) and a financial institution. OFX is currently described in SGML format, but will be available soon in XML format.

XML Namespaces

XML Namespaces handle cases in which XML tags can have multiple meanings. For example, to a music store, the tag <GROUP> could mean the group that recorded an audio compact disc (CD), but to a large corporation, the tag <GROUP> might indicate the division of the company an employee belongs to. XML Namespaces allow a single document to contain elements from multiple vocabularies and to handle cases in which the same name is applied to elements that are defined differently in different vocabularies.

XML and Security

Currently XML is as secure as HTML. Security may be added by having the server encrypt the data before transmission and having the client decrypt the data. Another option is for the client and server to communicate over a secure channel; for example, using S-HTTP. These are technologies that exist today. Technologies that might evolve in the future include a technology somewhat similar to MIME Object Security Services (MOSS). The idea is that XML consists of a number of elements and that a number of elements constitute an object. The contents of sensitive objects could be transmitted using a variety of different security technologies.

Extensible Style Language

Dynamic HTML (see "Dynamic HTML, Scriptlets, and the Document Object Model" later in this chapter) is closely related to XML in the sense that both enable a client to dynamically view data in different ways and to do so without repeated requests to the server. The Cascading Style Sheet (CSS) mechanism forms an integral part of Dynamic HTML. CSS as it stands can handle simple XML data but is inadequate for taking advantage of the full range of XML possibilities (adding a new data item, for example). *Extensible Style Language* (XSL), which is based on the SGML-related Document Style Semantics and Specification Language (DSSSL), is a CSS-compatible style sheet language being developed under the auspices of W3C as a means of applying formatting to XML elements. An example of functionality provided by XSL is the ability to extract a data item from an XML document, format it, and display it multiple times on a different document.

Scripting

One of the most powerful innovations for Web protocols has been the ability to add a *script,* written in a *scripting language,* to an HTML document. A script expands a static HTML document to include client-side interactivity.

JavaScript

JavaScript is a relatively simple object-oriented scripting language, designed to create and manipulate script objects. It was created by Netscape, and was originally called LiveScript. JavaScript is not Java, although aspects of the JavaScript language were designed to look and feel like Java.

JavaScript source code is inserted into an HTML document using the <SCRIPT LANGUAGE="JavaScript"> tag. When rendering the HTML document, the browser passes the code to the JavaScript interpreter.

JavaScript has basic language operators: *assignment, comparison, arithmetic, bitwise, logical, string,* and *special.* It supports these statements: *break, comment, continue, delete, do...while, export, for, for...in, function, if...else, import, return, switch, var, while,* and *with.*

JavaScript has the ability to access the properties and methods of objects. It comes with a set of core objects: Array, Boolean, Date, Function, Math, Number, RegExp, and String. Browsers expose an additional object model in order to expose the safe functionality of the browser to JavaScript-enabled Web pages. The Document and Form objects deal with the HTML document. The Window and Browser objects deal with the browser's window, frames, history, MIME types, and related functionality.

For interactive programming, JavaScript provides event objects and event handlers. There are events named onXXX, where XXX includes events such as: Abort, Click, DblClick, DragDrop, Error, Focus, KeyDown, KeyPress, KeyUp, Load, MouseDown, MouseMove, MouseOut, MouseOver, MouseUp, Move, Reset, Resize, Select, Submit, and Unload.

ECMAScript

ECMAScript is JavaScript standardized by a committee of the European standards body ECMA; the committee includes Netscape, Microsoft, Sun Microsystems, IBM, Borland International, and others. The effort began as an attempt to create a standard scripting language for the Web.

The ECMAScript standard defines the language and a core set of objects. ECMAScript does not define all the host-specific object interfaces. For example, a browser that supports an ECMAScript-compliant script language may also include a superset of object interfaces to the browser that would not be available in other browsers.

ActiveX Scripting and JScript

Faced with the popularity of JavaScript on the Web and the popularity of Microsoft Visual Basic as a Windows development tool, Microsoft developed a script engine abstraction layer to allow for a variety of script engines to be plugged into a script host.

Thus, Internet Explorer supports multiple script languages. The Internet Explorer implementation of JavaScript/ECMAScript is called JScript. Other languages, such as Perl, Tcl, and REXX, can also be used.

VBScript

Microsoft Visual Basic, Scripting Edition (VBScript) is essentially a subset of the Microsoft Visual Basic language. It is implemented as a fast, portable, lightweight interpreter for use in Web browsers. VBScript provides for the manipulation of ActiveX controls and Java applets.

Similar to JavaScript, VBScript source code is inserted into an HTML document by using the <SCRIPT LANGUAGE="VBScript"> tag. When rendering the HTML document, the browser passes the code to the VBScript interpreter.

As an alternative to JavaScript, VBScript is useful in that it allows the large Windows developer community to employ their Visual Basic development skills in the creation of interactive Web content.

Extending the Web Server

Like the Web client, the Web server has evolved from a basic HTTP server with CGI extensibility. There have been a few replacements of CGI, each with different goals. And as in the above section on HTML scripting used on the client, scripting is now an option for server-side HTML creation. Initially, Dynamic HTML was created by CGI applications (often written in the Perl language using one of the Internet modules). Later, client-side scripting languages moved to servers.

Netscape Server API

One of the first interfaces designed to improve on CGI was the Netscape Server API (NSAPI). CGI requires a separate process for each server application, and process startup and shutdown can be expensive. In addition, each separate CGI process is somewhat isolated in its access to resources and has to individually initialize each resource (such as a database) that it uses. These problems are magnified for frequently accessed CGI applications.

A server that implements NSAPI breaks down the HTTP request-response process into a series of logical steps. When a Web client sends a request to a Web server, it goes through common steps during the response. These steps include authorization, name translation, path checking, object type checking, request response, and transaction logging. NSAPI allows these server layers to be replaced by third-party developer modules. This layering can occur on a global, per-directory, or per-file basis. NSAPI applications are faster than CGI applications. They are tightly integrated with the Web server, having access to some of the servers functions and data and the ability to replace the server layers with new ones. New functionality can be added, such as specialized error handling, customized logging, and customized authentication schemes.

NSAPI is still used for programs that must be closely tied to the Web server and that require high performance. However, with newer technologies available, many developers use some form of Dynamic HTML for higher-level development of server-side applications.

WinCGI

CGI depends on applications to be able to access stdin/stdout handles for I/O. Win16 (mainly Visual Basic) applications have difficulty obtaining this information. So WinCGI was developed to allow HTTP applications to be written in Visual Basic. To achieve this, WinCGI stores the input and output data in a specified .ini file.

Many early Windows-based Web sites used server applications written with WinCGI. Multiple Windows-based Web server vendors supported WinCGI. However, with Win16 being replaced by the more capable Win32, and Visual Basic programmers moving to newer methods of writing server applications using Dynamic HTML, WinCGI has largely been replaced by other forms of Web server extensions.

Internet Server API

Internet Server API (ISAPI), developed by Process Software and Microsoft, is another server-side interface alternative to CGI applications that has performance and other benefits. There are two kinds of ISAPI interfaces: ISAPI applications and ISAPI filters. These work on a few Web server products, including Microsoft Internet Information Server (IIS).

For the benefit of people who are familiar with Novell NetWare, here is a rough analogy: ISAPI is similar to NetWare Loadable Modules (NLMs) in that the application runs as part of the system software (the Web server in this case). A faulty NLM can crash the system, and a faulty ISAPI DLL can crash the Web server. The analogy breaks down in the sense that NLMs execute in kernel mode, whereas ISAPI does not execute in kernel mode. Also, development and debugging tools for ISAPI are much more pervasive than those for NLMs.

ISAPI Applications

ISAPI applications are similar to CGI applications. A CGI application lives in its own process space, but process creation is an expensive operation especially for a frequently accessed application. On a Windows system, an ISAPI application is implemented as a Win32 dynamic-link library (DLL) that is loaded in the context of the Web server. Thus, the process-creation overhead is incurred only once. Similar performance benefits can occur on other operating systems that have similar process primitives.

ISAPI applications are based on a model similar to that of CGI applications. The HttpExtensionProc procedure is the equivalent of the main procedure, and the ReadClient and WriteClient procedures replace I/O with stdin and stdout. A data structure called Extension Control Block (ECB) contains most of the commonly accessed HTTP headers and variables; other HTTP headers can be obtained using GetServerVariable.

High-performance, low-level server application gateways use this interface. For less performance and more portability, CGI remains an option. For higher-level programming, scripts that use Dynamic HTML to manipulate existing objects are gaining popularity.

ISAPI Filters

An ISAPI filter is a process (implemented on a Windows system as a Win32 DLL) that intercepts HTTP I/O between the HTTP client and the HTTP server. ISAPI filters are able to read and alter HTTP I/O after it leaves the client and before it reaches the server. They are also able to read and alter HTTP I/O after it leaves the server and before it reaches the client. When a filter is invoked for a request going from the client to the server, it has three options: it can simply pass the unmodified request onward, it can process the request and pass it to the server to act on, or it can process and complete the request (so the server does not act on it).

ISAPI filters are intended for specialized server-side applications that need to monitor HTTP activity, including application categories such as custom authentication schemes, browser statistical analysis, custom URL/file remapping, encryption, and compression.

Examples of ISAPI filter implementations include the following:

- A filter that replaces the basic client authentication mechanism with a custom mechanism
- A filter that allows HTML content to be transferred in a compressed form
- A filter that encrypts the HTML data being transferred and provides privacy for that content
- A filter to perform logging and traffic analysis

Web Database Gateways

Web database gateways are one of the most common devices found on HTTP servers, providing dynamic, Web-based access to information stored in a database. Rather than having every developer implement his or her own CGI application to provide Web database gateway functionality, multiple solutions have been created so that developers don't have to reinvent the wheel.

Internet Database Connector

One Web database gateway is the Internet Database Connector (IDC), which is implemented as an ISAPI application and is included with IIS and other Web servers. IDC is a simple method that obviates the need for a new CGI application to act as a gateway between a database and a Web server. IDC is a single program that uses *open database connectivity* (ODBC) to query any ODBC-compliant database. Instead of writing a database application, a Web site developer uses a text file (.idc extension) to store the database information. The file is similar to an HTML document but includes additional variables to store the database name, user credentials, ODBC query to the database server, and HTML template on formatting the resultant output data that is returned to the user.

Active Server Pages

Microsoft Active Server Pages (ASP) is a technology that provides the server-side equivalent to using a scripting language and objects on the client. An ASP page is an HTML document containing a script that can manipulate ActiveX controls. The script runs on the server, and the client receives any output. Normally, the script on an ASP page drives an object, producing Dynamic HTML results that are unique for that client.

ASP technology is available primarily for the Windows-based Web servers—IIS and Personal Web Server (PWS)—but is also available for other Web servers running on other operating systems.

ASP comes with various low-level ActiveX controls, such as ODBC database controls that allow easy access to database-driven content. By providing low-level objects as ActiveX controls, ASP allows developers to write only high-level code in the form of scripts that manipulate these objects. When the Web server uses the ActiveX script engine interface, a variety of script languages can be used. Thus, scripts in JavaScript, VBScript, Perl, Tcl, and other languages can be employed.

One of the most common tasks required to create customized HTML is determining the browser's capabilities. ASP comes with a browscap.ini file, which is a browser capabilities database, so ASP scripts can easily check this file rather than the browser's HTTP User Agent header string for the existence of a feature.

In summary, here is a comparison of ASP and other server interfaces: CGI is good for low-performance, portable applications. ISAPI filters are good for applications that need to intercept HTTP I/O. ISAPI applications are best for low-level, high-performance applications that do not have ActiveX controls available, while ASP is best for creating high-level scripts that manipulate existing ActiveX controls.

Active Server Pages ships with a number of built-in building blocks that are based on ActiveX. These include:

- A request object, which provides access to information provided by the client in the HTTP request.
- A response object, which is used to generate the response, for example, set a cookie.
- A session object, which is used to store variables across an entire site on a per-user basis. These variables persist when the user moves between pages on the same site.

- An application object, which enables information to be shared among all users within a site.
- A server object, which allows new instances of ActiveX objects to be generated.

The advantages of Active Server Pages can be summarized as follows:

- ASP allows Dynamic HTML content to be generated using any programming or scripting language—VBScript, JScript, REXX, Perl, Tcl, Java, Visual Basic, C++, and even COBOL.
- ASP simplifies the task of generating a Dynamic HTML page and allows the page to be generated with no coding at all (only scripting).
- ASP allows the data access logic that is required for generating a Web page to be separated from the logic required for presenting the content of the page. This makes development, debugging, and maintenance simpler.
- ASP allows changes to be made without immediate compilation. The compilation is done automatically when the file is accessed by a browser (client).
- ASP caters to all flavors of browsers. ASP has built-in components that recognize the capabilities of a browser and act accordingly. The browser is simply expected to display the dynamic HTML generated by execution within the ASP environment at the server.

More details can be obtained from http://www.microsoft.com/iis/default.asp.

Proxy Servers

Proxy servers offer a convenient means of centralizing access to the Internet in a secure and efficient manner. Proxy servers are used by corporations to interface a local area network (LAN) with the Internet. A proxy server typically connects to the Internet at a different speed, using a different ISO data-link layer protocol than the LAN. A proxy server can also act as a firewall for security.

A client sends a request for a particular document to a Web proxy server. The proxy server retrieves the document using an appropriate protocol (HTPP, FTP, Gopher, and so on). The server then sends the document to the client. It is worthwhile noting that a client sends requests to the proxy server using HTTP, no matter what the nature of the document requested is. The request includes full details of the document involved, including the nature of the document and the protocol involved. The proxy server performs the necessary work to resolve the request to an address to which the request should be sent (in other words, resolving a domain name to an IP address.)

Proxy servers are implemented based on the CERN proxy protocol. This protocol was developed at the European Laboratory for Particle Physics (CERN).

Web Proxy Server Caching

Given that a number of clients might request the same document independently, it makes sense to cache documents at the proxy servers. This is in the interest of efficiency. The waiting time for a client is reduced if the document is located in the cache. Internet traffic is also reduced.

However, not all documents can be cached. Some Web documents can be accessed only by paying subscriber fees. These and other documents that should not be cached include the tags WWW-Authenticate, Pragma:no-cache, Cache-control:private, Cache-control:no-cache, and Set-Cookie. These are just some of the conditions indicating that a particular document should not be cached. Other conditions, such as the document being out of date or access to the object requiring authentication, also indicate the document is not suitable for caching.

Caching can be accomplished using a number of different means. One technique is called *passive caching*. Passive caching occurs when the proxy server simply waits for a client to send a request, then retrieves the required document, and then evaluates whether the document should be cached.

Another technique is called *active caching*. With active caching, the proxy server uses periods of low activity to fetch documents that it believes are likely to be requested by clients.

Large corporations have multiple proxy servers. A number of protocols have evolved to handle the caching done by a farm, or multitude of proxy servers. The following subsections discuss these caching protocols. Note that the descriptions for Internet Cache Protocol and Cache Array Routing Protocol generally cover communications between proxy servers and clients. These do not preclude the use of passive caching and active caching; indeed they require that one or both be used.

Internet Cache Protocol

Internet Cache Protocol (ICP) was originally developed at the University of Southern California and is described in RFC 2168. ICP specifies a message format for Web proxy servers to communicate with each other. The messages are typically used to exchange information about the presence or absence of a particular Web page in a proxy server cache. ICP messages are also used to decide on a particular Web server cache as the possible source of a particular Web page. RFC 2168 specifies the format of ICP messages. RFC 2187 provides details of how ICP is implemented using the messages described in RFC 2168. ICP extensions have been developed for IPv6 as well, but these have not been standardized.

Web proxy servers implementing ICP typically use three different ports. One port is HTTP based and is used by clients to query a cache server. Another port is User Datagram Protocol (UDP) based and is used to exchange ICP messages. The third port is Transmission Control Protocol (TCP) based and is used to retrieve Web pages from a proxy server cache. The ICP RFCs do not specify the transport protocol for exchanging ICP messages, but typically UDP is used.

ICP is useful, but some problems have been discovered now that it has been implemented widely. One drawback is the lack of scalability, because the number of ICP messages exchanged between proxy servers climbs rapidly as the number of proxy servers increases. Another problem is that the data on the proxy server caches becomes redundant over time. This redundancy occurs because when a proxy server receives a query for a Web page, it performs the following functions:

- The proxy server inspects the local cache
- If the requested information is not found in the local cache, the proxy server sends an ICP query message
- If a positive ICP reply is received, the proxy server retrieves the requested information from the neighboring proxy server cache and places the information in the local cache
- The proxy server satisfies the request using the freshly retrieved data

Cache Array Routing Protocol

Cache Array Routing Protocol (CARP) provides a means of using multiple proxy servers in a single unified cache in an extremely efficient manner. CARP was invented to address deficiencies with existing caching protocols such as Internet Cache Protocol. CARP eliminates the need for server-to-server communication (between the proxy servers). CARP also avoids a situation in which the cache contents of the various proxy servers simply become mirror images of each other. A simplified explanation of the basic functioning of CARP is presented here.

Using CARP, proxy servers are organized into an array. The array is periodically updated to reflect proxy servers that may have come on line or that may have crashed or been withdrawn from service. For each proxy server, a hash function based on the name of the proxy server is computed. When a client queries for a URL, a computation involving a hash function of the URL and the hash function for each proxy server is performed. The computation that results in the highest value identifies the proxy server that becomes the owner for that URL. This proxy server will either have the relevant page in its cache or will download the page to its cache if the Web page can be downloaded successfully. Note that this computation is per server, per URL. This means that it is possible that http://www.company.com/page1.html is owned by one proxy server while http://company.com/page2.html can be owned by a different proxy server. Once the client has identified the owner of a particular Web page, it queries that particular proxy server. The proxy server retrieves the relevant page from its cache, if the page is present in its cache. If the page is not present in the cache, the proxy server retrieves the page from the Web and adds it to its cache.

CARP is often referred to as *queryless distributed caching*. This name simply refers to the fact that the Web pages are cached in a number of proxy servers and no queries are performed to determine which server might happen to have a cached copy of a particular Web page. CARP has been submitted to the IETF for consideration as a draft standard. The latest specification (at the time this book goes to press) is available at http://www.microsoft.com/proxy/guide/CarpSpec.asp. A white paper on CARP is also available at http://www.microsoft.com/proxy/guide/CarpWP.asp. CARP is supported in Microsoft and Netscape products.

ActiveX

ActiveX provides a framework for dynamically extending capabilities of Web clients (browsers) as well as Web servers. In fact, more recent versions of Internet Explorer are relying more and more on a set of ActiveX controls. For example, Internet Explorer versions 3.0 and later use an ActiveX control to display HTML code. This ActiveX object can also be used by other, totally unrelated applications, such as a financial program or an application that provides stock market quotations. No specific programming language is required to create an ActiveX control. As the technology stands, ActiveX controls can be implemented using Visual C++, Visual Basic, or Java. In addition, ActiveX support is available on a variety of platforms, including Windows, Macintosh, and some flavors of UNIX.

ActiveX is based on a technology from Microsoft called the Component Object Model (COM). COM itself has gone through a series of revisions. It began as OLE, short for Object Linking and Embedding. OLE version 1.0 introduced OLE compound documents. OLE 2 introduced COM. The term ActiveX has become favored as a replacement for OLE, although there are some technological differences between the two (which I'll describe later in this section).

COM supports communication between two objects on the same computer. These objects might be part of the same process or they might belong to different processes. Distributed COM (DCOM) supports the same paradigm, but the two objects can be on different computers. An object continues to use the same interface to communicate with the other object no matter whether the second object is located on the local computer or a remote computer.

Another important part of OLE was the concept of *monikers*. A moniker is an OLE object that understands how to initialize another OLE object. A moniker itself has to be initialized by the OLE object that creates the moniker. Depending on the moniker (and what it does), it might be simpler to create the moniker rather than to create the OLE object the moniker would have created in the first place.

Prior to ActiveX, OLE Controls (OCXs) were used to accomplish a specific objective, such as displaying HTML. ActiveX controls are similar to OLE controls but with some important differences:

- ActiveX controls are more lightweight. An ActiveX control doesn't need to implement all the interfaces that an OCX must. An ActiveX control has less communications overhead than an OCX.

- ActiveX allows for the use of asynchronous monikers in an effort to provide higher efficiency.

- ActiveX controls allow for the use of security and code signing.

ActiveX consists of several underlying technologies. Some of these technologies apply only to the Web client, some apply only to the Web server, and some apply to both. In the following sections, I'll describe these technologies in more detail.

ActiveX Controls

ActiveX controls constitute the basic building blocks of ActiveX. When someone refers to ActiveX, he or she is usually referring to ActiveX controls. An ActiveX control is a software module that cannot stand by itself. It must run within the framework of an ActiveX container, such as a Web browser, a word processor, or a spreadsheet. An ActiveX container provides a specified functionality. The functionality of an ActiveX control can be almost anything the creator of the ActiveX control wants—database access, file access, time (value) retrieval, user interface display, and so on. An ActiveX control can communicate with another ActiveX control, an ActiveX container, or the operating system.

A number of prebuilt ActiveX controls are available. One example is NetMasters' FastNet ActiveX (formerly the Internet ActiveX Control Pack), which packages Internet communications technologies such as TCP, UDP, FTP, and Simple Mail Transfer Protocol (SMTP) as ActiveX controls. These controls enable applications to communicate using the protocols without knowing the gory details.

ActiveX Scripting

ActiveX scripting allows code to exist in the HTML file itself instead of being precompiled and then embedded into the HTML code. The code is interpreted and executed. In some cases, the code must first be downloaded.

ActiveX scripting includes support for JavaScript as well as VBScript, which is a subset of the scripting capabilities in Visual Basic. The subset has been defined with an eye toward maintaining security. ActiveX scripting also includes support for the

ActiveScript API, which provides a smooth migration for existing OCX container applications so that they can be converted easily to ActiveX scripting containers.

Strictly speaking, ActiveX scripting consists of two major technologies:

- An ActiveX scripting host, which can be a Web browser, a server, or some other application, such as an authoring tool or spreadsheet.
- An ActiveX scripting engine, which interprets the script. A variety of scripts are supported, including Perl, VBScript, JavaScript, Lisp, and others.

ActiveX Documents

ActiveX documents are not a particularly important part of the ActiveX technology. They are based on OLE DocObjects and are displayed and edited within an ActiveX container.

ActiveX Security

ActiveX uses a series of technologies, such as Authenticode and public key cryptography, to ensure the quality and the identity of code that's dynamically downloaded and executed. (See Chapter 5, "Cryptography and Security Basics," for more information on security issues.) The ActiveX control can be signed by the company that developed the control. The company has to acquire an X.509 certificate from VeriSign and sign the ActiveX control by using its private key and Public Key Cryptography Standards (PKCS) 7 and 10. (See Chapter 5 for information about PKCS). When the ActiveX container downloads the control, it invokes Authenticode to verify the signature and executes the ActiveX control only if the signature can be verified. A user can choose to bypass this process by trusting the ActiveX control, but doing so can be dangerous.

ActiveX and Java

ActiveX controls can be coded using a variety of languages, including Java. Thus a Java applet can itself be an ActiveX control. ActiveX Controls, Java Applets, and JavaBeans can all be dynamically downloaded and executed. ActiveX uses a paradigm of verifying the ActiveX control before executing it. Java prefers the paradigm of a "sandbox" within which the Java applet or JavaBeans component can "play." The sandbox restricts what an application executing within the sandbox is allowed to do. For example, all disk input and output is prohibited.

ActiveX Ownership

ActiveX is primarily developed by Microsoft. Representatives from a number of companies, including Microsoft, have formed a group called the *Active Group*. The Active Group makes suggestions for ActiveX technology, and Microsoft bases some decisions about how to evolve ActiveX on this feedback. Microsoft has also transferred what appear to be limited rights to ActiveX to the Open Group. The Open Group, with the blessing of Microsoft, licenses COM to any interested party.

Dynamic HTML, Scriptlets, and the Document Object Model

Dynamic HTML (DHTML) is the name given to a combination of CSS, scripting languages, and HTML. The objective of DHTML is to generate HTML pages dynamically rather than have statically defined HTML pages. However, DHTML is not used just to generate the contents of an HTML page dynamically. It is also used to present a different view of the same page based on user feedback without asking the server to regenerate the page from scratch.

Microsoft and Netscape implement Dynamic HTML differently. Both companies have vowed to abide by standards established in HTML 4.0, which was finalized in December 1997.

One difference is that the Netscape implementation allows style sheet changes only when an HTML page loads. The Microsoft implementation, on the other hand, allows the style to change even after an HTML page has been loaded. Netscape permits the generation of DHTML using only JavaScript, whereas Microsoft permits the use of JavaScript or VBScript. Yet another difference is how the two companies handle downloadable or embedded fonts. The fonts with which an HTML page is displayed can make the difference between the page looking well laid out or being unreadable. To address this, the fonts to be used are associated with the document itself. Netscape has a font definition file that can have a "pointer" to a Web page. Microsoft extends CSS to add a reference to font files. An extension to the existing scripting methods started with JavaScript/JScript/ECMAScript, VBScript, and other client-side and server-side scripting languages. Normally these lightweight programming languages are embedded into HTML documents and are interpreted by the browser or the server. The main purpose of these scripts is to invoke objects built-in to the browser or server or to call local objects (ActiveX Controls, Java applets or servlets, and so on).

Existing scripting solutions have only moderate interactivity with the HTML content that contains them. They give developers the basic ability to create HTML content. Server-side scripting solutions are normally a little more powerful in this area because they are often used to create content for a client.

In addition to HTML page access, DHTML provides new multimedia controls that are available for scripting in an HTML document: Audio Mixer Control, Path Control,

Sequencer Control, Sprite Control, and Structured Graphics Control. DHTML also provides Transitions effects and Visual Filters effects.

DHTML also introduces the concept of an event object. The event object is fired when a certain event occurs—for example, when the mouse is clicked at certain locations on the HTML page and when the mouse is positioned over certain locations on the HTML page. Microsoft browsers allow event handlers to be written in VBScript or JavaScript, whereas Netscape requires the event handlers to be written in JavaScript.

Scriptlets

DHTML also introduces the concept of a *scriptlet*. A scriptlet is an HTML document that behaves more like an object and less like a document. Written in a scripting language, the scriptlet can act like a normal scripted HTML document. It can also expose methods for other scripted Web pages to invoke. Scriptlets are useful when a scripted HTML document would be insufficiently powerful yet the task involved is not complex enough to merit developing a new ActiveX control or Java class.

For more information on scriptlets, see http://www.microsoft.com/scripting.

Document Object Model

The Document Object Model (DOM) is a relatively new technology in the process of being defined by the World Wide Web Consortium. The purpose of DOM is to provide a standard set of objects that are platform-independent and language-independent that will allow programs to dynamically update documents. The expectation is that DOM will interface with Java and ECMAScript, COM, Perl, VBScript, and C++.

Java

In the following sections, I'll describe Java-based technologies and Java's relationship to other protocols.

Java Remote Method Invocation and Object Serialization

Java Remote Method Invocation (RMI) is used to extend a Java application so that it can run on systems other than the local one. RMI provides basic distributed computing for Java classes, so that a Java program residing on one machine can be executed on another. RMI is similar in concept to Remote Procedure Call (RPC) functionality, but it uses Java's object model instead of procedures and requires both systems to be running Java.

RMI uses object serialization to extend the Java I/O classes over the network, encoding object parameters into a stream of bytes and then back again.

Java and CORBA

Common Object Request Broker Architecture (CORBA) is an infrastructure that pro- vides the ability to run objects located anywhere on a network. CORBA includes an Object Management Group Interface Definition Language (OMG IDL) for writing language-specific bindings for objects. These bindings use an Object Request Bro- ker (ORB), which is a language-specific helper routine, to facilitate the interface definition abstractions. CORBA works over the Internet via the OMG's Inter-ORB Protocol (IIOP).

With the use of a Java IDL and a Java ORB, objects written in Java are able to oper- ate with other objects written in a variety of languages.

Java IDL is a tool that generates client stubs and server skeletons that are needed by CORBA ORBs.

Java provides RMI as the native Java-to-Java interface.

Java and COM

An application written in the Java language runs on a single system by default. A Java application can use the java.net class to speak with another network program via sockets. A Java application can use RMI to talk to another Java application. A Java application can use CORBA to talk to other CORBA objects.

Another way that a Java application can communicate with other processes (locally and over the network) is through COM. COM provides a language-independent method for objects to interact. Originally, COM was a Windows-specific platform, but COM is moving to a variety of other platforms.

With COM integrated into the design of the Java VM, COM support can be made transparent. Within VM, a COM object appears to a Java application as another Java class. Outside VM, a Java class appears to a COM object as another COM object. Via DCOM, this can span systems. With COM support included in the Java VM design (as in the Microsoft Java VM), the language-independent interface definition layer is transparent.

JavaBeans

JavaBeans is a technology that allows Java-based applications to abstract the various object model interfaces (CORBA, COM, OpenDoc, and so on). JavaBeans provides a Java-centric object model, in which Java applications write to the Beans object model and assume bindings for the appropriate object model will be taken care of. The JavaBeans API provides methods to obtain and publish interface information (about their properties and bindings), which can be passed to the interface definition lay- ers of the various object systems and used by application builder tools. Additionally, the API provides event handling methods, component storage, and layout control.

Java Naming and Directory Interface

Java Naming and Directory Interface (JNDI) allows Java applications access to naming and directory services. JNDI gives developers unified access to namespaces from a heterogeneous enterprise network. Service providers included with the system use Lightweight Directory Access Protocol (LDAP) (versions 2 and 3) and Network Information Service (NIS). Developers can use JNDI to provide their own services to other directory service protocols.

Java Web Server and Servlets

Java got its start on the client side, in the Web browser. The applet was a small application that ran in the context of the client-side browser. However, Java is also used for server-side development.

Some Internet servers written in Java, primarily Sun's Java Web Server, provide a new Java-centric Servlet API, for running Java *servlets*. Similar conceptually to CGI, servlets are Java classes run by the Web server. The Servlet API is a small interface that provides no user interface (UI) and is protocol-independent. Servlets are often run from the server's local file system, are more trustworthy than foreign applets, and use the digital signature abilities of Java. The Security Manager allows the server administrator to set a servlet's access privileges (such as local file I/O). As with other post-CGI interfaces to Web servers, servlets are dynamically loaded and can remain loaded—to avoid the performance cost of process setup and shutdown.

Servlets can be used with Web servers as well as with other kinds of servers; for example mail servers. Assuming the server in question supports the required interface, servlets offer a convenient means of adding proprietary processing to a wide range of server products.

HotJava Browser and HotJava Views

The HotJava Browser is a Web browser written in Java. Developers are able to plug in new content and protocol handlers, extending the ability of the browser to handle different media and network types.

HotJava Views uses the HotJava Browser as the desktop (or "Webtop"), targeting the network computer thin client market. As the graphical user interface (GUI) front end to a Java-based Webtop, HotJava Views includes basic e-mail and a calendar name directory among its applications, a Selector (process manager), and the HotJava Browser Web client. HotJava Views enables application developers to write Java applications and integrate them into the Webtop, through interfaces provided by HotJava.

JavaSpace

JavaSpace is a technology for exchanging data and objects among Java programs. The data is distributed and persistent. JavaSpace is used by Java applications to save and restore state in a distributed manner. Although it might be considered vaguely similar to a database on a network, Javaspace is not a relational or object database.

Java Management API

The Java Management API (JMAPI) is a set of interfaces that allows developers to create network management applications on Java-based platforms.

Developers write to Java-based APIs that speak Simple Network Management Protocol (SNMP). New management applications write to the UI of the Java-based Admin View Module (AVM), to integrate with other network management solutions. Other base object interfaces provide access to other code and data needed to write a complete network management module.

References

http://info.internet.isi.edu/in-notes/rfc/files/rfc2187.txt

http://info.internet.isi.edu/in-notes/rfc/files/rfc2186.txt

http://www.netscape.com/newsref/std/cookie_spec.html

http://home.netscape.com/assist/net_sites/pushpull.html

http://www.macromedia.com/shockwave/

http://www.javasoft.com/

http://www.microsoft.com/com/default.htm

http://www.w3.org/PICS/

http://www.w3.org/XML/

http://www.w3.org/

http://www.sgml.org/

http://www.microcsoft.com/standards/xml

http://www.microsoft.com/standards/cdf-f.htm

http://www.microsoft.com/standards/osd/osdspec-f.htm

http://www.w3.org/metadata/rdf/overview.html

http://www.microsoft.com/xml/cdf/

http://developer.netscape.com/one/javascript/

http://www.ecma.ch/stand/ecma-262.htm

http://www.microsoft.com/scripting/

http://www.microsoft.com/vbscript/

http://www.netscape.com/newsref/std/server_api.html

http://tech.west.ora.com/win-httpd/httpddoc/wincgi.htm

http://www.microsoft.com/iis/

http://www.microsoft.com/scripting

http://www.javasoft.com/products/jdk/rmi/index.html

http://www.javasoft.com/

http://www.microsoft.com/java/

http://jserv.javasoft.com/products/java-server/documentation/webserver1.1/
  servlets/intro.html

14

Electronic Commerce

ELECTRONIC COMMERCE ENCOMPASSES ALL financial transactions on the Internet. In addition to the information in this chapter, you should study the cryptographic fundamentals in Chapter 5, "Cryptography and Security Basics," because of the confidential nature of financial transactions. And since much of Internet commerce takes place via Web pages, you should learn the Web protocol fundamentals described in Chapter 12, "World Wide Web Basics," and Chapter 13, "Advanced Web."

Web Merchant Servers

There are a variety of server side protocols involved in electronic commerce transactions on the Internet. In this section, we will cover several of the more important ones.

Shopping Cart Applications

Early Web commerce was rudimentary. Web merchants created Hypertext Markup Language (HTML) versions of their order forms that customers could fill out, print, and return via ordinary mail. The merchants' catalogs were online, but the ordering process was not.

Next merchants created order forms that customers could submit on line. This required front-end HTML forms for customer information and a back-end Common Gateway Interface (CGI) and related applications on the Web server to receive the data and process it. Simple order forms required users to enter data in one or more HTML forms. The HTML front end was often dynamically generated, based on a database of merchandise.

Then came more sophisticated applications that allowed users to browse online catalogs and add items from multiple pages to virtual shopping carts. The back-end system remembered all the items selected and gathered them up for purchase at the end of the virtual shopping session. These applications are known as *shopping cart applications*.

To save information about the selected items, shopping cart applications use Hypertext Transfer Protocol (HTTP) cookies and HTTP headers. Remember that HTTP is stateless (see Chapter 12, "World Wide Web Basics") in the sense that an HTTP command is executed without reference to any prior command. Since HTTP is stateless, some kind of token that can span HTTP transactions is usually needed. This customer transaction token is included as a parameter on subsequent URLs of dynamically created HTML pages or is included in another HTTP header for the shopping cart back end to access.

Cleartext HTTP

A Web-based transaction can take place using normal Web protocols and using normal credit cards to fulfill payment. A client can send payment information to the merchant using HTML pages and HTML forms. However, HTTP is a cleartext (ASCII text) protocol, leaving an opportunity for network analyzers to capture plain text data and obtain billing information, such as credit card numbers.

Secure HTTP

Secure HTTP (S-HTTP), produced by Enterprise Integration Technology (EIT), is an extension of the HTTP protocol. S-HTTP enables browsers and servers to sign, authenticate, and encrypt an HTTP network packet. It uses the Multipurpose Internet Mail Extensions (MIME) infrastructure used by HTTP to add headers indicating required processing, and it includes additional data to store certificate and key information. Negotiation between an S-HTTP–enabled browser and server is a little more complicated than normal HTTP authentication. S-HTTP is not widely used today because it has been largely replaced by Secure Sockets Layer.

HTTP and Secure Sockets Layer

Secure Sockets Layer (SSL) is an encryption method developed by Netscape Communications for Transmission Control Protocol/Internet Protocol (TCP/IP) sockets. Similar to S-HTTP, SSL offers the ability to secure an HTTP network packet. But while S-HTTP works only at the HTTP protocol level, SSL works at the sockets level, providing the ability to secure a variety of other socket-based Internet protocols. The negotiation between an SSL-aware client and server is similar to the socket negotiation process; SSL includes messages between the client and server to negotiate the encryption algorithm type and to exchange certificate and key information.

When using SSL with HTTP, a Web browser uses the HTTPS:// *URL* type instead of the normal HTTP:// *URL* type that is used for cleartext HTTP. Many Web browsers indicate to the user that an HTTPS-based transaction is more secure than a normal HTTP transaction (by the use of dialog boxes during transitions, the use of graphical icons to show keys and broken or unbroken links, and so forth).

SSL is widely used and has basically replaced S-HTTP for general-purpose secure Web transactions. The Internet Engineering Task Force (IETF) working group on Transport Level Security (TLS) is working on extending SSL (and ideas from related transport-level protocols) in a variety of ways.

Merchant-Server Systems

Today most Web commerce employs traditional Web protocols and uses SSL-encrypted HTTP to transfer sensitive billing information. A variety of shopping cart applications remain available that provide similar functionality. Dedicated back-end systems are being replaced with commercial merchant-server products. These products often include tools to help integrate product information from a database server with the Web by using scripting and HTML page generation. They also include modular systems to handle taxing, shipping, and integration with other business computer systems.

More sophisticated systems include real-time payment validation, which requires integration with merchant systems that talk to the merchant's acquiring bank. Less sophisticated systems can postpone payment validation until the requested transaction is moved to the merchant's normal billing system.

Examples of large commercial products include Microsoft Site Server, Netscape Merchant System, Open Market Commerce Server, IBM's Net Commerce, and Electronic Commerce Suite from iCat.

Secure Electronic Transaction

The Secure Electronic Transaction (SET) protocol is an electronic bankcard payment protocol that was developed by a consortium of companies led by MasterCard and Visa. It "virtualizes" the financial transaction method for credit card purchases.

Using physical credit cards, cardholders interact with merchants to purchase items, merchants interact with acquiring banks to validate the transaction, and the issuing banks interact with the cardholders to receive payment for the transactions. To leverage this existing and familiar infrastructure for electronic transactions, MasterCard, Visa, and other companies produced the SET protocol. It uses the same basic process but replaces the physical credit card with an online protocol. With SET, the same hierarchies of trust exist between the merchant and acquiring bank, and between the cardholder and issuing bank. On line, these hierarchies of trust are formalized by digital certificates and a certificate authority hierarchy that follows the economy's financial system.

SET replaces two separately proposed technologies: Secure Transaction Technology (STT, developed by Visa and Microsoft) and Secure Electronic Payment Protocol (SEPP, developed by MasterCard and IBM). Luckily, the benefits of a single infrastructure were clear enough that the two protocols were merged into a single protocol, SET.

In some ways, SET is better than the existing credit card infrastructure, especially in terms of added privacy for the consumer. Transactions are encrypted so that merchants see information only about items purchased—they do not see personal account information. Likewise, banks do not see information about items purchased—they see only requests for credit from the merchant.

SET is not tied to HTTP and Web-based commerce. It can be used in a variety of protocols. It is not a simple protocol: its messages and structures are designed with Abstract Syntax Notation One (ASN.1). Unlike SSL, SET uses message-based encryption, not channel-based encryption. As a result, forms of encryption that are stronger than general-purpose forms are allowed.

SET structures break down a request into two basic parts—the order information (OI) and the payment information (PI). The PI is used by the bank; the merchant doesn't need to see it. (All the merchant needs to see is the bank's authorization that the payment is valid.) The whole transaction is tied together using the concept of *dual signatures*.

Dual signatures generate two different messages, one addressed to the merchant and the other to the bank. The two are linked so that the bank can associate the payment with the order without having complete details of the order. The merchant is guaranteed payment for a particular order and its value but does not have access to any other information (such as the customer account number—the equivalent of the 16-digit credit card number).

Each message runs through a message digest algorithm that generates a 160-bit message digest. The two message digests are then concatenated, and the result is also run through the message digest algorithm. The resulting message digest is signed using the customer's private key. The customer then sends two messages. One goes to the merchant, specifying the details of the order and including a message digest of the message sent to the bank. The other goes to the bank, specifying the amount of the transaction and including the message digest of the message sent to the merchant.

The bank and merchant can each verify that the message received is authentic by generating the digest of the message and concatenating it with the message digest of the other message. The computed overall message digest should be identical to the decrypted dual signature (using the sender's public key). Note that this method also allows a customer to submit bids for items. The merchant submits the message to the bank for processing in case the merchant accepts the bid. The message digest associates a merchant/customer transaction with a bank/customer message authorizing payment.

SET obviously uses both symmetric and asymmetric encryption. It also uses certificates to associate a pair of public and private keys. Various software companies are providing APIs to access this protocol. Most applications that use SET—such as merchant-server systems and the analogous browser-side object (a kind of virtual wallet)—will use these libraries.

Digital Currency

In addition to electronic payment methods patterned after existing forms of currency such as credit cards, new forms of digital currency are being developed. Some are software-only, and some require new hardware—mainly smartcards.

Most types of digital currency have their own protocols to exchange financial requests among customer, merchant, and issuer. The protocol is implemented with back-end server software as well as client-side "wallet" software.

Some examples of existing digital currency technologies include:

- CyberCash and CyberCoin from CyberCash Inc. (http://www.cybercash.com)
- eCash by DigiCash Inc. (http://www.digicash.com)
- MilliCent from Digital Equipment (http://www.millicent.digital.com)
- Internet Keyed Payment Protocols (iKP) from IBM (http://www.zurich.ibm.ch/Technology/Security/extern/ecommerce/iKP.html)
- NetCheque from the University of Southern California's Information Sciences Institute (http://www.netcheque.org)
- NetBill from Carnegie Mellon University's Information Networking Institute, Mellon Bank, and CyberCash (http://www.netbill.com)
- Mondex from Mondex International (http://www.mondex.com)
- Interactive Messaging Platform from First Virtual (http://www.firstvirtual.com/services/imp/index.html)
- Netscape LivePayment from Netscape (http://live.netscape.com/comprod/products/iapps/livepayment.html)
- MiniPay from IBM (http://www.hrl.il.ibm.com/mpay/)

Micropayments

An advantage of digital currency over existing currency is the ability to use *micro-payments*—payments that are smaller than normal currency allows. In the case of the U.S. currency system, this usually means values of less than one cent. For credit card systems, however, the value is larger than one cent because the infrastructure assumes that transactions will be larger. Micropayments are often associated with "nontangible goods" on line—for example, access to a Web page or an online chat room for a five-cent charge. Existing payment systems that define micropayments in larger values don't work well with such small charges.

Wallets

Most forms of digital currency in development require some form of digital "wallet" on the client side—software that sends information about the financial transaction to the server using a specific protocol. Some software companies are creating wallet APIs so that various digital money solutions can use a single wallet, much like an actual wallet can contain multiple cards that use different payment methods.

Other types of companies are also interested in such a wallet. Some Web sites include "guest books" to sign, ask for personal information, and ask for your personal preferences to create dynamic user-specific content. Some of this information can be stored in wallets. When this information is stored in a central location with well-established procedures for requesting private information and well-defined methods for providing that information, the use of a common wallet or electronic wallet (a small client-side database that contains data such as credit card numbers, information about digital signatures, and identification and authentication information) for nonfinancial information becomes valuable.

Smartcards

Smartcards are similar in size to credit cards and contain a microprocessor that stores information. One of the primary uses of a smartcard is for financial purposes. Smartcards can use digital signatures and other forms of cryptography, which makes them more tamper-resistant than normal credit cards.

A variety of smartcard standards exist. The International Organization for Standardization (ISO) has developed the ISO 7816 standards, for integrated circuit cards with contacts, which define smartcard interoperability at the hardware and data-link protocol levels. Europay, MasterCard, and Visa have defined a smartcard specification that extends ISO 7816 standards with additional data types and encoding rules for use by the financial services industry. The European telecommunications industry's Global System for Mobile Communications (GSM) has defined a smartcard specification to identify and authenticate mobile phone users. The Personal Computer/Smart Card (PC/SC) workgroup has defined a smartcard framework and APIs for personal computer platforms. The OpenCard Framework has defined a smartcard framework and APIs for OpenCard-compliant platforms (including network computers).

Java Commerce

Java Commerce is a collection of technologies that bring electronic commerce to the Java platform. The Java Electronic Commerce Framework (JECF) is an extension to the Java platform that enables electronic commerce applications, including the Java Wallet. The Java Commerce APIs implement commerce interfaces for Java platforms. The Java Commerce APIs are extended using a cassette, an object similar to a JavaBean.

Looking Ahead

The future of digital currency remains uncertain. A technology that controls the flow of money will be developed with more care than many other technologies. Because of privacy and authentication requirements, it is difficult to implement a common solution for governments, corporations, and individuals. Encryption and the use of certificate authorities adds to the complexity, as do the choices about products and software that support certain servers and clients but not others.

References

For more information on electronic commerce, see *Understanding Electronic Commerce* by David Kosiur (Microsoft Press, 1997).

http://test.team2it.com/rsa/q133.html

http://home.netscape.com/assist/security/ssl/index.html

http://www.ietf.org/html.charters/tls-charter.html

http://www.mastercard.com/set or http://www.visa.com/set

http://www.smartcardsys.com

http://www.opencard.org

http://java.sun.com/commerce

http://www.w3.org/ECommerce

Multimedia

P
A
R
T

V

15

Multimedia on the Internet

THIS CHAPTER DESCRIBES THE TECHNICAL DETAILS of how multimedia is implemented on the Internet. The intent is to describe standards and proprietary products and techniques.

Table 15-1 illustrates the bandwidth requirements of some multimedia applications.

Table 15-1 Multimedia Applications and Bandwidth Requirements

Application	Bandwidth Requirement (Without Compression)	Possible Transmission Technology
Phone conversation	64 Kbps	Integrated Services Digital Network (ISDN)
Compact disc (CD)-quality audio	Just above 700 Kbps	Ethernet, xDSL (Digital Subscriber Line)
High-definition television (HDTV)	2 Gbps	Asynchronous Transfer Mode (ATM)

Given the limited bandwidth available on the Internet (and more important, the bandwidth in one's individual connection to the Internet), *compression* plays a big role on the Internet. The only way to transmit multimedia over the Internet is to use compression. Not just any compression technique will suffice, however. I'll give you a quick outline of the requirements.

The compression algorithm must be real-time in order to be used for video tele-conferencing products and real-time video such as a live sportscast or a live televi-sion news report. Both the compression and decompression must be achieved in real-time computing; that is, the time for compression and decompression must be small. (Special situations such as broadcast of movies that were prerecorded and precompressed may permit a compression algorithm that is CPU-intensive and time-intensive for compression, but simple for decompression.)

The compression algorithm must have robust error handling because data packets can be lost on the Internet. The compression algorithm must not depend on the receipt of a previous or subsequent packet.

The algorithm should have acceptable "loss." Some compression algorithms work by dropping unimportant data—the decompressed data is not identical to data that was present before the compression was begun. While some loss is acceptable, there is a limit. In the case of a video transmission, too much loss of data in the compres-sion/decompression algorithm would result in a poor-quality picture. A compression/decompression algorithm or technique is often called a *codec*.

To illustrate the effectiveness of codecs, Table 15-2 lists the bandwidth requirements when codecs are used for the same applications that were mentioned in Table 15-1.

Table 15-2   Multimedia Applications and Bandwith Requirements with Codecs

Application	Bandwidth Requirement (with Compression)	Possible Transmission Technology
Phone conversation	Less than 5 Kbps	Modem
CD-quality audio	64 Kbps	ISDN
HDTV	30 Mbps	FDDI (Fiber Distributed Data Interface), ATM

Codecs may be implemented using software or hardware. Hardware implementations of codecs are extremely fast, and the work is accomplished without loading the main CPU. The disadvantage is that the special hardware can be expensive and the codec may not be dynamically negotiated. The advantages of having software implemen-tations of codecs is that the codec may be changed easily and one can even use vari-ous codecs. In addition, software codecs are cheaper than hardware codecs. The disadvantage of software codecs is that implementation is usually slower than hard-ware codecs and keeps the CPU busier.

Streaming

Another important technique to make multimedia usable on the Internet is streaming. The Web began as a TeX-mode tool. Files were (and are) completely downloaded by a client before they can be viewed. This works for files of reasonable size, but multimedia files tend to be huge. Streaming is the name given to the technique whereby a client downloads a portion of a file, decompresses that portion, and starts playing the contents (audio/video) before the rest of the file arrives. A buffer of data is built up before the playback is begun. Subsequent portions of the multimedia file are downloaded while the previously downloaded portion is playing. The portion that is playing is also periodically delayed. Thus, at no point in time is the complete multimedia file available to the client.

Sound and the Internet

With both the worsening congestion and somewhat limited available bandwidth on the Internet, audio products have flourished compared to video products. This is not surprising given that the bandwidth capacity requirements for carrying sound are far lower than for carrying video.

Sound also compresses well. Human conversations have a fair number of gaps that can simply be ignored. In addition, the high and low ends of the audio spectrum can be disregarded without producing a noticeable effect on the transmission of human speech. In other words, human conversations can be compressed using an algorithm that "loses" some of the original data.

The compressed data is then transmitted over the Internet using Transmission Control Protocol (TCP) or User Datagram Protocol (UDP). Each has its proponents and advantages. VocalTec's Internet Wave product uses TCP. The advantage to using TCP is that it has a built-in mechanism for flow control, ensuring that the network does not get bogged down with multimedia data. The disadvantage is that playback of the multimedia stream of TCP packets may be interrupted when a packet is lost or delayed. At times, it might be better not to wait for a missing packet to arrive but to simply play back the sound using whatever packets have arrived because the lost packet may not have a noticeable effect. The RealAudio product from RealNetworks, Inc. (formerly Progressive Networks) uses UDP to transmit compressed multimedia data. The advantage of using UDP is that it is simpler (and perhaps faster) than TCP. The fact that delivery is not guaranteed does not matter, as long as the delivery to loss ratio is rather small.

Different techniques are used to compensate for packets lost in transmission. VocalTec uses a predictive caching algorithm that attempts to "guess" the contents of lost packets. RealAudio uses a technique called interleaving or mincing. For example, 48 milliseconds worth of data is minced into a millisecond each. Instead of putting the first four milliseconds of data into the first packet, the next four into the second packet, and so on, the first packet contains the first, thirteenth, twenty-fifth, and thirty-seventh millisecond of data. The second packet contains the data for the second, fourteenth, twenty-sixth, and thirty-eigth millisecond of data. A process such as this is illustrated in Figure 15-1.

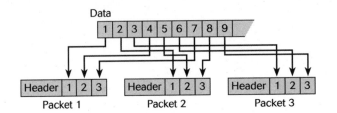

Figure 15-1 *The interleaving method of controlling packet loss.*

The result is that if a packet is lost, only one millisecond of data is lost every four milliseconds, rather than a continuous gap of four milliseconds.

WARNING

These numbers are for illustrative purposes only and are not necessarily the exact values and numbers used by RealAudio. The numbers used are only to provide a concrete explanation of the technique.

VocalTec

Internet Wave (I-Wave) technology developed by VocalTec uses TCP rather than UDP as the transport mechanism. One advantage here is the flow and congestion control applied to TCP packets automatically, which ensures that a network does not get bogged down because of multimedia data transmission.

RealAudio

RealAudio is a streaming technology for sending voice data over the Internet. Real-Audio uses UDP rather than TCP as a transport mechanism. Obviously, UDP is more "lightweight" than TCP, with lower overheads. RealAudio has its own algorithm for taking care of lost UDP packets. A disadvantage of TCP is that it will wait for a single lost or delayed packet to present the data in sequence. If there are four packets of voice data delivererd but a fifth packet of voice data is lost or delayed, it is better for the transport mechanism to deliver the data as it is rather than wait beyond a certain time interval, especially if the amount of voice data within each data packet is small.

RealAudio was defined as a proprietary client/server architecture with a proprietary protocol. The proprietary protocol was later submitted to the Internet Engineering Task Force (IETF) as a draft standard and is described later in this chapter in the section "Real-Time Streaming Protocol." The Real-Time Streaming Protocol (RTSP) allows bidirectional communication between client and server. (Remember that Hypertext Transfer Protocol [HTTP] does not allow this.) The bidirectional protocol allows the client to implement functionality such as fast-forward or rewind. The RealAudio implementation actually consists of two different servers, as illustrated in Figure 15-2.

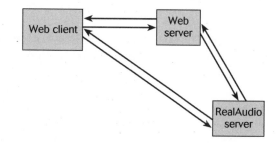

Figure 15-2   *The RealAudio client/server interaction.*

When files are downloaded for viewing off line, the client sends a request to the Web server and receives a response back from the server. The assumption is that the files are complete in themselves and do not have pointers to other files. When files are viewed on line (for example, for a live broadcast such as a baseball game), the Web server returns information about where the data lives. The client then sends a request to the RealAudio multimedia server, receives the data, and then decodes and plays the data.

There might be messages exchanged between the Web server and the RealAudio multimedia server. For example, when a client sends a request to the Web server, the Web server might inquire where the data can be found, at which time the RealAudio multimedia server could initiate the required action. However, the details of this exchange are proprieatry and do not constitute a part of any standard.

With RealAudio, one can develop products that are the equivalent of a slide show with background voice, as well as other interesting products. Live sportscasts using RealAudio are increasingly popular. Just visit a baseball team's homepage (for example, http://www.mariners.org) and you will see a link to RealAudio and details of game broadcasts on the Internet.

Telephone Products for the Internet

Products that implement the equivalent of a telephone conversation over the Internet are available from a number of companies, including DigiPhone, VocalTec, NetSpeak, and Quarterdeck. (Some freeware versions exist as well.) These products are known as *Web phones*. Web phones allow people to conduct voice conversations across the Internet. The main advantage of using a Web phone is that a long distance call can be made for the cost of a local connection to an Internet Service Provider. Web phones also offer additional features, such as graphical user interface (GUI) and integration with Web browsers. Web phones are not yet very popular for a number of reasons. These include:

- The network bandwidth available to most people (over a 28.8 Kbps modem) is not good enough to deliver a smooth continuous sound stream. To solve the bandwidth problem, the voice data is compressed before sending and decompressed before being played back. Different companies use different compression/decompression (codec) algorithms. This tends to mean that a person with a Web phone package from Company A can talk only to people having a Web phone package from the same company. WebPhone (from NetSpeak Corporation) uses a technique called TrueSpeech on Pentium CPU-based machines for compression/decompression. TrueSpeech can achieve a compression ratio of 18:1. On 486 CPU-based machines, WebPhone uses Global System for Mobile Communications (GSM), a standard defined for use in cellular telephone conversations. GSM can achieve compression ratios of 5:1. Different companies use different protocols to transmit the data. In addition, the compression algorithms and the line bandwidth can result in conversations that are not as distinct as normal telephone conversations.

- Many computers today have a half-duplex sound card. This means that one needs a CB-radio kind of protocol for talking (where the talking party indicates when the listener may talk by saying "over"). This is a nuisance and something people are not accustomed to when using a phone.

- To set up a phone conversation over a computer, one needs to know the Internet Protocol (IP) address of the party being called. Many users connect to the Internet and have their ISP dynamically assign an IP address. This address obviously differs in different dial-in sessions. Web phone companies and vendors work around this problem by providing a central server. When the Web phone package is running on the user PC, the software sends its IP address (assigned on a temporary basis by the ISP) to the central server. The server provides a list of people who are on line and willing to receive a Web phone call. This is the plan adopted by VocalTec with its Internet Phone product. Quarterdeck uses a similar approach, providing a network of servers that provide directory services for its WebTalk product. DigiPhone has a different process whereby a directory that is updated daily is electronically mailed to registered users. This brings us to yet another potential problem: Web phone users need to have their PC powered up and ready to receive a call.

A controversy is brewing over telephone products that use the Internet. The long-distance carriers have petitioned to have these products banned or regulated as long-distance telephone companies. However, there is a market for such products, and thus a number of people who do not agree with the long-distance carriers.

Video Compression Basics

Multimedia transmission consists of transmitting and displaying a series of images. When images are not "stand alone" and are parts of a movie clip, the image is often called a *frame*. Video compression is required, simply to reduce the amount of video data to a manageable size. Some techniques of compression can be used to compress data within one frame, without any reference to another frame. This is called *Intraframe coding*. Video compression is based on leveraging the redundancy in video images. This redundancy occurs in three areas:

- *Spatial redundancy.* Pixels within an image share a spatial relationship with each other; for example, a pixel is next to another pixel. Spatial redundancy occurs when neighboring pixels have the same color and sometimes the same intensity values. This happens quite often. Spatial redundancy is leveraged using intraframe coding. One technique of intraframe coding is discrete cosine transform (DCT), described in the following section.

- *Spectral redundancy.* Spectral information consists of light intensity and color. Spectral redundancy in movie frames occurs because bright pixels tend to be bright in all colors, rather than just a single or couple of colors. In addition, the human eye is more sensitive to brightness than color; that is, a human eye is more likely to notice that a pixel has the wrong brightness than the right color.

- *Temporal redundancy.* Movies show frames at a rate of about 30 times per second. Even in "action" movies, only some parts of a frame are different from the succeeding frame when the frames shown at this speed are "sampled." One technique that is employed to leverage temporal redundancy is Motion Vector Encoding. The idea is to divide the frame into a number of blocks. The encoding effectively says, "Everything is the same as the previous frame except that there was momement within this block." (For example, in a block representing an eye, the video shows an eyewink.)

The usual simple frame that shows a complete image does not suffice to take advantage of temporal redundancy. To deal with the different types of redundancy, three kinds of frames are used. The first is the original simple frame that shows the complete image. This is the *I-frame,* or *intracode frame,* named to emphasize the fact that the frame is described without reference to any other frame. The second type of frame is called a *P-frame,* or *predicted frame.* A P-frame is constructed using the previous B-frame, a motion vector, and an error picture that adjusts for errors in the motion vector. The last type of frame is a *B-frame,* or *Bi-Directional* predicted frame. B-frames consist of a forward motion vector, a backward motion vector, and an error. B-frames are used when a P-frame has a newly introduced object. (Motion vectors exist in many forms and describing them is beyond the scope of this book.)

Discrete Cosine Transform

Compression can use an equation to represent data rather than sampling the data repeatedly and transmitting the actual values. Consider a case in which you want to draw a straight line. Beginning algebra teaches us that a line can be represented by the equation y=mx+c. This means you can compress a line into just two values, *x* and *c*.

Obviously, compression is not this simple. The trick is to dynamically figure an equation that can represent the data of interest. And the equation is usually a lot more complex than that for a straight line. One technique used with video compression is called *discrete cosine transform* (DCT). DCT attempts to represent the data as a series of cosine waves. Only some of the cosine waves (corresponding to the principal frequencies) are retained. The cosine waves that are discarded result in loss of data.

DCT is used within the Moving Picture Experts Group (MPEG) standards (described in the next section). DCT is also referred to as an intraframe coding technique because it operates on a single video frame at a time.

Video Standards

Various standards exist for video encoding and video conferencing. This section briefly describes some of the prominent ones.

Moving Picture Experts Group

Moving Pictures Experts Group (MPEG) is an informal name given to an industry panel that develops multimedia standards. The official designation is ISO/IEC JTC1 SC29 WG11, which stands for "International Organization for Standardization/International Electro-Technical Commission, Joint Technical Committee 1, Subcommittee 29, Work Group 11." MPEG meets about four times a year to plan work activities and adopt resolutions.

MPEG has adopted three standards so far, known as MPEG-1, MPEG-2, and MPEG-3. The panel is working on MPEG-4 and MPEG-7.

MPEG-1

MPEG-1 is primarily used for compressing video images on CD-ROMs and is detailed in ISO/IEC Standard 11172-2.

MPEG-1 is based on the principles of spatial, spectral, and temporal redundancy described in the previous section. Each frame is divided into macroblocks consisting of 16 by 16 pixels. The uncompressed data for each macroblock consists of 16 blocks, 4 blocks representing data for the color green, 4 for red, 4 for blue, and 4 blocks for the chrominance (or brightness) of each pixel. MPEG-1 reduces these 16 blocks to 4 blocks, 2 to represent the chrominance and 1 each for the colors red and blue. MPEG-1 uses DCT for compression. MPEG-1 uses motion vectors and the three types of frames—I-frames, P-frames, and B-frames—described earlier.

MPEG-1 data is more computationaly intensive to compress than to decompress. MPEG-1 compression ratios typically fall in the 50:1 range, although a 200:1 ratio is theoretically possible. Ironically MPEG-1 is gaining popularity now, after the MPEG committee has defined MPEG-2 and MPEG-3 and is well on its way toward defining new MPEG standards. Part of the reason may be that MPEG-2 is not as popular as might have been expected. Another reason may be that MPEG-1 was slightly ahead of its time in the sense that the computing power available has only recently caught up to the requirements of MPEG-1.

MPEG-2

MPEG-2 makes MPEG-1 suitable for digital television. MPEG-2 is a superset of MEPG-1. The notable features in MPEG-2 are support for interlaced frames (a frame depicts half the image), support for multiplexing of video streams, and different algorithms for compressing the chrominance and luminance fields.

Support for MPEG-2 is still sketchy, but that may change with the advances in computing power, such as the Intel MMX.

MPEG-3

MPEG-3 was intended to upgrade MPEG-2 from a compression standard that could be applied to digital TV to one that could be used for high-defintion television (HDTV). Subsequently, it was realized that all functionality specified by MPEG-3 could be accomplished using MPEG-2. So MPEG-3 has become a footnote to the history of multimedia technology.

MPEG-4

Work continues on MPEG-4, which might become an international standard in mid-to-late 1998. Currently proposed features of MPEG-4 include support for two-way video traffic, support for lower bandwidth lines, and support for user interactivity that allows one to select parts of a program and ignore others.

MPEG-7

I have found no explanation of what happened to MPEG-5 and MPEG-6. Work continues on MPEG-7; one goal is to establish standards for a multimedia search engine.

International Telecommunications Union

The International Telecommunications Union (ITU) is engaged in, among other things, defining standards for audio and video communications and teleconferencing.

ITU H.320

In 1990, ITU defined H.320, a series of specifications that define standards for video conferencing, including multipoint conferencing (conferencing between more than two sites). H.320 assumes ISDN as the digital transmission system. (See Chapter 3, "More About Transports," for a description of ISDN.)

ITU H.323

ITU H.323 has been described as an umbrella recommendation and covers several areas, including codecs and call control. H.323 extends H.320 to work over TCP/IP, Ethernet, and an analog phone line in addition to ISDN. H.323 thus allows for low-cost conferencing. Two commercial products that have implemented H.323 are Microsoft NetMeeting and CU-SeeMe from White Pine Software. (See the next section, "Internet Video Products" for more information about CU-SeeMe.)

H.323 uses two TCP connections and UDP for a single conferencing session. Actually, up to five UDP ports are used while the session is being established. Configuring firewalls to allow these connections is tricky and may require intervention by the administrator.

ITU H.261

ITU H.261 is a standard for teleconferencing applications. By nature, teleconferencing applications involve limited movement (compared to general purpose and entertainment movies) and the H.261 standard leverages that by limiting the range of motion vectors to 15 pixels. Unlike MPEG standards, H.261 does not include any B-frames. H.261 is not necessarily the most efficient standard for teleconferencing. PictureTel, which owns a majority of the video teleconferencing market, has a proprietary algorithm that is superior to H.261. PictureTel uses H.261 when a session is set up with non-PictureTel equipment at one end, but uses its proprietary algorithm when both ends of a session employ PictureTel equipment.

ITU H.260

ITU H.260 is concerned with multipoint document sharing and conferencing applications. ITU H.260 is intended to lay standards for applications such as teleconferencing, whiteboard sharing, and file transfer. ITU H.260 is a work in progress, and more protocols that deal with conferencing reservations are expected.

Internet Video Products

The following sections describe various products that implement video over the Internet. One important problem with these products is that the level of interoperability is rather low. At times, the IBM personal computer version of a product will not operate with its Macintosh counterpart. Interoperability is an even bigger obstacle when products are dissimilar.

CU-SeeMe

CU-SeeMe is a video conferencing and videophone product that works over the Internet. CU-SeeMe was developed at Cornell University and is available free for the IBM PC as well as Macintosh. White Pine Software sells an enhanced version of CU-SeeMe. The most prominent feature supported by the enhanced version but not the basic version is a teleconferencing electronic chalkboard.

CU-SeeMe uses UDP to transmit data and a proprietary technique for leveraging temporal redundancy. (For more information about temporal redundancy, see "Video Compression Basics" earlier in this chapter.) The technique starts in a way similar to the MPEG-1 standard and divides the frame into 8-by-8-pixel macroblocks. The blocks are then compared to the corresponding block in the previous frame. Only the blocks that have changed significantly are transmitted. The advantage is that compression can be achieved without the intensive computing power that motion vector encoding requires. The disadvantage is that when some frames are lost in transmission, the picture on the screen is a jumble of updated frames and old frames.

CU-SeeMe also implements a flow-control mechanism. The receiver periodically transmits information about packet loss and the sender adjusts the amount of data sent accordingly.

CU-SeeMe implements multiparty conferencing by means of reflectors. A *reflector* is a server that acts as a central resource for clients wanting to have a multipoint conference. To begin with, the server acts as a directory service that lists the conferences and subconferences available. This allows clients to locate the conference of interest. Once the session is established, the reflector acts to conserve network bandwidth. Normally, if there are n clients involved in a multipoint conference, each client has to send n-1 copies of the audio/video data. In addition, some clients may have to do this at 28 Kbps. But by using reflectors, each client sends only a single copy of the data. The reflector sends out n-1 copies to the other clients. And the reflector has a higher network bandwidth available than the client. The disadvantage is that the reflector still needs to ship $n^*(n$-1) copies of the data. A free version of the reflector runs on UNIX.

Reflectors exist on the Internet and one may be "borrowed" if the lender is willing. White Pine uses Four11 (http://www.four11.com) as a directory server for clients to find other clients to initiate a conference.

MeetingPoint

White Pine sells a commercial version of the reflector for Microsoft Windows NT called MeetingPoint. MeetingPoint acts as a directory server, allowing clients to locate and initiate conferences they want to join. The server also reduces network traffic by supporting IP multicast. MeetingPoint also supports the H.323 protocol. Thus, MeetingPoint can act as a server to any H.323 client, including the Microsoft and Netscape browsers (the appropriate versions that support H.323).

VideoPhone and QuickTime

VideoPhone is available from Connectix Corporation. The software is similar to the QuickTime product available from Apple and is bundled with QuickCam (also from Connectix), a video capture device. Both VideoPhone and QuickTime support multi-point conferencing and IP multicast. Both products also support advanced features such as electronic conferencing whiteboards. However, the Macintosh (QuickTime) and Windows (VideoPhone) versions are incompatible and contain different features. Connectix has pledged to synchronize the Macintosh and Windows versions.

Microsoft NetShow 3.0

Microsoft literature describes NetShow as a platform for delivering multimedia content over networks. The content may consist of video, audio, audio synchronized with still images, text, URLs, and so forth. The NetShow product has several components. The NetShow player is a client-side component that plays multimedia files. The NetShow server runs on a Windows NT platform and streams audio, video, and other files to clients. An extensive set of services to administer the server exists, as well as a number of content authoring tools. Microsoft also provides a number of SDKs to administer NetShow servers, and to encode and edit content.

The most important aspect of NetShow is the variety of codecs it supports. This allows NetShow to be used in many different situations and also allows interoperability with a wide range of applications. Table 15-3 enumerates the various codecs supported by NetShow.

Table 15-3   Codecs Supported by Microsoft NetShow 3.0

Codec	Audio/Video	Comments
Lernout & Hauspie CELP	Audio	Compresses all audio to constant bit rate of 4.8 Kbps; used for low end audio applications
Microsoft G.723.1	Audio	General purpose audio codec
Voxware MetaSound	Audio	General purpose audio codec that compresses to a bit rate of 8–28 Kbps
Fraunhofer Institut Integrierte	Audio	Codec for CD-quality audio Schaltungen MPEG-3
Voxware MetaVoice	Audio	Compresses audio to constant bit rate of 2.4 Kbps

Table 15-3 **Codecs Supported by Microsoft NetShow 3.0**

Codec	Audio/Video	Comments
Sipro Lab Telecom ACELP.net	Audio	General purpose audio that compresses at a low bit rate
MSN Audio	Audio	General purpose audio that compresses at a low bit rate
Microsoft MPEG-4	Video	Compresses video to a form that requires a bit rate of 28.8–300 Kbps
VDOnet	Video	Low to medium bit rate codec; 28.8–150 Kbps
Intel H.263	Video	Codec for streaming video over low band width networks (such as 28.8 Kbps)
Duck TrueMotion RT	Video	Codec that requires high transmission rates of the order of 1–2 Mbps

NetShow works with content that has been rendered into a file format called *Advanced Streaming Format* (ASF). ASF is an open (nonproprietary, standards-based) file format that allows different types of data, such as audio, video, still images, text, and HTML pages to be combined and delivered in a single stream. ASF files are stored on a variety of servers, including HTTP servers or traditional file servers. ASF data can be streamed using a variety of transport protocols, including Real-Time Transport Protocol (RTP), UDP, TCP, and so forth.

Multimedia Protocols

A number of protocols have evolved for transporting multimedia across the Internet. These protocols are in various stages of adoption. The sections that follow describe each protocol in detail.

MBone

The multicast backbone (MBone) is a network that exists within the Internet. In existence since early 1992, the MBone consists of Class D IP addresses and a set of routers that are IP multicast–aware. The MBone has a number of routers that run IP multicast–aware routing protocols. Some of these routers are really just workstations running as routers. Others are commercial routers running modified software. When IP multicast packets need to be sent through portions of the Internet that are not

IP multicast–aware, the IP packets are tunneled within IP packets; that is, the IP multicast packets are sent as the data portion of IP packets that are addressed to a router at the other end of the tunnel. This is illustrated in Figure 15-3.

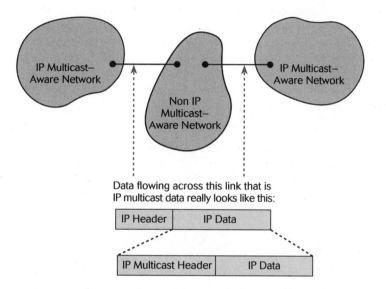

Figure 15-3   *IP Multicast Tunneling.*

The MBone is used to test new routing protocols and IP multicast software, as well as multimedia protocols such as RTP. Audio/video transmissions are done over the MBone on a semi-regular basis. Announcements of the transmission schedule are made on the IETF mailing list. One can join the IETF mailing list by sending a request to ietf-request@ietf.org. Free software to receive MBone transmissions, including audio applications, is available from a number of Web sites. More details may be obtained from the MBone Frequently Asked Questions (FAQ) at ftp.isi.edu/mbone/faq.txt.

Real-Time Transport Protocol

Real-Time Transport Protocol (RTP) provides delivery services for multimedia applications and also provides the means for multimedia applications to work over networks. RTP does not provide guaranteed or in-sequence delivery but does give a sequence number that allows multimedia applications to detect missing and out-of-sequence packets. RTP is defined to work in a one-to-one or one-to-many transmission situation.

RTP usually carries data using UDP as the delivery mechanism, but RTP is defined to be transport-protocol independent and can also work over other protocols, such as TCP or Asynchronous Transfer Mode (ATM). RTP assumes that one RTP packet is encapsulated within one protocol data unit of the underlying transport; for example, one UDP packet. When RTP is used with a non-message-based mechanism, such as TCP, a pseudoheader is used that consists of the RTP header preceded by a Length field.

When an application starts an RTP session, it uses two ports: one for RTP and another for Real-Time Control Protocol (RTCP), described later in this chapter. Multimedia data is transmitted using two sessions—one for audio and another for video. Here are some of the fields included in the RTP header:

- Payload Type. The Payload Type field indicates the type of data carried by the RTP packet. This allows applications to use the correct codec to play the contents of the packet. Applications can adaptively switch the payload type based on network conditions and can do so in the middle of an RTP session. An example of this type is described in RFC 1889. RFC 1890 enumerates the values for the payload type and their meaning; for example, a value of 3 denotes GSM encoded data, 26 denotes Joint Photographic Experts Group (JPEG) data, and 31 denotes H.261 data.

- Sequence Number. The Sequence Number field is 16 bits in length and allows applications to detect missing and out-of-sequence packets.

- Timestamp. The Timestamp field is 32 bits long and provides a means for applications to synchronize the audio and video streams. The Timestamp field is set to a random initial value and increases monotonically. Two or more packets may have the same timestamp value; for example, two audio packets that correspond to the same video frame.

RTP does not provide a reliable transport mechanism for delivering packets in sequence. RTP also does not provide flow control or congestion control and depends upon RTCP to provide these services.

The current version of RTP is version 2. Version 1 was used only experimentally and version 2 is not backward-compatible. RTP is described in detail in RFCs 1889 and 1890.

Real-Time Control Protocol

Real-Time Control Protocol works in conjunction with RTP to provide flow-control and congestion-control services. Participants in an RTP session periodically transmit RTCP packets. The packets carry statistics such as the number of packets sent, the number of packets lost, and so on. The idea is that the sender can use this information to dynamically vary the rate of transmission and even change the payload type. Using RTCP, a receiver can advise a sender that the transmission rate needs to be modified if one media stream is being received too fast compared with another stream.

RTCP packets also carry an identifier called the canonical name (CNAME). The CNAME is used along with the transport address and port (for example, IP address and UDP port number) to uniquely identify a media stream.

Real-Time Streaming Protocol

The proposed Real-Time Streaming Protocol (RTSP) is a joint effort by RealNetworks and Netscape Communications Corporation that defines how multimedia data can be efficiently delivered over IP networks for one-to-many applications. RTSP is architecturally located above RTP and RTCP, which were described earlier. Just as HTTP transports HTML, RTSP transports multimedia data. The difference is that while with HTTP the client makes requests and the server services those requests, with RTSP, both the server and client can issue requests; that is, RTSP is bidirectional. RTSP accomplishes data transfer using TCP or RTP. RTP itself can use TCP or UDP.

RTSP includes methods to establish a connection, manage the connection, and make requests for objects. As an example, the SET_TRANSPORT message is used to communicate port addresses and also the IP multicast address (if multicast is being used). The PLAY_RANGE message is used to make a request to the server to send a specified amount of multimedia data (in milliseconds). The client can send a STOP message, which is like pushing the pause button on a video cassette recorder. The SEND_REPORT message provides an example of the bidirectional nature of the RTSP protocol. This message is sent by the server to a client to ask the client about the reception quality of data.

The protocol has been proposed to the IETF as a draft standard. RTSP is intended to allow clients and servers from different vendors to interoperate. RTSP adds control mechanisms that are missing from RTP; for example, RTSP permits selection of a delivery mechansim such as UDP, TCP, and the like. RTSP is expected to help provide a smooth transition path to IP multicast. RTSP is a work in progress, and mechanisms for session establishment and control are some of the issues under consideration.

Resource Reservation Setup Protocol

Resource Reservation Setup Protocol (RSVP) is an Internet signaling protocol that is used to reserve network transmission and router resources. RSVP is initiated by recipients rather than senders, and scales well with a network that has a large number of nodes. RSVP depends on multicast and unicast routing protocols to determine a path from sender to recipient. RSVP packets are sent along this path from the recipient toward the sender. Routers merge requests from multiple recipients before propagating the reservation requests upstream to the sender. The routers maintain a "soft state;" that is, routers depend on recipients to periodically refresh the reservation request.

Architecturally, RSVP runs above IP, but it is similar to Internet Control Message Protocol (ICMP) and Internet Group Membership Protocol (IGMP) rather than a transport protocol. RSVP messages are initiated by a host node on behalf of applications. Each node that receives an RSVP message takes two actions. The first action is to evaluate the RSVP message and decide whether the requested resource reservation can be granted. The evaluation depends on availability of resources (also referred to as admission control) as well as whether the requesting user has administrative permission (referred to as policy control). If the request is granted, the second action takes place, which is to update the required state information at the node. The request is also forwarded to the next node on the reverse path from sender to receiver. The state information at each node is considered "soft"—the requesting node is expected to periodically refresh the request. Otherwise the state is timed out. The periodic refresh messages may flow along different paths. This way, if the routing path changes, the state along the old path is timed out and new resources are allocated along the new routing path.

References

http://www.digiphone.com (DigiPhone)

http://www.vocaltec.com (VocalTec Inc., vendor of Internet Phone)

http://www.itelco.com (NetSpeak, vendor of WebPhone)

http://www.quarterdeck.com (Quarterdeck Corp., vendor of WebTalk)

http://www.imtc.org (International Multimedia Teleconferencing Consortium)

http://www.connectix.com (Connectix, vendor of VideoPhone)

http://www.wpine.com (White Pine, vendor of Enhanced CU-SeeMe)

http://www.apple.com (Apple)

http://www.cornell.edu (Cornell University)

http://www.four11.com (Internet White Pages by Yahoo!, the White Pine CU-SeeMe directory server)

http://www.ietf.cnri.reston.va.us/html.charters/rsvp-charter.html (RSVP)

http://huntleyl.prognet.com/prognet/rt/ (RTSP)

http://www.mediadesign.co.at/newmedia/more/mbone-faq.html

http://www.mbone.com

http://www.mpeg.org (MPEG resources—NOT the official MPEG home page)

http://drogo.cselt.stet.it/mpeg/ (Official MPEG home page)

http://www.itu.ch/

http://web.ansi.org

RFC 1890, "RTP Profile for Audio and Video Conferences with Minimal Control"

RFC 1889, "RTP: A Transport Protocol for Real-Time Applications"

RFC 1112, "Host Extensions for IP Multicasting"

16

Virtual Reality Modeling Language

AS WORLD WIDE WEB PROTOCOLS HAVE gained in popularity, support has grown for converting the user interface from two-dimensional (2-D), using HTML for text and images, to three-dimensional (3-D), using Virtual Reality Modeling Language (VRML).

VRML is a file format for describing interactive 3-D objects and worlds on the Internet. It uses existing Web protocols and works within the Web infrastructure. A user views a VRML world with a VRML browser or viewer. Some VRML browsers are stand-alone programs, others are extensions of existing Web browsers.

VRML worlds are normally entered via HTML Web pages, obtained through HTTP-based uniform resource locators (URLs), and retrieved by standard Web servers. (VRML worlds can also be located on a local file system.) VRML worlds can reference standard media formats—such as those of the Joint Photographic Experts Group (JPEG), Moving Picture Experts Group (MPEG), Portable Network Graphics (PNG), and Musical Instrument Digital Interface (MIDI)—that have been glued into VRML by using Multipurpose Internet Mail Extensions (MIME). The media formats can be programmatically scripted within the VRML world via Java and JavaScript and externally by using another Java application.

VRML is intended for both content authors and programmers. VRML worlds can be created using authoring tools, with no coding required, and they can be programmed to be more interactive than most computer-aided design (CAD) databases or other 3-D objects.

VRML Versions

VRML version 1, developed in 1994, specified static VRML worlds with only a limited interactive model. Its ASCII file format (.wrl files) had its origins in Silicon Graphics' OpenInventor computer-aided design. Version 1 .wrl files can be specified in Unicode UTF8 format. VRML version 1 worlds can contain static 3-D objects and hyperlinks to other types of media.

VRML version 2 (established in 1996) allows for more complex behaviors. VRML version 2 worlds support dynamic objects and can be programmatically scripted using Java and JavaScript.

The VRML 97 specification, which is the Draft International Standard (DIS) version of VRML, is based on the August 1996 draft of VRML version 2. The International Organization for Standardization (ISO) and the International Electrotechnical Commission (IEC) cooperated in this effort. The work was done in the Joint Technical Committee 1 (JTC 1) in Subcommittee 24 (SC24), which specializes in computer graphics and image processing. The ISO/IEC JTC1/SC24 VRML 97 specification is ISO/IEC DIS 14772-1.

File Format Basics

A VRML world is a scene graphic, which is a hierarchical, directed acyclic graphic of one or more objects. A scene consists of multiple nodes; there are nodes for a variety of characteristics—shape, color, texture, lighting, and so forth. A node can have one or more fields containing specific information about the node.

VRML worlds have event generators and event receivers. Most event generators are sensor nodes. Sensor nodes enable interactivity within a VRML world—time, collisions, proximity, touching, visibility, and so forth. VRML has an event architecture to enable nodes to communicate by sending or receiving events.

Another form of node that helps to generate events is a script node. The bindings that the script nodes define are used by code in programming languages (such as Java and JavaScript) to trigger events that affect the VRML world.

The nodes of a VRML world can be contained within a single file or within different files, pointed to URLs. VRML nodes are described in Table 16-1.

Table 16-1   VRML Nodes

Node	Description
Anchor	Retrieves the URL that the user activates
Appearance	Specifies the visual characteristics of an object
AudioClip	Specifies an audio media object
Background	Specifies the backdrop (ground, sky, and so forth) of a world
Billboard	A form of the Transform node with a rotation view that follows the user
Box	Defines a box object
Collision	Collision detection properties for child nodes
Color	The colors (RGB) used in the fields of a node
ColorInterpolator	Produces a color based on a changed event
Cone	Defines a conical object
Coordinate	Defines a set of 3-D coordinates
CoordinateInterpolator	Produces a set of 3-D coordinates based on a changed event
Cylinder	Defines a cylindrical object
CylinderSensor	Maps pointer motion into rotation on a cylinder
DirectionalLight	Defines a directional light source
ElevationGrid	Defines a rectangular grid
Extrusion	Extrudes 2-D shapes along a 3-D spine
Fog	Simulates fog
FontStyle	Defines font information for text nodes
Group	Combines multiple child nodes into a logical grouping
ImageTexture	Defines the texture map of an image
IndexedFaceSet	Represents a 3-D shape by constructing multiple polygons
IndexedLineSet	Represents a 3-D shape by constructing multiple lines
Inline	A grouping node that reads child data from a URL
LOD	Defines level-of-detail data for an object at various distances
Material	Defines the surface material property of a geometry node

Table 16-1   VRML Nodes

Node	Description
MovieTexture	Defines the synchronization data for a movie file and a texture map
NavigationInfo	Describes the characteristics of the user's viewing model
Normal	Defines the set of 3-D surface normal vectors to be used with a geometry node
NormalInterpolator	Interpolates a list of normal vector sets
OrientationInterpolator	Interpolates a set of rotation values
PixelTexture	Defines the 2-D texture map
PlaneSensor	Maps pointing-device motion into a 2-D plane translation
PointLight	Specifies the 3-D location of a light source
PointSet	Defines a set of 3-D points
PositionInterpolator	Linearly interpolates a list of 3-D vectors
ProximitySensor	Sensor for when an object moves within a region
ScalarInterpolator	Linearly interpolates a list of floating point values
Script	Scripting language interface node
Shape	Defines the appearance and geometry of an object
Sound	Defines the spatial representation of a sound in a scene
Sphere	Defines a spherical object
SphereSensor	Maps pointer motion into rotation on a sphere
SpotLight	Defines a light source from a specific point
Switch	Conditional grouping node that traverses a specified node
Text	Specifies text
TextureCoordinate	Specifies a set of 2-D texture coordinates
TextureTransform	Defines a 2-D transform node applied to textural coordinates
TimeSensor	Generates events as time passes
TouchSensor	Tracks the state of a pointing device when it points at an object
Transform	Grouping node that defines the coordinate system of its children
Viewpoint	Defines a location for the user to view the scene
VisibilitySensor	Detects visibility changes of an object
WorldInfo	Defines basic information about the VRML world

VRML Scripting in Java and JavaScript

The VRML Browser Scripting Interface uses Script nodes to provide an interface for programming a VRML world. Scripts have access to many of the nodes, fields, and events in a VRML file. The Browser Scripting Interface exposes other interfaces to interact with the nodes, fields, and events of a VRML scene and to interact with the VRML browser. The VRML version 2 specification defines interfaces for Java and JavaScript.

VRML External Authoring Interface

VRML version 2 provides an interface for programs external to the VRML browser, which lets them communicate with the VRML browser and interface with a VRML world. The VRML External Authoring Interface (EAI) provides programmatic access to the VRML browser. This is accomplished in a manner similar to the internal VRML scripting interface, by providing an interface to VRML nodes, events, and the Browser Scripting Interface.

The EAI is not yet final; the interface proposed by the EAI working group is for the Java language, implemented via a vrml.external package.

Future Developments

A number of VRML working groups are extending the capabilities of VRML. Current efforts include the following:

- The VRML object-oriented extensions working group is creating object-oriented extensions for VRML.

- The VRML database working group is working on providing database functionality within VRML.

- The VRML compressed binary format working group is creating a method for encoding VRML files to reduce the file size for faster network transfer and to provide a simple file format for efficient parsing.

- The VRML color fidelity working group is working on color quality assurance methods for VRML browsers.

- The VRML keyboard input working group is working on updating VRML to better accept keyboard input for VRML worlds, which are now predominantly mouse driven.

- The VRML widgets working group is creating a set of VRML widgets that will provide a common set of user interface building blocks.

- The VRML universal media libraries working group is creating a set of media elements—including images, sounds, and VRML objects—for local VRML browsers, which will decrease network traffic and increase content richness.

- The VRML humanoid animation working group is creating a method of representing humanoid forms in VRML worlds.

- The VRML biota working group is creating tools for representation of living systems in VRML worlds.

- The VRML metaforms working group is creating a methodology for specifying formal grammars that map to VRML, to enable the representation of the structure and growth of digital life forms.

- The living worlds working group is working on a set of interfaces to provide VRML worlds with multiuser functionality.

- The distributed interactive simulation working group is working on the integration of VRML, Java, and Distributed Interactive Simulation (DIS) to provide large-scale virtual environments. DIS is probably best known for its use in multiuser military simulations.

References

http://www.vrml.org.

http://www.bsi.org.uk/sc24.

Appendixes

P
A
R
T

VI

A

Internet Standards

THIS APPENDIX LISTS REQUESTS FOR COMMENTS (RFCs) that have been approved by the Internet Architecture Board (IAB) and published separately as standards. They have been assigned numbers that are distinct from the RFC numbers. Some standards may be defined by more than one RFC. The idea is that the underlying protocol can be developed and clarified by publishing a new RFC, while the standard number remains the same. The standard will then reference the new RFC. An example is Standard 1 (Internet Official Protocol Standards), whose underlying RFC has changed more than ten times. The following table lists Internet standards numbers, the name of the standard, and the underlying RFCs.

Internet Standards

Standard Number	Title	RFC Number
0001	Internet Official Protocol Standards	2200
0002	Assigned Numbers	1700
0003	Host Requirements	1123, 1122
0004	Gateway Requirements	1009
0005	Internet Protocol (IP)	1112, 950, 922, 919, 792, 791
0006	User Datagram Protocol (UDP)	768

Internet Standards

Standard Number	Title	RFC Number
0007	Transmission Control Protocol (TCP)	793
0008	Telnet Protocol (TP)	855, 854
0009	File Transfer Protocol (FTP)	959
0010	Simple Mail Transfer Protocol (SMTP) Service Extensions	1869, 821
0011	Standard for the Format of Advanced Research Project Agency (ARPA) Internet Text Messages	822
0012	Network Time Protocol (NTP)	1119
0013	Domain Name System (DNS)	1035, 1034
0014	Mail Routing and the Domain System	974
0015	Simple Network Management Protocol (SNMP)	1157
0016	Structure of Management Information	1212, 1155
0017	Management Information Base	1213
0018	External Gateway Protocol (EGP)	904
0019	NetBIOS Service Protocols; NetBIOS Working Group	1002, 1001
0020	Echo Protocol	862
0021	Discard Protocol	863
0022	Character Generator Protocol	864
0023	Quote of the Day Protocol	865
0024	Active Users Protocol	866
0025	Daytime Protocol	867
0026	Time Server Protocol	868
0027	Binary Transmission Telnet Option	856
0028	Echo Telnet Option	857
0029	Suppress Go Ahead Telnet Option	858
0030	Status Telnet Option	859
0031	Timing Mark Telnet Option	860
0032	Extended Options List Telnet Option	861
0033	Trivial File Transfer Protocol	1350
0034	Routing Information Protocol	1058
0035	ISO Transport Service on Top of the TCP (Version3)	1006

Internet Standards

Standard Number	Title	RFC Number
0036	Transmission of IP and Address Resolution Protocol (ARP) over Fiber Distributed Data Interface (FDDI) Networks	1390
0037	An Ethernet Address Resolution Protocol	826
0038	A Reverse Address Resolution Protocol	903
0039	Interface Message Processor: Specifications for the Interconnection of a Host and an IMP (Revised)	None
0040	Host Access Protocol Specification	1221
0041	Standard for the Transmission of IP Datagrams over Ethernet Networks	894
0042	Standard for the Transmission of IP Datagrams over Experimental Ethernet Networks	895
0043	Standard for the Transmission of IP Datagrams over Institute of Electrical and Electronics Engineers (IEEE) 802 Networks	1042
0044	DCN Local-Network Protocols	891
0045	Internet Protocol on Network System's HYPERchannel: Protocol Specification	1044
0046	Transmitting IP Traffic over ARCNET Networks	1201
0047	Nonstandard for Transmission of IP Datagrams over Serial Lines: Serial Line Internet Protocol (SLIP)	1055
0048	Standard for the Transmission of IP Datagrams over NetBIOS Networks	1008
0049	Standard for the Transmission of 802.2 Packets over Internetwork Packet Exchange (IPX) Networks	1132
0050	Definitions of Managed Objects for the Ethernet-like Interface Types	1643
0051	Point-to-Point Protocol (PPP)	1662
0052	The Transmission of IP Datagrams over the Switched Multimegabit Data Services (SMDS) Service	1209
0053	Post Office Protocol (POP) Version 3	1939
0054	Open Shortest Path First (OSPF) Version 2	2328

B

Draft Standard RFCs

DRAFT STANDARD REQUESTS FOR COMMENTS (RFCs) are those RFCs that will be incorporated earliest into the Internet Standards listed in Appendix A. The following draft standard RFCs have advanced beyond the RFCs proposed as standards, listed in Appendix C.

RFC 2289, "A One-Time Password System"

RFC 2197, "SMTP Service Extension for Command Pipelining"

RFC 2178, "OSPF Version 2"

RFC 2132, "DHCP Options and BOOTP Vendor Extensions"

RFC 2131, "Dynamic Host Configuration Protocol"

RFC 2115, "Management Information Base for Frame Relay DTEs Using SMIv2"

RFC 2067, "IP over HIPPI"

RFC 2049, "Multipurpose Internet Mail Extensions (MIME) Part Five: Conformance Criteria and Examples"

RFC 2047, "MIME (Multipurpose Internet Mail Extensions) Part Three: Message Header Extensions for Non-ASCII Text"

RFC 2046, "Multipurpose Internet Mail Extensions (MIME) Part Two: Media Types"

RFC 2045, "Multipurpose Internet Mail Extensions (MIME) Part One: Format of Internet Message Bodies"

RFC 1994, "PPP Challenge Handshake Authentication Protocol (CHAP)"

RFC 1990, "The PPP Multilink Protocol (MP)"

RFC 1989, "PPP Link Quality Monitoring"

RFC 1908, "Coexistence between Version 1 and Version 2 of the Internet-Standard Network Management Framework"

RFC 1907, "Management Information Base for Version 2 of the Simple Network Management Protocol (SNMPv2)"

RFC 1906, "Transport Mappings for Version 2 of the Simple Network Management Protocol (SNMPv2)"

RFC 1905, "Protocol Operations for Version 2 of the Simple Network Management Protocol (SNMPv2)"

RFC 1904, "Conformance Statements for Version 2 of the Simple Network Management Protocol (SNMPv2)"

RFC 1903, "Textual Conventions for Version 2 of the Simple Network Management Protocol (SNMPv2)"

RFC 1902, "Structure of Management Information for Version 2 of the Simple Network Management Protocol (SNMPv2)"

RFC 1864, "The Content-MD5 Header Field"

RFC 1850, "OSPF Version 2 Management Information Base"

RFC 1832, "XDR: External Data Representation Standard"

RFC 1779, "A String Representation of Distinguished Names"

RFC 1778, "The String Representation of Standard Attribute Syntaxes"

RFC 1777, "Lightweight Directory Access Protocol"

RFC 1772, "Application of the Border Gateway Protocol in the Internet"

RFC 1771, "A Border Gateway Protocol 4 (BGP-4)"

RFC 1762, "The PPP DECnet Phase IV Control Protocol (DNCP)"

RFC 1757, "Remote Network Monitoring Management Information Base"

RFC 1748, "IEEE 802.5 MIB Using SMIv2"

RFC 1743, "IEEE 802.5 MIB Using SMIv2"

RFC 1725, "Post Office Protocol—Version 3"

RFC 1724, "RIP Version 2 MIB Extension"

RFC 1723, "RIP Version 2—Carrying Additional Information"

RFC 1722, "RIP Version 2 Protocol Applicability Statement"

RFC 1694, "Definitions of Managed Objects for SMDS Interfaces Using SMIv2"

RFC 1660, "Definitions of Managed Objects for Parallel-Printer-Like Hardware Devices Using SMIv2"

RFC 1659, "Definitions of Managed Objects for RS-232-Like Hardware Devices Using SMIv2"

RFC 1658, "Definitions of Managed Objects for Character Stream Devices Using SMIv2"

RFC 1657, "Definitions of Managed Objects for the Fourth Version of the Border Gateway Protocol (BGP-4) Using SMIv2"

RFC 1653, "SMTP Service Extension for Message Size Declaration"

RFC 1652, "SMTP Service Extension for 8bit-MIMEtransport"

RFC 1651, "SMTP Service Extensions"

RFC 1629, "Guidelines for OSI NSAP Allocation in the Internet"

RFC 1583, "OSPF Version 2"

RFC 1575, "An Echo Function for CLNP (ISO 8473)"

RFC 1559, "DECnet Phase IV MIB Extensions"

RFC 1549, "PPP in HDLC Framing"

RFC 1548, "The Point-to-Point Protocol (PPP)"

RFC 1542, "Clarifications and Extensions for the Bootstrap Protocol"

RFC 1534, "Interoperation Between DHCP and BOOTP"

RFC 1522, "MIME (Multipurpose Internet Mail Extensions) Part Two: Message Header Extensions for Non-ASCII Text"

RFC 1521, "MIME (Multipurpose Internet Mail Extensions) Part One: Mechanisms for Specifying and Describing the Format of Internet Message Bodies"

RFC 1516, "Definitions of Managed Objects for IEEE 802.3 Repeater Devices"

RFC 1497, "BOOTP Vendor Information Extensions"

RFC 1493, "Definitions of Managed Objects for Bridges"

RFC 1490, "Multiprotocol Interconnect over Frame Relay"

RFC 1460, "Post Office Protocol—Version 3"

RFC 1398, "Definitions of Managed Objects for the Ethernet-Like Interface Types"

RFC 1395, "BOOTP Vendor Information Extensions"

RFC 1356, "Multiprotocol Interconnect on X.25 and ISDN in the Packet Mode"

RFC 1305, "Network Time Protocol (Version 3) Specification, Implementation"

RFC 1288, "The Finger User Information Protocol"

RFC 1247, "OSPF Version 2"

RFC 1225, "Post Office Protocol: Version 3"

RFC 1196, "Finger User Information Protocol. December 1, 1990 (Format: TXT= 24799) (Obsoletes RFC1194, 742)"

RFC 1194, "Finger User Information Protocol. November 1, 1990 (Format: TXT= 24626 bytes) (Obsoletes RFC0742)"

RFC 1191, "Path MTU Discovery"

RFC 1188, "Proposed Standard for the Transmission of IP Datagrams over FDDI Networks"

RFC 1184, "Telnet Linemode Option"

RFC 1171, "Point-to-Point Protocol for the Transmission of Multiprotocol Datagrams over Point-to-Point Links"

RFC 1158, "Management Information Base for Network Management of TCP/IP-Based Internets: MIB-II"

RFC 954, "NICNAME/WHOIS"

C

Proposed Internet Standards

THIS APPENDIX LISTS REQUESTS FOR COMMENTS (RFCs) that have been proposed for incorporation into the Internet standards described in Appendix A. Only time will tell whether the following RFCs will become part of the standards.

RFC 2327, "SDP: Session Description Protocol"

RFC 2320, "Definitions of Managed Objects for Classical IP and ARP over ATM Using SMIv2 (IPOA-MIB)"

RFC 2308, "Negative Caching of DNS Queries (DNS NCACHE)"

RFC 2305, "A Simple Mode of Facsimile Using Internet Mail"

RFC 2304, "Minimal FAX Address Format in Internet Mail"

RFC 2303, "Minimal PSTN Address Format in Internet Mail"

RFC 2302, "Tag Image File Format (TIFF)—Image/TIFF MIME Sub-Type Registration"

RFC 2301, "File Format for Internet Fax"

RFC 2298, "An Extensible Message Format for Message Disposition Notifications"

RFC 2294, "Representing the O/R Address Hierarchy in the X.500 Directory Information Tree"

RFC 2293, "Representing Tables and Subtrees in the X.500 Direc"

RFC 2290, "Mobile-IPv4 Configuration Option for PPP IPCP"

RFC 2287, "Definitions of System-Level Managed Objects for Applications"

RFC 2284, "PPP Extensible Authentication Protocol (EAP)"

RFC 2283, "Multiprotocol Extensions for BGP-4"

RFC 2280, "Routing Policy Specification Language (RPSL)"

RFC 2279, "UTF-8, a Transformation Format of ISO 10646"

RFC 2275, "View-Based Access Control Model (VACM) for the Simple Network Management Protocol (SNMP)"

RFC 2274, "User-Based Security Model (USM) for Version 3 of the Simple Network Management Protocol (SNMPv3)"

RFC 2273, "SNMPv3 Applications"

RFC 2272, "Message Processing and Dispatching for the Simple Network Management Protocol (SNMP)"

RFC 2271, "An Architecture for Describing SNMP Management Frameworks"

RFC 2266, "Definitions of Managed Objects for IEEE 802.12 Repeater Devices"

RFC 2265, "View-Based Access Control Model (VACM) for the Simple Network Management Protocol (SNMP)"

RFC 2264, "User-Based Security Model (USM) for Version 3 of the Simple Network Management Protocol (SNMPv3)"

RFC 2263, "SNMPv3 Applications"

RFC 2262, "Message Processing and Dispatching for the Simple Network Management Protocol (SNMP)"

RFC 2261, "An Architecture for Describing SNMP Management Frameworks"

RFC 2257, "Agent Extensibility (AgentX) Protocol Version 1"

RFC 2256, "A Summary of the X.500(96) User Schema for Use with LDAPv3"

RFC 2255, "The LDAP URL Format"

RFC 2254, "The String Representation of LDAP Search Filters"

RFC 2253, "Lightweight Directory Access Protocol (v3): UTF-8 String Representation of Distinguished Names"

RFC 2252, "Lightweight Directory Access Protocol (v3): Attribute Syntax Definitions"

RFC 2251, "Lightweight Directory Access Protocol (v3)"

RFC 2250, "RTP Payload Format for MPEG1/MPEG2 Video"

RFC 2249, "Mail Monitoring MIB"

RFC 2248, "Network Services Monitoring MIB"

RFC 2247, "Using Domains in LDAP/X.500 Distinguished Names"

RFC 2245, "Anonymous SASL Mechanism"

RFC 2244, "ACAP—Application Configuration Access Protocol"

RFC 2243, "OTP Extended Responses"

RFC 2242, "NetWare/IP Domain Name and Information"

RFC 2241, "DHCP Options for Novell Directory Services"

RFC 2239, "Definitions of Managed Objects for IEEE 802.3 Medium Attachment Units (MAUs) Using SMIv2"

RFC 2238, "Definitions of Managed Objects for HPR Using SMIv2"

RFC 2236, "Internet Group Management Protocol, Version 2"

RFC 2234, "Augmented BNF for Syntax Specifications: ABNF"

RFC 2233, "The Interfaces Group MIB Using SMIv2"

RFC 2232, "Definitions of Managed Objects for DLUR Using SMIv2"

RFC 2231, "MIME Parameter Value and Encoded Word Extensions: Character Sets, Languages, and Continuations"

RFC 2228, "FTP Security Extensions"

RFC 2227, "Simple Hit-Metering and Usage-Limiting for HTTP"

RFC 2226, "IP Broadcast over ATM Networks"

RFC 2225, "Classical IP and ARP over ATM"

RFC 2222, "Simple Authentication and Security Layer (SASL)"

RFC 2221, "IMAP4 Login Referrals"

RFC 2218, "A Common Schema for the Internet White Pages Service"

RFC 2215, "General Characterization Parameters for Integrated Service Network Elements"

RFC 2214, "Integrated Services Management Information Base Guaranteed Service Extensions using SMIv2"

RFC 2213, "Integrated Services Management Information Base Using SMIv2"

RFC 2212, "Specification of Guaranteed Quality of Service"

RFC 2211, "Specification of the Controlled-Load Network Element Service"

RFC 2210, "The Use of RSVP with IETF Integrated Services"

RFC 2207, "RSVP Extensions for IPSEC Data Flows"

RFC 2206, "RSVP Management Information Base using SMIv2"

RFC 2205, "Resource ReSerVation Protocol (RSVP)—Version 1 Functional Specification"

RFC 2203, "RPCSEC_GSS Protocol Specification"

RFC 2198, "RTP Payload for Redundant Audio Data"

RFC 2195, "IMAP/POP AUTHorize Extension for Simple Challenge/Response"

RFC 2193, "IMAP4 Mailbox Referrals"

RFC 2192, "IMAP URL Scheme"

RFC 2190, "RTP Payload Format for H.263 Video Streams"

RFC 2184, "MIME Parameter Value and Encoded Word Extensions: Character Sets, Languages, and Continuations"

RFC 2183, "Communicating Presentation Information in Internet Messages: The Content-Disposition Header Field"

RFC 2181, "Clarifications to the DNS Specification"

RFC 2177, "IMAP4 IDLE command"

RFC 2165, "Service Location Protocol"

RFC 2164, "Use of an X.500/LDAP Directory to Support MIXER Address Mapping"

RFC 2163, "Using the Internet DNS to Distribute MIXER Conformant Global Address Mapping (MCGAM)"

RFC 2160, "Carrying PostScript in X.400 and MIME"

RFC 2159, "A MIME Body Part for FAX"

RFC 2158, "X.400 Image Body Parts"

RFC 2157, "Mapping Between X.400 and RFC-822/MIME Message Bodies"

RFC 2156, "MIXER (Mime Internet X.400 Enhanced Relay): Mapping Between X.400 and RFC 822/MIME"

RFC 2155, "Definitions of Managed Objects for APPN Using SMIv2"

RFC 2147, "TCP and UDP over IPv6 Jumbograms"

RFC 2142, "Mailbox Names for Common Services, Roles, and Functions"

RFC 2141, "URN Syntax"

RFC 2138, "Remote Authentication Dial-In User Service (RADIUS)"

RFC 2137, "Secure Domain Name System Dynamic Update"

RFC 2136, "Dynamic Updates in the Domain Name System (DNS UPDATE)"

RFC 2128, "Dial Control Management Information Base Using SMIv2"

RFC 2127, "ISDN Management Information Base Using SMIv2"

RFC 2126, "ISO Transport Service on Top of TCP (ITOT)"

RFC 2125, "The PPP Bandwidth Allocation Protocol (BAP)/The PPP Bandwidth Allocation Control Protocol (BACP)"

RFC 2122, "VEMMI URL Specification"

RFC 2113, "IP Router Alert Option"

RFC 2112, "The MIME Multipart/Related Content-Type"

RFC 2111, "Content-ID and Message-ID Uniform Resource Locators"

RFC 2110, "MIME E-mail Encapsulation of Aggregate Documents, Such as HTML (MHTML)"

RFC 2109, "HTTP State Management Mechanism"

RFC 2108, "Definitions of Managed Objects for IEEE 802.3 Repeater Devices Using SMIv2"

RFC 2097, "The PPP NetBIOS Frames Control Protocol (NBFCP)"

RFC 2096, "IP Forwarding Table MIB"

RFC 2095, "IMAP/POP AUTHorize Extension for Simple Challenge/Response"

RFC 2091, "Triggered Extensions to RIP to Support Demand Circuits"

RFC 2088, "IMAP4 Nonsynchronizing Literals"

RFC 2087, "IMAP4 QUOTA Extension"

RFC 2086, "IMAP4 ACL Extension"

RFC 2085, "HMAC-MD5 IP Authentication with Replay Prevention"

RFC 2082, "RIP-2 MD5 Authentication"

RFC 2080, "RIPng for IPv6"

RFC 2079, "Definition of an X.500 Attribute Type and an Object Class to Hold Uniform Resource Identifiers (URIs)"

RFC 2078, "Generic Security Service Application Program Interface, Version 2"

RFC 2077, "The Model Primary Content Type for Multipurpose Internet Mail Extensions"

RFC 2074, "Remote Network Monitoring MIB Protocol Identifiers"

RFC 2073, "An IPv6 Provider-Based Unicast Address Format"

RFC 2070, "Internationalization of the Hypertext Markup Language"

RFC 2069, "An Extension to HTTP: Digest Access Authentication"

RFC 2068, "Hypertext Transfer Protocol—HTTP/1.1"

RFC 2065, "Domain Name System Security Extensions"

RFC 2062, "Internet Message Access Protocol—Obsolete Syntax"

RFC 2060, "Internet Message Access Protocol—Version 4rev1"

RFC 2058, "Remote Authentication Dial-In User Service (RADIUS)"

RFC 2056, "Uniform Resource Locators for Z39.50"

RFC 2051, "Definitions of Managed Objects for APPC Using SMIv2"

RFC 2038, "RTP Payload Format for MPEG1/MPEG2 Video"

RFC 2037, "Entity MIB Using SMIv2"

RFC 2035, "RTP Payload Format for JPEG-Compressed Video"

RFC 2034, "SMTP Service Extension for Returning Enhanced Error Codes"

RFC 2032, "RTP Payload Format for H.261 Video Streams"

RFC 2029, "RTP Payload Format of Sun's CellB Video Encoding"

RFC 2025, "The Simple Public-Key GSS-API Mechanism (SPKM)"

RFC 2024, "Definitions of Managed Objects for Data Link Switching Using SMIv2"

RFC 2023, "IP Version 6 over PPP"

RFC 2022, "Support for Multicast over UNI 3.0/3.1–based ATM Networks"

RFC 2021, "Remote Network Monitoring Management Information Base Version 2 Using SMIv2"

RFC 2020, "IEEE 802.12 Interface MIB"

RFC 2019, "Transmission of IPv6 Packets Over FDDI"

RFC 2018, "TCP Selective Acknowledgment Options"

RFC 2017, "Definition of the URL MIME External-Body AccessType"

RFC 2015, "MIME Security with Pretty Good Privacy (PGP)"

RFC 2013, "SNMPv2 Management Information Base for the User Datagram Protocol using SMIv2"

RFC 2012, "SNMPv2 Management Information Base for the Transmission Control Protocol Using SMIv2"

RFC 2011, "SNMPv2 Management Information Base for the Internet Protocol Using SMIv2"

RFC 2006, "The Definitions of Managed Objects for IP Mobility Support Using SMIv2"

RFC 2005, "Applicability Statement for IP Mobility Support"

RFC 2004, "Minimal Encapsulation Within IP"

RFC 2003, "IP Encapsulation Within IP"

RFC 2002, "IP Mobility Support"

RFC 2001, "TCP Slow Start, Congestion Avoidance, Fast Retransmit, and Fast Recovery Algorithms"

RFC 1997, "BGP Communities Attribute"

RFC 1996, "A Mechanism for Prompt Notification of Zone Changes (DNS NOTIFY)"

RFC 1995, "Incremental Zone Transfer in DNS"

RFC 1985, "SMTP Service Extension for Remote Message Queue Starting"

RFC 1982, "Serial Number Arithmetic"

RFC 1981, "Path MTU Discovery for IP Version 6"

RFC 1973, "PPP in Frame Relay"

RFC 1972, "A Method for the Transmission of IPv6 Packets over Ethernet Networks"

RFC 1971, "IPv6 Stateless Address Autoconfiguration"

RFC 1970, "Neighbor Discovery for IP Version 6 (IPv6)"

RFC 1968, "The PPP Encryption Control Protocol (ECP)"

RFC 1964, "The Kerberos Version 5 GSS-API Mechanism"

RFC 1962, "The PPP Compression Control Protocol (CCP)"

RFC 1961, "GSS-API Authentication Method for SOCKS Version 5"

RFC 1960, "A String Representation of LDAP Search Filters"

RFC 1959, "An LDAP URL Format"

RFC 1938, "A One-Time Password System"

RFC 1933, "Transition Mechanisms for IPv6 Hosts and Routers"

RFC 1929, "Username/Password Authentication for SOCKS V5"

RFC 1928, "SOCKS Protocol Version 5"

RFC 1914, "How to Interact with a Whois++ Mesh"

RFC 1913, "Architecture of the Whois++ Index Service"

RFC 1894, "An Extensible Message Format for Delivery Status Notifications"

RFC 1893, "Enhanced Mail System Status Codes"

RFC 1892, "The Multipart/Report Content Type for the Reporting of Mail System Administrative Messages"

RFC 1891, "SMTP Service Extension for Delivery Status Notifications"

RFC 1890, "RTP Profile for Audio and Video Conferences with Minimal Control"

RFC 1889, "RTP: A Transport Protocol for Real-Time Applications"

RFC 1886, "DNS Extensions to Support IP Version 6"

RFC 1885, "Internet Control Message Protocol (ICMPv6) for the Internet Protocol Version 6 (IPv6)"

RFC 1884, "IP Version 6 Addressing Architecture"

RFC 1883, "Internet Protocol, Version 6 (IPv6) Specification"

RFC 1866, "Hypertext Markup Language—2.0"

RFC 1854, "SMTP Service Extension for Command Pipelining"

RFC 1848, "MIME Object Security Services"

RFC 1847, "Security Multiparts for MIME: Multipart/Signed and Multipart/Encrypted"

RFC 1835, "Architecture of the Whois++ Service"

RFC 1833, "Binding Protocols for ONC RPC Version 2"

RFC 1831, "RPC: Remote Procedure Call Protocol Specification Version 2"

RFC 1829, "The ESP DES-CBC Transform"

RFC 1828, "IP Authentication Using Keyed MD5"

RFC 1827, "IP Encapsulating Security Payload (ESP)"

RFC 1826, "IP Authentication Header"

RFC 1825, "Security Architecture for the Internet Protocol"

RFC 1812, "Requirements for IP Version 4 Routers"

RFC 1808, "Relative Uniform Resource Locators"

RFC 1798, "Connectionless Lightweight X.500 Directory Access Protocol"

RFC 1793, "Extending OSPF to Support Demand Circuits"

RFC 1784, "TFTP Timeout Interval and Transfer Size Options"

RFC 1783, "TFTP Block-Size Option"

RFC 1782, "TFTP Option Extension"

RFC 1781, "Using the OSI Directory to Achieve User-Friendly Naming"

RFC 1767, "MIME Encapsulation of EDI Objects"

RFC 1766, "Tags for the Identification of Languages"

RFC 1764, "The PPP XNS IDP Control Protocol (XNSCP)"

RFC 1763, "The PPP Banyan Vines Control Protocol (BVCP)"

RFC 1759, "Printer MIB"

RFC 1755, "ATM Signaling Support for IP over ATM"

RFC 1752, "The Recommendation for the IP Next Generation Protocol"

RFC 1749, "IEEE 802.5 Station Source Routing MIB Using SMIv2"

RFC 1747, "Definitions of Managed Objects for SNA Data Link Control (SDLC) Using SMIv2"

RFC 1745, "BGP4/IDRP for IP—OSPF Interaction"

RFC 1742, "AppleTalk Management Information Base II"

RFC 1740, "MIME Encapsulation of Macintosh Files—MacMIME"

RFC 1738, "Uniform Resource Locators (URLs)"

RFC 1734, "POP3 AUTHentication Command"

RFC 1731, "IMAP4 Authentication Mechanisms"

RFC 1730, "Internet Message Access Protocol—Version 4"

RFC 1717, "The PPP Multilink Protocol (MP)"

RFC 1697, "Relational Database Management System (RDBMS) Management Information Base (MIB) using SMIv2"

RFC 1696, "Modem Management Information Base (MIB) using SMIv2"

RFC 1695, "Definitions of Managed Objects for ATM Management Version 8.0 Using SMIv2"

RFC 1692, "Transport Multiplexing Protocol (TMux)"

RFC 1666, "Definitions of Managed Objects for SNA NAUs Using SMIv2. August 1994. (Format: TXT=134385 Bytes) (Obsoletes RFC1665)"

RFC 1665, "Definitions of Managed Objects for SNA NAUs Using SMIv2. July 1994. (Format: TXT=133381 Bytes) (Obsoleted by RFC1666)"

RFC 1663, "PPP Reliable Transmission"

RFC 1656, "BGP-4 Protocol Document Roadmap and Implementation Experience"

RFC 1655, "Application of the Border Gateway Protocol in the Internet"

RFC 1654, "A Border Gateway Protocol 4 (BGP-4)"

RFC 1650, "Definitions of Managed Objects for the Ethernet-Like Interface Types using SMIv2"

RFC 1648, "Postmaster Convention for X.400 Operations"

RFC 1647, "TN3270 Enhancements"

RFC 1638, "PPP Bridging Control Protocol (BCP)"

RFC 1628, "UPS Management Information Base"

RFC 1626, "Default IP MTU for Use over ATM AAL5"

RFC 1619, "PPP over SONET/SDH"

RFC 1618, "PPP over ISDN"

RFC 1612, "DNS Resolver MIB Extensions"

RFC 1611, "DNS Server MIB Extensions"

RFC 1604, "Definitions of Managed Objects for Frame Relay Service"

RFC 1598, "PPP in X.25"

RFC 1596, "Definitions of Managed Objects for Frame Relay Service"

RFC 1595, "Definitions of Managed Objects for the SONET/SDH Interface Type"

RFC 1587, "The OSPF NSSA Option"

RFC 1584, "Multicast Extensions to OSPF"

RFC 1582, "Extensions to RIP to Support Demand Circuits"

RFC 1577, "Classical IP and ARP over ATM"

RFC 1573, "Evolution of the Interfaces Group of MIB-II"

RFC 1572, "Telnet Environment Option"

RFC 1570, "PPP LCP Extensions"

RFC 1567, "X.500 Directory Monitoring MIB"

RFC 1566, "Mail Monitoring MIB"

RFC 1565, "Network Services Monitoring MIB"

RFC 1553, "Compressing IPX Headers over WAN Media (CIPX)"

RFC 1552, "The PPP Internetworking Packet Exchange Control Protocol (IPXCP)"

RFC 1544, "The Content-MD5 Header Field"

RFC 1541, "Dynamic Host Configuration Protocol"

RFC 1533, "DHCP Options and BOOTP Vendor Extensions"

RFC 1532, "Clarifications and Extensions for the Bootstrap Protocol"

RFC 1531, "Dynamic Host Configuration Protocol"

RFC 1525, "Definitions of Managed Objects for Source Routing Bridges"

RFC 1519, "Classless Inter-Domain Routing (CIDR): an Address Assignment and Aggregation Strategy"

RFC 1518, "An Architecture for IP Address Allocation with CIDR"

RFC 1517, "Applicability Statement for the Implementation of Classless Inter-Domain Routing (CIDR)"

RFC 1515, "Definitions of Managed Objects for IEEE 802.3 Medium Attachment Units (MAUs)"

RFC 1514, "Host Resources MIB"

RFC 1513, "Token Ring Extensions to the Remote Network Monitoring MIB"

RFC 1512, "FDDI Management Information Base"

RFC 1510, "The Kerberos Network Authentication Service (V5)"

RFC 1509, "Generic Security Service API: C-Bindings"

RFC 1508, "Generic Security Service Application Program Interface"

RFC 1507, "DASS—Distributed Authentication Security Service"

RFC 1502, "X.400 Use of Extended Character Sets"

RFC 1496, "Rules for Downgrading Messages from X.400/88 to X.400/84 When MIME Content Types are Present in the Messages"

RFC 1495, "Mapping Between X.400 and RFC-822 Message Bodies"

RFC 1494, "Equivalences Between 1988 X.400 and RFC-822 Message Bodies"

RFC 1488, "The X.500 String Representation of Standard Attribute Syntaxes"

RFC 1487, "X.500 Lightweight Directory Access Protocol"

RFC 1485, "A String Representation of Distinguished Names (OSI-DS 23 v5)"

RFC 1483, "Multiprotocol Encapsulation over ATM Adaptation Layer 5"

RFC 1479, "Inter-Domain Policy Routing Protocol Specification: Version 1"

RFC 1478, "An Architecture for Inter-Domain Policy Routing"

RFC 1477, "IDPR as a Proposed Standard"

RFC 1474, "The Definitions of Managed Objects for the Bridge Network Control Protocol of the Point-to-Point Protocol"

RFC 1473, "The Definitions of Managed Objects for the IP Network Control Protocol of the Point-to-Point Protocol"

RFC 1472, "The Definitions of Managed Objects for the Security Protocols of the Point-to-Point Protocol"

RFC 1471, "The Definitions of Managed Objects for the Link Control Protocol of the Point-to-Point Protocol"

RFC 1469, "IP Multicast over Token-Ring Local Area Networks"

RFC 1461, "SNMP MIB Extension for Multiprotocol Interconnect over X.25"

RFC 1452, "Coexistence between Version 1 and Version 2 of the Internet-Standard Network Management Framework"

RFC 1450, "Management Information Base for Version 2 of the Simple Network Management Protocol (SNMP-V2)"

RFC 1449, "Transport Mappings for Version 2 of the Simple Network Management Protocol (SNMP-V2)"

RFC 1448, "Protocol Operations for Version 2 of the Simple Network Management Protocol (SNMP-V2)"

RFC 1444, "Conformance Statements for Version 2 of the Simple Network Management Protocol (SNMP-V2)"

RFC 1443, "Textual Conventions for Version 2 of the Simple Network Management Protocol (SNMP-V2)"

RFC 1442, "Structure of Management Information for Version 2 of the Simple Network Management Protocol (SNMP-V2)"

RFC 1441, "Introduction to Version 2 of the Internet-Standard Network Management Framework"

RFC 1427, "SMTP Service Extension for Message Size Declaration"

RFC 1426, "SMTP Service Extension for 8bit-MIMEtransport"

RFC 1425, "SMTP Service Extensions"

RFC 1424, "Privacy Enhancement for Internet Electronic Mail: Part IV: Key Certification and Related Services"

RFC 1423, "Privacy Enhancement for Internet Electronic Mail: Part III: Algorithms, Modes, and Identifiers"

RFC 1422, "Privacy Enhancement for Internet Electronic Mail: Part II: Certificate-Based Key Management"

RFC 1421, "Privacy Enhancement for Internet Electronic Mail: Part I: Message Encryption and Authentication Procedures"

RFC 1420, "SNMP over IPX"

RFC 1419, "SNMP over AppleTalk"

RFC 1418, "SNMP over OSI"

RFC 1415, "FTP-FTAM Gateway Specification"

RFC 1414, "Identification MIB"

RFC 1413, "Identification Protocol"

RFC 1407, "Definitions of Managed Objects for the DS3/E3 Interface Type"

RFC 1406, "Definitions of Managed Objects for the DS1 and E1 Interface Types"

RFC 1403, "BGP OSPF Interaction"

RFC 1397, "Default Route Advertisement in BGP2 and BGP3 Version of the Border Gateway Protocol"

RFC 1389, "RIP Version 2 MIB Extensions"

RFC 1388, "RIP Version 2 Carrying Additional Information"

RFC 1382, "SNMP MIB Extension for the X.25 Packet Layer"

RFC 1381, "SNMP MIB Extension for X.25 LAPB"

RFC 1378, "The PPP AppleTalk Control Protocol (ATCP)"

RFC 1377, "The PPP OSI Network Layer Control Protocol (OSINLCP)"

RFC 1376, "The PPP DECnet Phase IV Control Protocol (DNCP)"

RFC 1374, "IP and ARP on HIPPI"

RFC 1372, "Telnet Remote Flow Control Option"

RFC 1370, "Applicability Statement for OSPF"

RFC 1369, "Implementation Notes and Experience for the Internet Ethernet MIB"

RFC 1368, "Definition of Managed Objects for IEEE 802.3 Repeater Devices"

RFC 1364, "BGP OSPF Interaction"

RFC 1354, "IP Forwarding Table MIB"

RFC 1353, "Definitions of Managed Objects for Administration of SNMP Parties"

RFC 1352, "SNMP Security Protocols"

RFC 1351, "SNMP Administrative Model"

RFC 1349, "Type of Service in the Internet Protocol Suite"

RFC 1341, "MIME (Multipurpose Internet Mail Extensions): Mechanisms for Specifying and Describing the Format of Internet Message Bodies"

RFC 1334, "PPP Authentication Protocols"

RFC 1333, "PPP Link Quality Monitoring"

RFC 1332, "The PPP Internet Protocol Control Protocol (IPCP)"

RFC 1331, "Point-to-Point Protocol (PPP) for the Transmission of Multiprotocol Datagrams over Point-to-Point Links"

RFC 1328, "X.400 1988 to 1984 Downgrading"

RFC 1327, "Mapping Between X.400 (1988)/ISO 10021 and RFC 822"

RFC 1323, "TCP Extensions for High Performance"

RFC 1318, "Definitions of Managed Objects for Parallel-Printer-Like Hardware Devices"

RFC 1317, "Definitions of Managed Objects for RS-232-Like Hardware Devices"

RFC 1316, "Definitions of Managed Objects for Character Stream Devices"

RFC 1315, "Management Information Base for Frame Relay DTEs"

RFC 1314, "A File Format for the Exchange of Images in the Internet"

RFC 1304, "Definitions of Managed Objects for the SIP Interface Type"

RFC 1294, "Multiprotocol Interconnect over Frame Relay"

RFC 1293, "Inverse Address Resolution Protocol"

RFC 1289, "DECnet Phase IV MIB Extensions"

RFC 1286, "Definitions of Managed Objects for Bridges"

RFC 1285, "FDDI Management Information Base"

RFC 1284, "Definitions of Managed Objects for the Ethernet-Like Interface Types"

RFC 1277, "Encoding Network Addresses to Support Operation over Non-OSI Lower Layers"

RFC 1276, "Replication and Distributed Operations Extensions to Provide an Internet Directory Using X.500"

RFC 1274, "The COSINE and Internet X.500 Schema"

RFC 1271, "Remote Network Monitoring Management Information Base"

RFC 1269, "Definitions of Managed Objects for the Border Gateway Protocol: Version 3"

RFC 1256, "ICMP Router Discovery Messages"

RFC 1253, "OSPF Version 2 Management Information Base"

RFC 1252, "OSPF Version 2 Management Information Base"

RFC 1248, "OSPF Version 2 Management Information Base"

RFC 1243, "AppleTalk Management Information Base"

RFC 1240, "OSI Connectionless Transport Services on Top of UDP: Version 1"

RFC 1239, "Reassignment of Experimental MIBs to Standard MIBs"

RFC 1237, "Guidelines for OSI NSAP Allocation in the Internet"

RFC 1234, "Tunneling IPX Traffic through IP Networks"

RFC 1233, "Definitions of Managed Objects for the DS3 Interface Type"

RFC 1232, "Definitions of Managed Objects for the DS1 Interface Type"

RFC 1231, "IEEE 802.5 Token Ring MIB"

RFC 1229, "Extensions to the Generic-Interface MIB"

RFC 1220, "Point-to-Point Protocol Extensions for Bridging"

RFC 1195, "Use of OSI IS-IS for Routing in TCP/IP and Dual Environments"

RFC 1172, "Point-to-Point Protocol (PPP) Initial Configuration Options"

RFC 1144, "Compressing TCP/IP Headers for Low-Speed Serial Links"

RFC 1139, "Echo Function for ISO 8473"

RFC 1134, "Point-to-Point Protocol: Proposal for Multiprotocol Transmission of Datagrams over Point-to-Point Links"

RFC 1131, "OSPF Specification"

RFC 1116, "Telnet Linemode Option"

RFC 1096, "Telnet X Display Location Option"

RFC 1091, "Telnet Terminal Type Option"

RFC 1079, "Telnet Terminal Speed Option"

RFC 1073, "Telnet Window Size Option"

RFC 1053, "Telnet X.3 PAD Option"

RFC 1043, "Telnet Data Entry Terminal Option: DODIIS Implementation"

RFC 1041, "Telnet 3270 Regime Option"

RFC 977, "Network News Transfer Protocol"

RFC 946, "Telnet Terminal Location Number Option"

RFC 933, "Output-Marking Telnet Option"

RFC 927, "TACACS User-Identification Telnet Option"

RFC 885, "Telnet End-of-Record Option"

RFC 779, "Telnet Send-Location Option"

RFC 749, "Telnet SUPDUP-Output Option"

RFC 736, "Telnet SUPDUP Option"

RFC 735, "Revised Telnet Byte Macro Option"

RFC 727, "Telnet Logout Option"

RFC 726, "Remote-Controlled Transmission and Echoing Telnet Option"

RFC 698, "Telnet Extended ASCII Option"

RFC 658, "Telnet Output Linefeed Disposition"

RFC 657, "Telnet Output Vertical Tab Disposition Option"

RFC 656, "Telnet Output Vertical Tab Stops Option"

RFC 655, "Telnet Output Form-Feed Disposition Option"

RFC 654, "Telnet Output Horizontal Tab Disposition Option"

RFC 653, "Telnet Output Horizontal Tab Stops Option"

RFC 652, "Telnet Output Carriage-Return Disposition Option"

Index

Note: Page numbers in italics refer to figures or tables.

V

W

X – Y

Z

THE MANUSCRIPT for this book was prepared using Microsoft Word 97. Pages were composed by Microsoft Press using Adobe PageMaker 6.52 for Windows, with text in Garamond and display type in Cosmos Medium. Composed pages were delivered to the printer as electronic prepress files.

Cover Designer
Greg Hickman

Interior Graphic Designer
Kim Eggleston

Compositors
Barb Runyan, Stuart Greenman

Principal Proofreader
Cheryl Penner

Indexer
Maro Riofrancos